THE ADVENTURE ZONE

Petals to the Metal

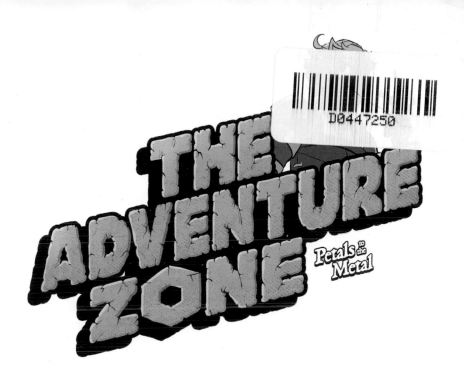

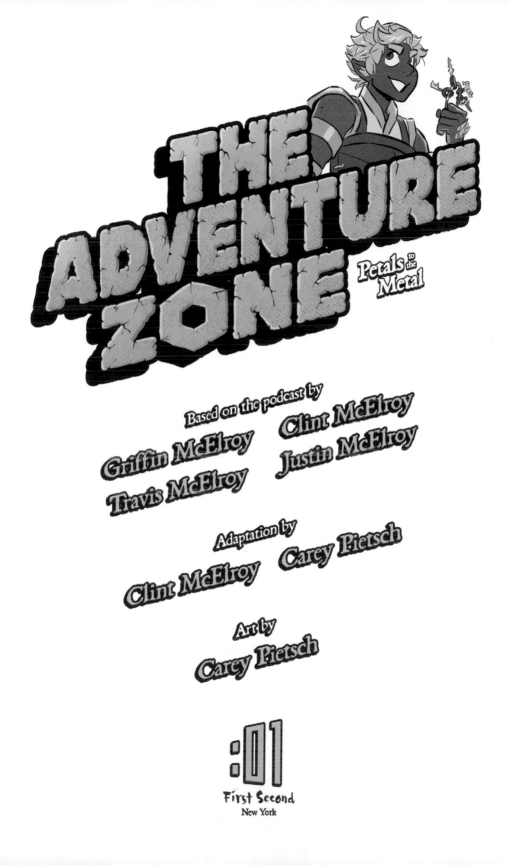

THE ADVENTURE ZONE

Petals to the Metal

Based on the podcast by

Griffin McElroy   Clint McElroy
Travis McElroy   Justin McElroy

Adaptation by

Clint McElroy   Carey Pietsch

Art by

Carey Pietsch

:01

First Second
New York

First Second

Text copyright © 2020 by Clint McElroy, Griffin McElroy, Justin McElroy, and Travis McElroy
Illustrations copyright © 2020 by Carey Pietsch

Letterer: Tess Stone
Flatters: Megan Brennan, Ensley Chau, Leigh Davis,
Suzanne Geary, Luke Healy, Hien Pham, and Cassandra Tassoni
Authenticity Readers: Mey Rude and Kori Michele Handwerker
Game board photo copyright © 2020 by Megan Brennan and Lisa Aurigemma
Fan art gallery copyright © 2020 by (respectively):
Andrew Soman
Angela Tong
April Leong
Emily K. Smith
Julia Maddalina
Gabriela Epstein
Kory Bing
Mhuyo
Myra Hild
Nathanael Whale
Nick Leerie
Pati Ćmak
Alexandra Maria Flis

Published by First Second
First Second is an imprint of Roaring Brook Press,
a division of Holtzbrinck Publishing Holdings Limited Partnership
120 Broadway, New York, NY 10271

Don't miss your next favorite book from First Second!
For the latest updates go to firstsecondnewsletter.com and sign up for our newsletter.

Library of Congress Control Number: 2019938061

ISBN: 978-1-250-23263-2 (Paperback)
ISBN: 978-1-250-23262-5 (Hardcover)
ISBN: 978-1-250-76215-3 (Special Edition)
ISBN: 978-1-250-76684-7 (Special Edition)
ISBN: 978-1-250-76216-0 (Special Edition)

Our books may be purchased in bulk for promotional, educational, or business use.
Please contact your local bookseller or the Macmillan Corporate and Premium Sales Department
at (800) 221-7945 ext. 5442 or by email at MacmillanSpecialMarkets@macmillan.com.

First edition, 2020
Edited by Calista Brill and Alison Wilgus
Cover design by Molly Johanson and Carey Pietsch
Series design by Andrew Arnold
Interior book design by Molly Johanson
Printed in China

Penciled with a 2B pencil-style tool in Procreate. Inked with a brush-style
digital nib in Clip Studio Paint and colored digitally in Photoshop.

Paperback: 10 9 8 7 6 5 4 3
Hardcover: 10 9 8 7 6 5 4 3 2 1

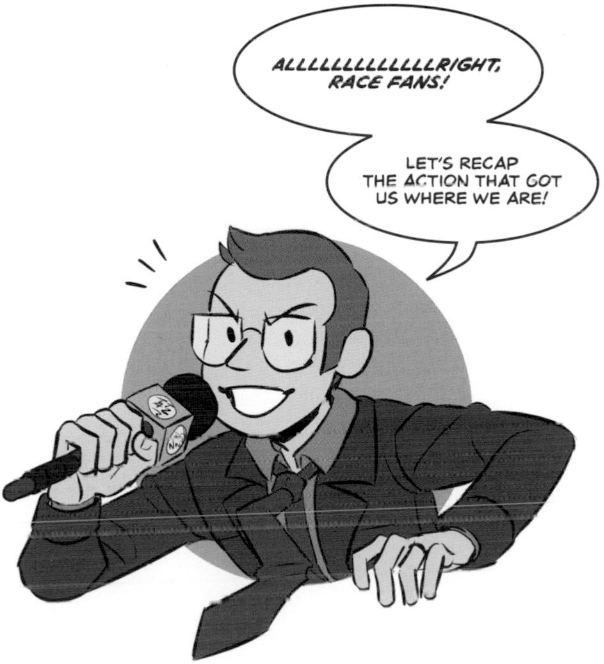
ALLLLLLLLLLLLLLLRIGHT, RACE FANS!
LET'S RECAP THE ACTION THAT GOT US WHERE WE ARE!

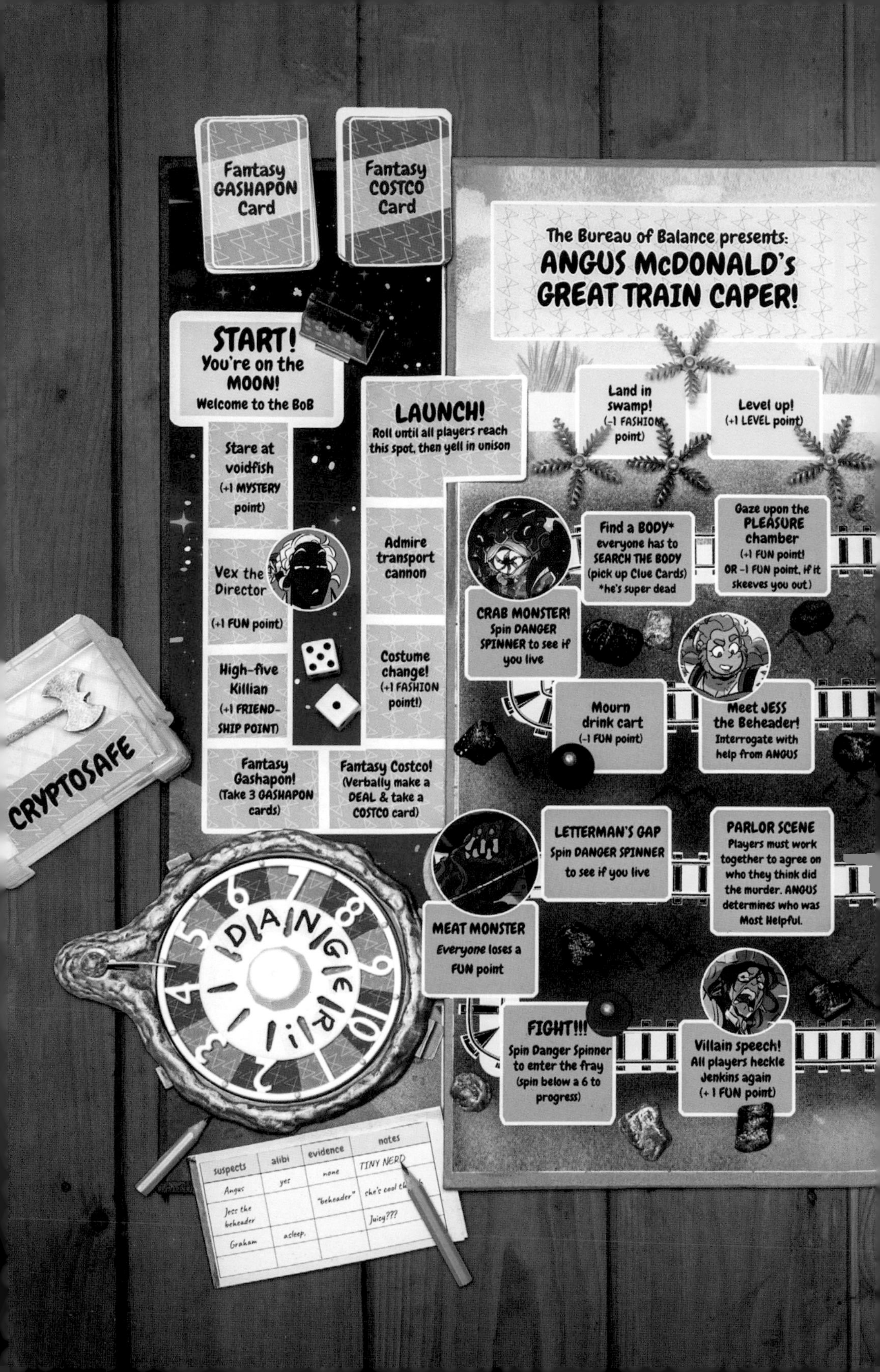

Fantasy GASHAPON Card
Fantasy COSTCO Card
The Bureau of Balance presents:
ANGUS McDONALD's GREAT TRAIN CAPER!
START! You're on the MOON! Welcome to the BoB
Stare at voidfish (+1 MYSTERY point)
Vex the Director (+1 FUN point)
High-five Killian (+1 FRIEND-SHIP POINT)
Fantasy Gashapon! (Take 3 GASHAPON cards)
Fantasy Costco! (Verbally make a DEAL & take a COSTCO card)
LAUNCH! Roll until all players reach this spot, then yell in unison
Admire transport cannon
Costume change! (+1 FASHION point!)
Land in swamp! (-1 FASHION point)
Level up! (+1 LEVEL point)
Find a BODY* everyone has to SEARCH THE BODY (pick up Clue Cards) *he's super dead
Gaze upon the PLEASURE chamber (+1 FUN point! OR -1 FUN point, if it skeeves you out)
CRAB MONSTER! Spin DANGER SPINNER to see if you live
Mourn drink cart (-1 FUN point)
Meet JESS the Beheader! Interrogate with help from ANGUS
LETTERMAN'S GAP Spin DANGER SPINNER to see if you live
PARLOR SCENE Players must work together to agree on who they think did the murder. ANGUS determines who was Most Helpful.
MEAT MONSTER Everyone loses a FUN point
FIGHT!!! Spin Danger Spinner to enter the fray (spin below a 6 to progress)
Villain speech! All players heckle Jenkins again (+1 FUN point)
CRYPTOSAFE
DANGER!
suspects | alibi | evidence | notes
Angus | yes | none | TINY NERD
Jess the beheader | | "beheader" | she's cool th
Graham | asleep. | | Juicy???

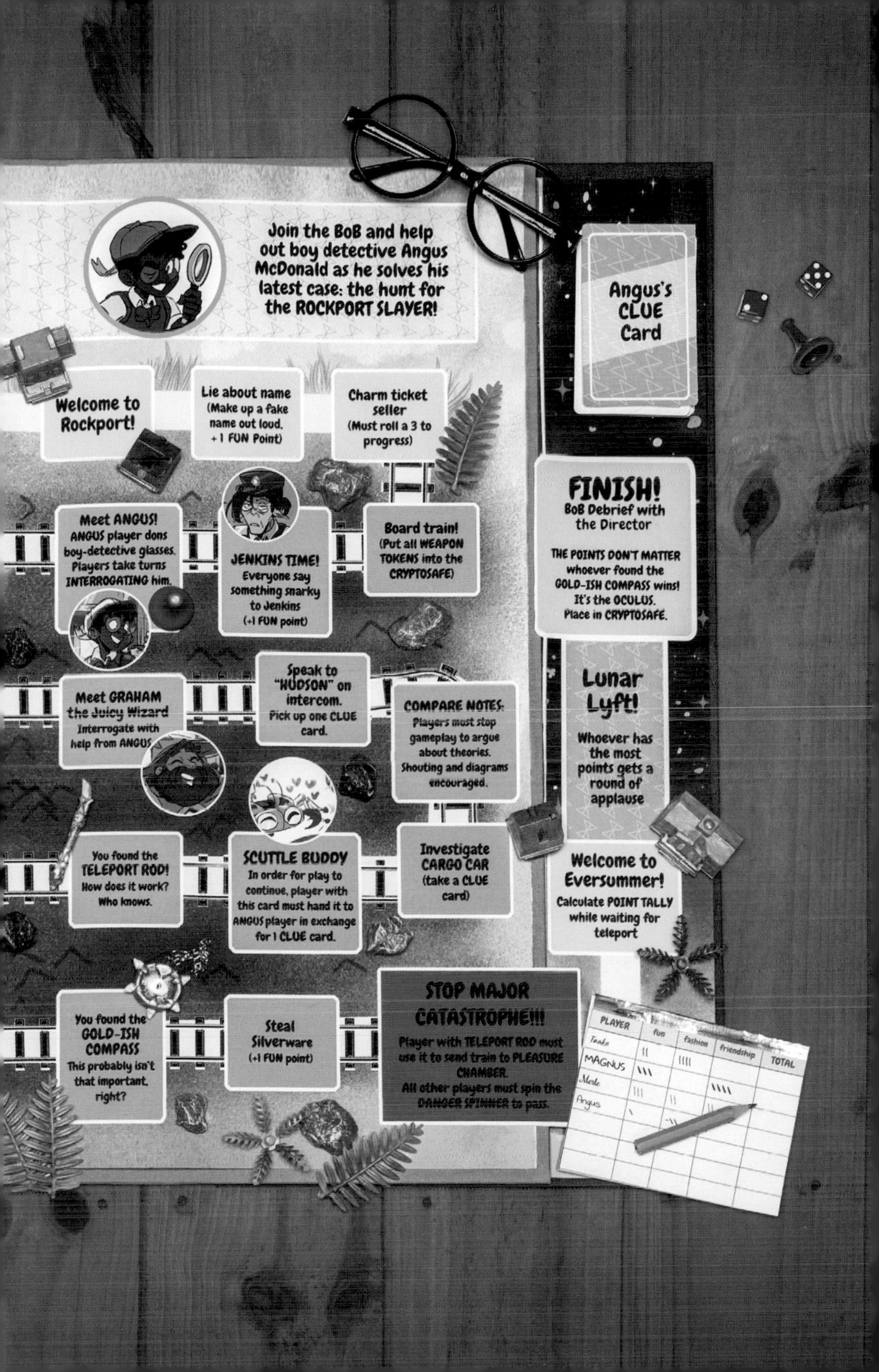
Join the BoB and help out boy detective Angus McDonald as he solves his latest case: the hunt for the ROCKPORT SLAYER!
Angus's CLUE Card
Welcome to Rockport!
Lie about name (Make up a fake name out loud, +1 FUN Point)
Charm ticket seller (Must roll a 3 to progress)
Meet ANGUS! ANGUS player dons boy-detective glasses. Players take turns INTERROGATING him.
JENKINS TIME! Everyone say something snarky to Jenkins (+1 FUN point)
Board train! (Put all WEAPON TOKENS into the CRYPTOSAFE)
FINISH! BoB Debrief with the Director
THE POINTS DON'T MATTER whoever found the GOLD-ISH COMPASS wins! It's the OCULUS. Place in CRYPTOSAFE.
Meet GRAHAM the Juicy Wizard Interrogate with help from ANGUS
Speak to "HUDSON" on intercom. Pick up one CLUE card.
COMPARE NOTES: Players must stop gameplay to argue about theories. Shouting and diagrams encouraged.
Lunar Lyft! Whoever has the most points gets a round of applause
You found the TELEPORT ROD! How does it work? Who knows.
SCUTTLE BUDDY In order for play to continue, player with this card must hand it to ANGUS player in exchange for 1 CLUE card.
Investigate CARGO CAR (take a CLUE card)
Welcome to Eversummer! Calculate POINT TALLY while waiting for teleport
You found the GOLD-ISH COMPASS This probably isn't that important, right?
Steal Silverware (+1 FUN point)
STOP MAJOR CATASTROPHE!!! Player with TELEPORT ROD must use it to send train to PLEASURE CHAMBER. All other players must spin the DANGER SPINNER to pass.
PLAYER
fun
fashion
friendship
TOTAL
Taako
MAGNUS
Merle
Angus

Chapter 1

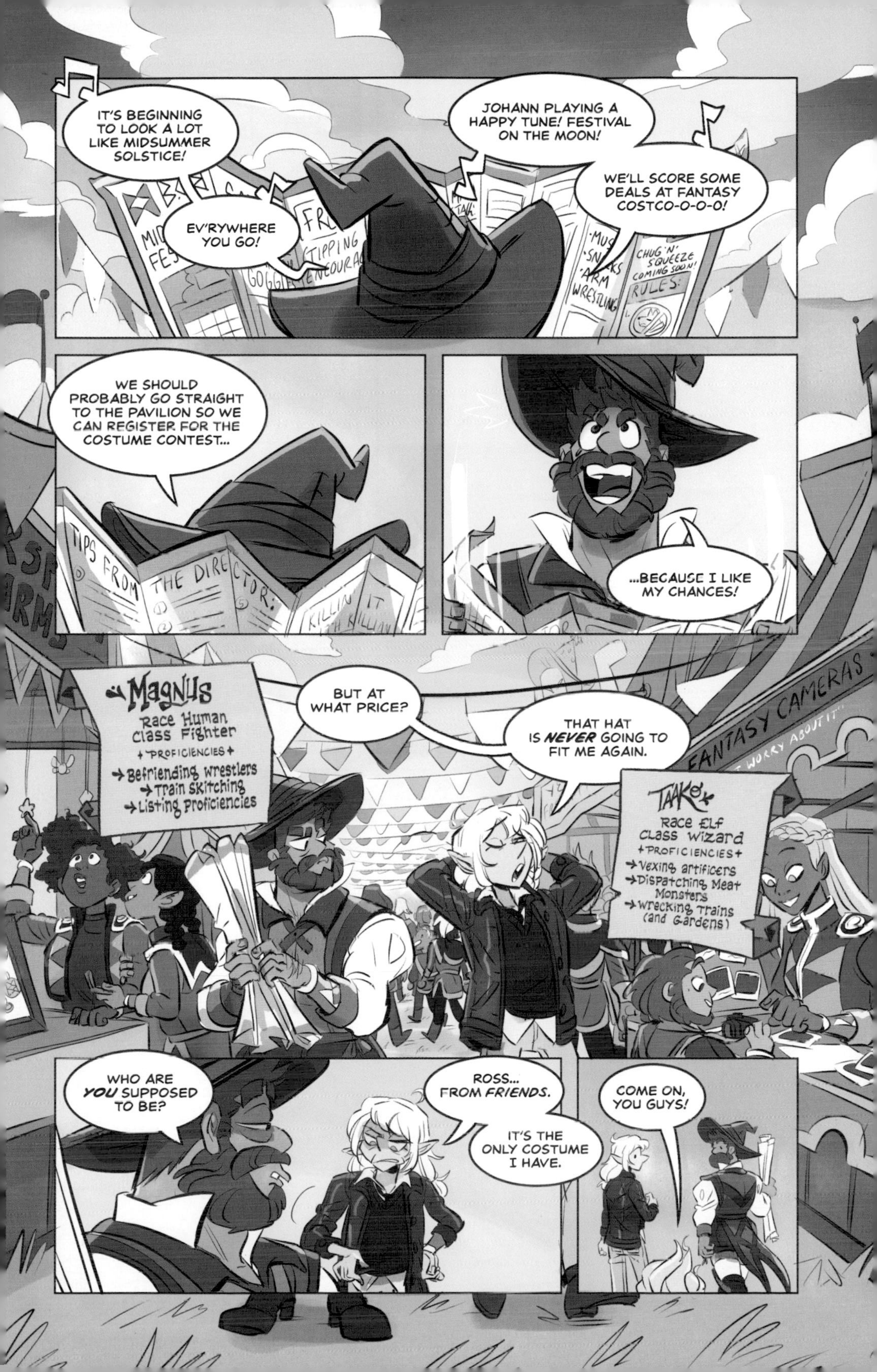
IT'S BEGINNING TO LOOK A LOT LIKE MIDSUMMER SOLSTICE!
EV'RYWHERE YOU GO!
JOHANN PLAYING A HAPPY TUNE! FESTIVAL ON THE MOON!
WE'LL SCORE SOME DEALS AT FANTASY COSTCO-O-O-O!
CHUG 'N' SQUEEZE COMING SOON!
RULES:
WE SHOULD PROBABLY GO STRAIGHT TO THE PAVILION SO WE CAN REGISTER FOR THE COSTUME CONTEST...
TIPS FROM THE DIRECTOR:
...BECAUSE I LIKE MY CHANCES!
Magnus
Race Human
Class Fighter
Proficiencies
Befriending wrestlers
Train Skitching
Listing Proficiencies
BUT AT WHAT PRICE?
THAT HAT IS NEVER GOING TO FIT ME AGAIN.
FANTASY CAMERAS
Taako
Race Elf
Class Wizard
Proficiencies
Vexing artificers
Dispatching Meat Monsters
Wrecking Trains (and Gardens)
WHO ARE YOU SUPPOSED TO BE?
ROSS... FROM FRIENDS.
IT'S THE ONLY COSTUME I HAVE.
COME ON, YOU GUYS!

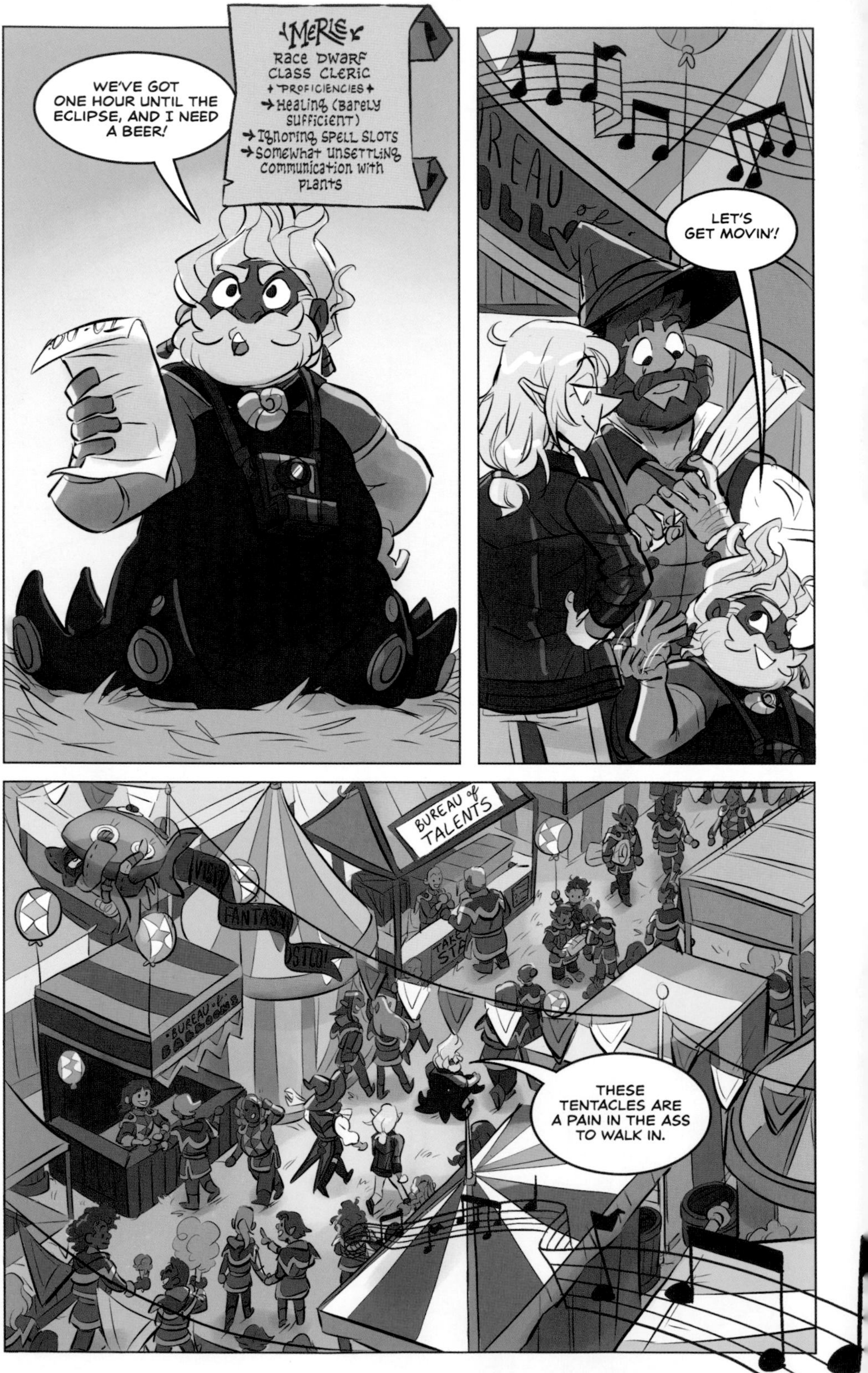
WE'VE GOT ONE HOUR UNTIL THE ECLIPSE, AND I NEED A BEER!
MERLE
Race Dwarf
Class Cleric
PROFICIENCIES
→Healing (barely sufficient)
→Ignoring spell slots
→Somewhat unsettling communication with plants
LET'S GET MOVIN'!
BUREAU of TALENTS
FANTASY
BUREAU of BALLOONS
THESE TENTACLES ARE A PAIN IN THE ASS TO WALK IN.

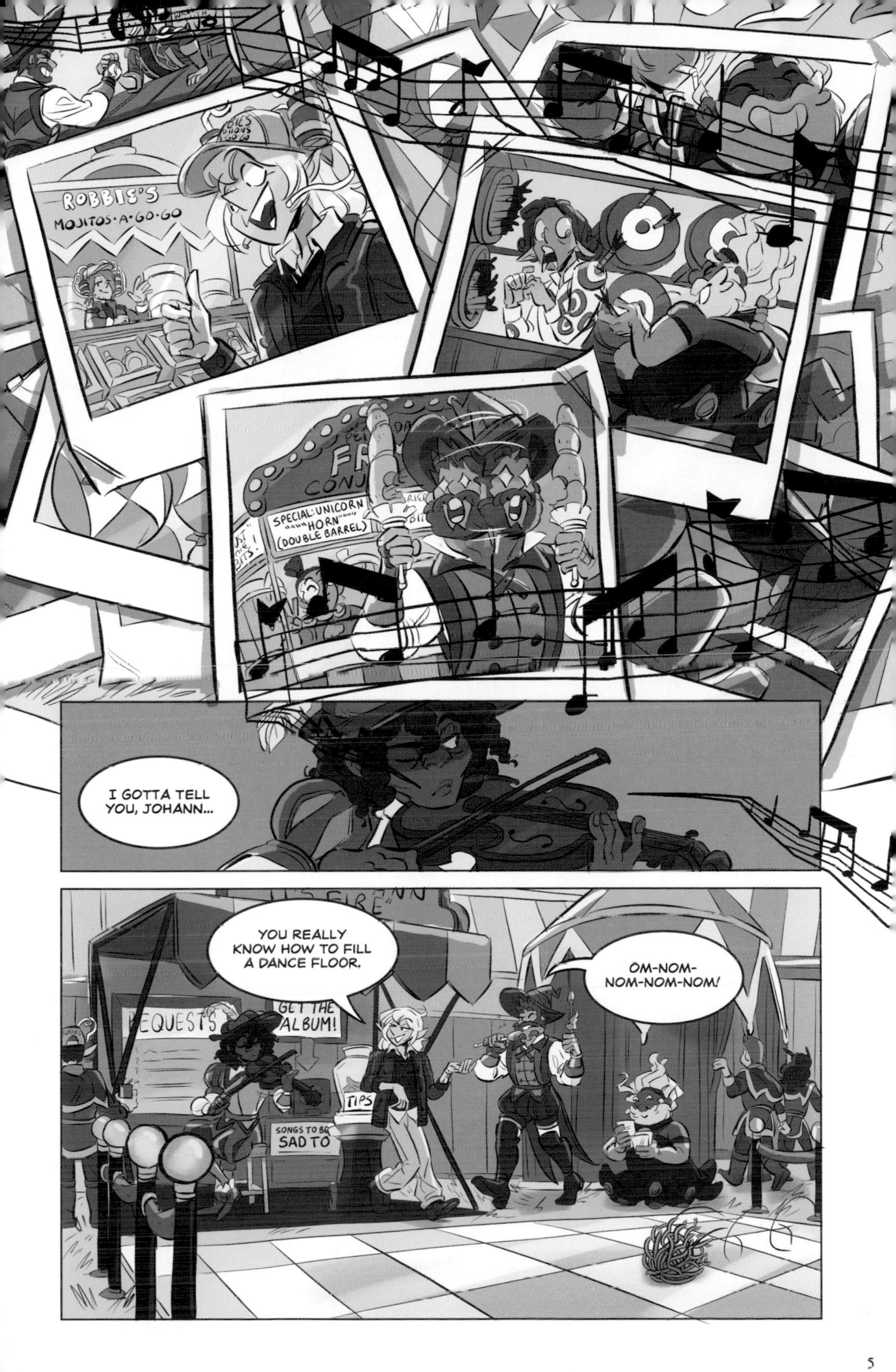
ROBBIE'S
MOJITOS·A·GO·GO
SPECIAL: UNICORN "HORN" (DOUBLE BARREL)
I GOTTA TELL YOU, JOHANN...
YOU REALLY KNOW HOW TO FILL A DANCE FLOOR.
OM-NOM-NOM-NOM-NOM!
REQUESTS
GET THE ALBUM!
TIPS
SONGS TO BE SAD TO

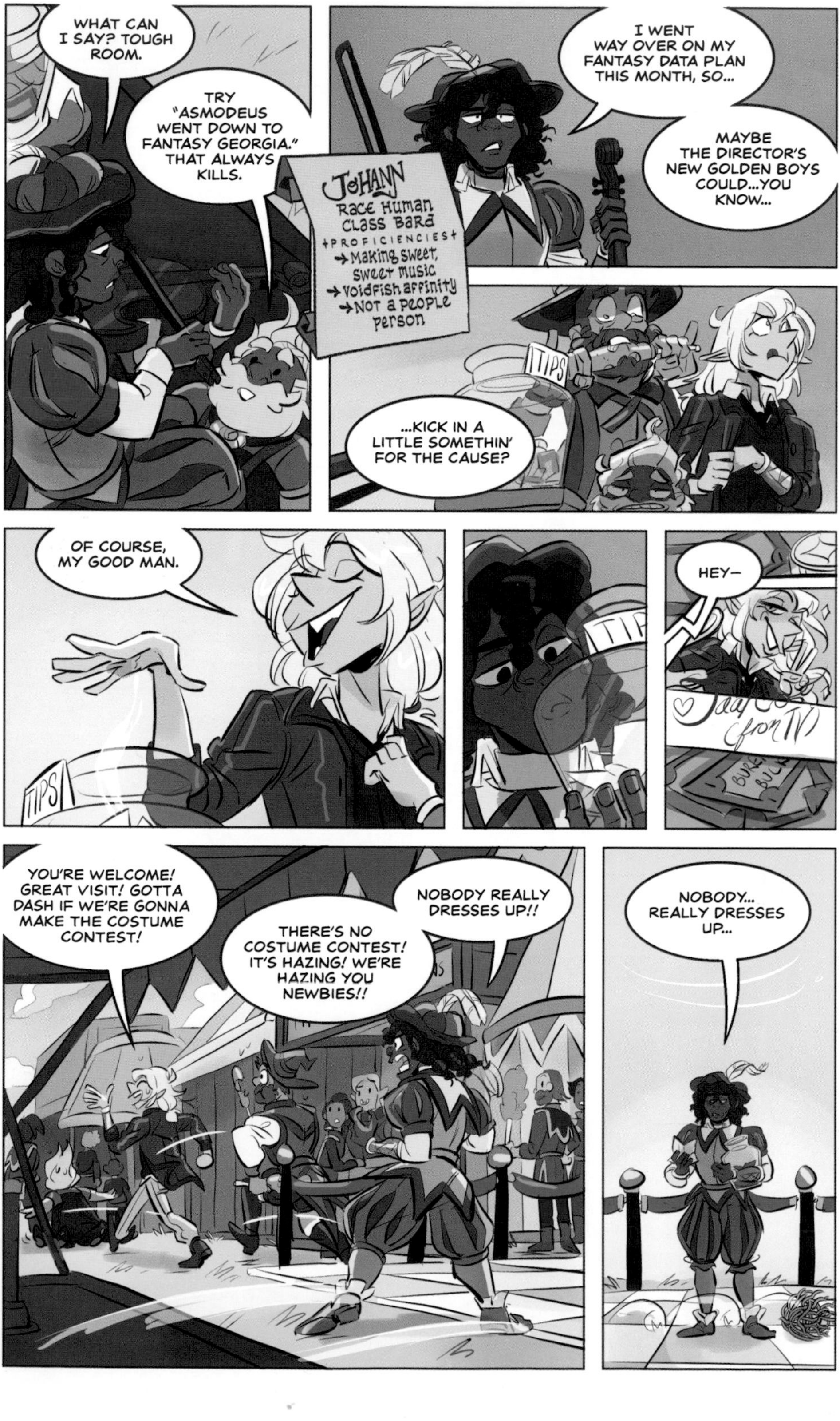
WHAT CAN I SAY? TOUGH ROOM.
TRY "ASMODEUS WENT DOWN TO FANTASY GEORGIA." THAT ALWAYS KILLS.
Johann
Race Human
Class Bard
PROFICIENCIES
→ Making sweet, sweet music
→ Voidfish affinity
→ Not a people person
I WENT WAY OVER ON MY FANTASY DATA PLAN THIS MONTH, SO...
MAYBE THE DIRECTOR'S NEW GOLDEN BOYS COULD...YOU KNOW...
TIPS
...KICK IN A LITTLE SOMETHIN' FOR THE CAUSE?
OF COURSE, MY GOOD MAN.
TIPS
TIPS
HEY—
YOU'RE WELCOME! GREAT VISIT! GOTTA DASH IF WE'RE GONNA MAKE THE COSTUME CONTEST!
THERE'S NO COSTUME CONTEST! IT'S HAZING! WE'RE HAZING YOU NEWBIES!!
NOBODY REALLY DRESSES UP!!
NOBODY... REALLY DRESSES UP...

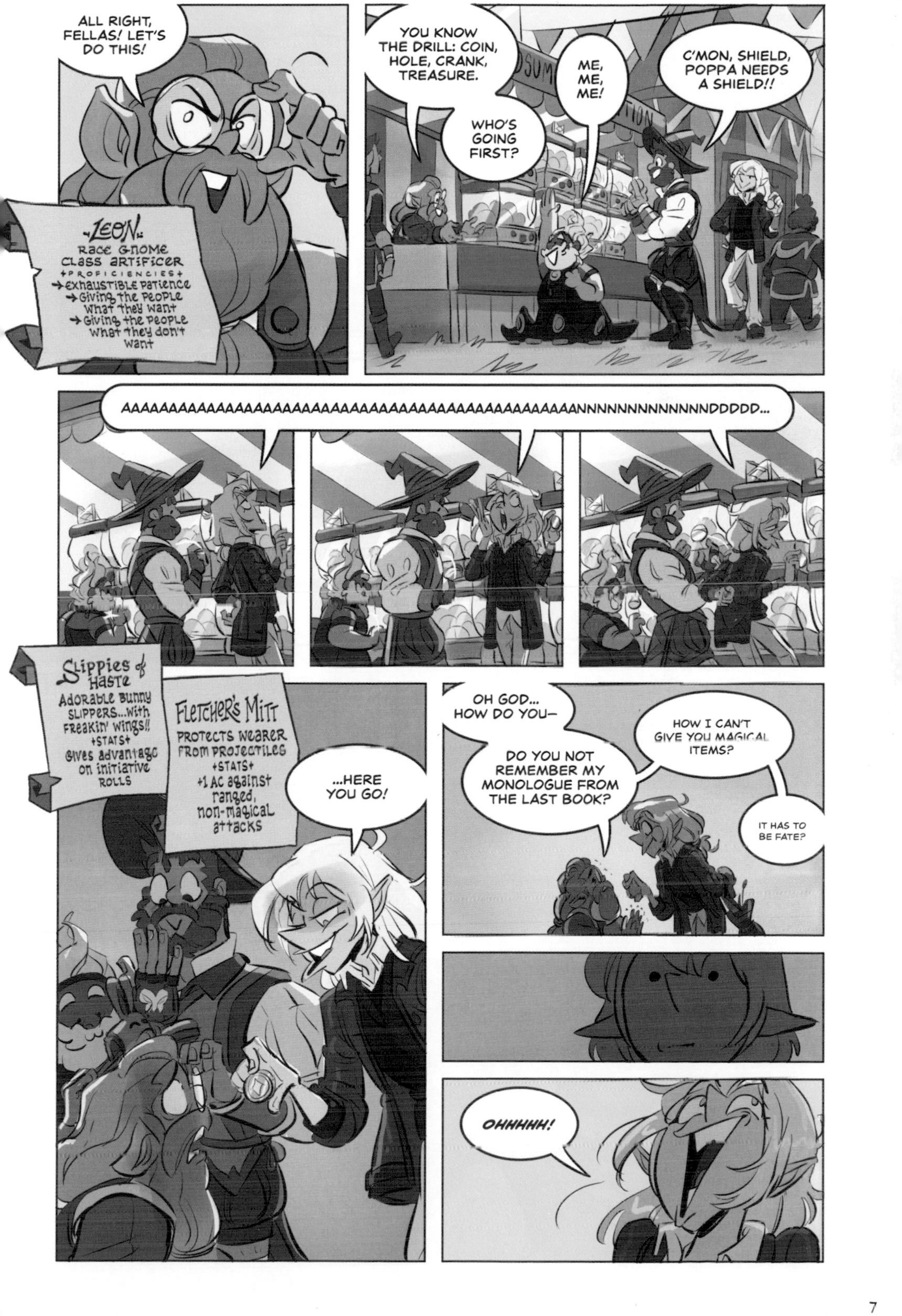
ALL RIGHT, FELLAS! LET'S DO THIS!
LEON
RACE GNOME
CLASS ARTIFICER
PROFICIENCIES
→EXHAUSTIBLE PATIENCE
→GIVING THE PEOPLE WHAT THEY WANT
→GIVING THE PEOPLE WHAT THEY DON'T WANT
YOU KNOW THE DRILL: COIN, HOLE, CRANK, TREASURE.
WHO'S GOING FIRST?
ME, ME, ME!
C'MON, SHIELD, POPPA NEEDS A SHIELD!!
AAAAAAAAAAAAAAAAAAAAAAAAAAAAAAAAAAAAAAAAAAAAAANNNNNNNNNNNNDDDDD...
Slippies of Haste
Adorable Bunny Slippers...with Freakin' Wings!!
STATS
Gives advantage on initiative rolls
FLETCHER'S MITT
PROTECTS WEARER FROM PROJECTILES
STATS
+1 AC against ranged, non-magical attacks
...HERE YOU GO!
OH GOD... HOW DO YOU—
DO YOU NOT REMEMBER MY MONOLOGUE FROM THE LAST BOOK?
HOW I CAN'T GIVE YOU MAGICAL ITEMS?
IT HAS TO BE FATE?
OHHHHH!

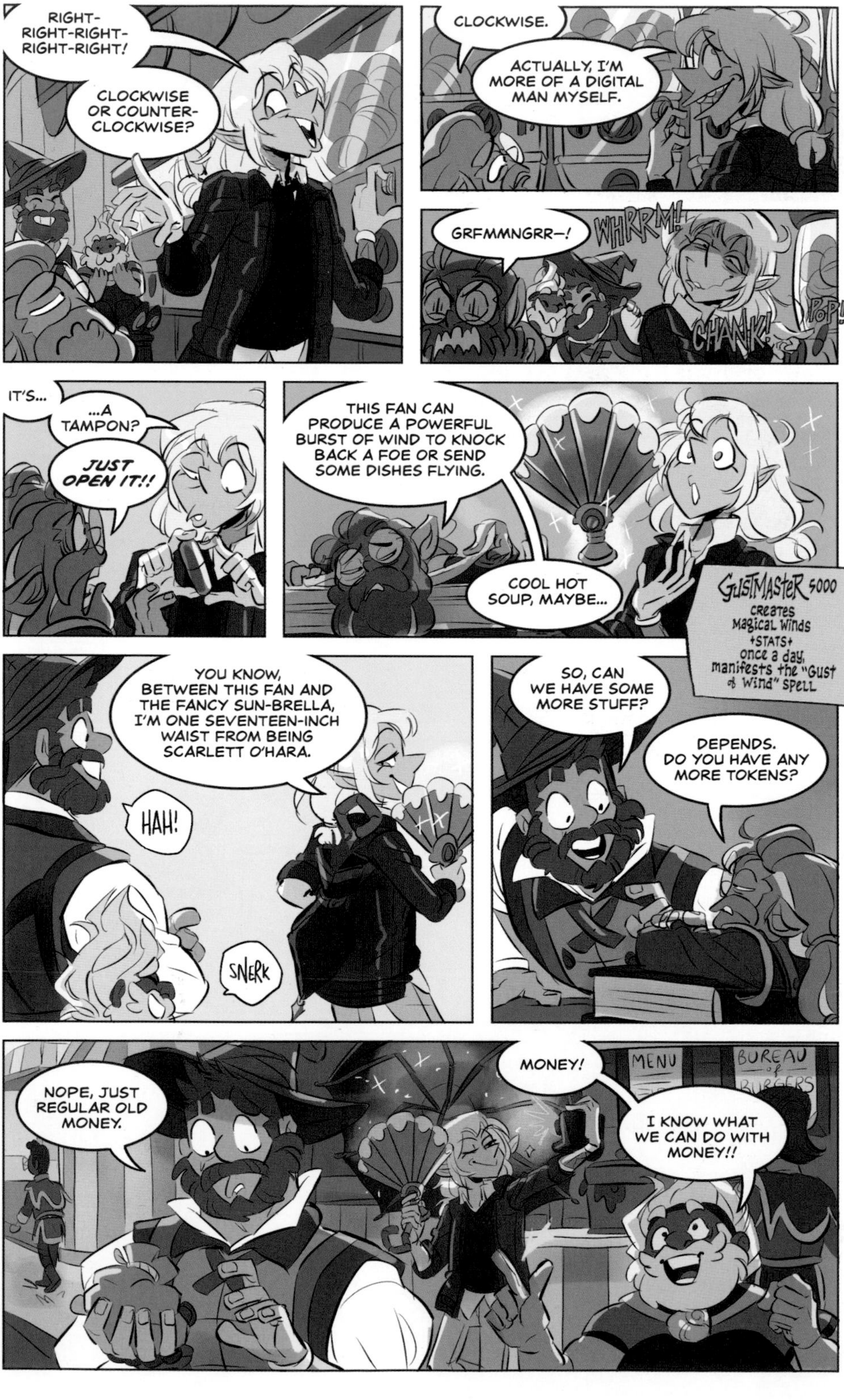
RIGHT-RIGHT-RIGHT-RIGHT-RIGHT!
CLOCKWISE OR COUNTER-CLOCKWISE?
CLOCKWISE.
ACTUALLY, I'M MORE OF A DIGITAL MAN MYSELF.
GRFMMNGRR–!
WHRRM!
CHANK!
POP!
IT'S...
...A TAMPON?
JUST OPEN IT!!
THIS FAN CAN PRODUCE A POWERFUL BURST OF WIND TO KNOCK BACK A FOE OR SEND SOME DISHES FLYING.
COOL HOT SOUP, MAYBE...
GUSTMASTER 5000
creates Magical winds
+STATS+
once a day, manifests the "Gust of Wind" spell
YOU KNOW, BETWEEN THIS FAN AND THE FANCY SUN-BRELLA, I'M ONE SEVENTEEN-INCH WAIST FROM BEING SCARLETT O'HARA.
HAH!
SNERK
SO, CAN WE HAVE SOME MORE STUFF?
DEPENDS. DO YOU HAVE ANY MORE TOKENS?
NOPE, JUST REGULAR OLD MONEY.
MONEY!
I KNOW WHAT WE CAN DO WITH MONEY!!
MENU
BUREAU of BURGERS

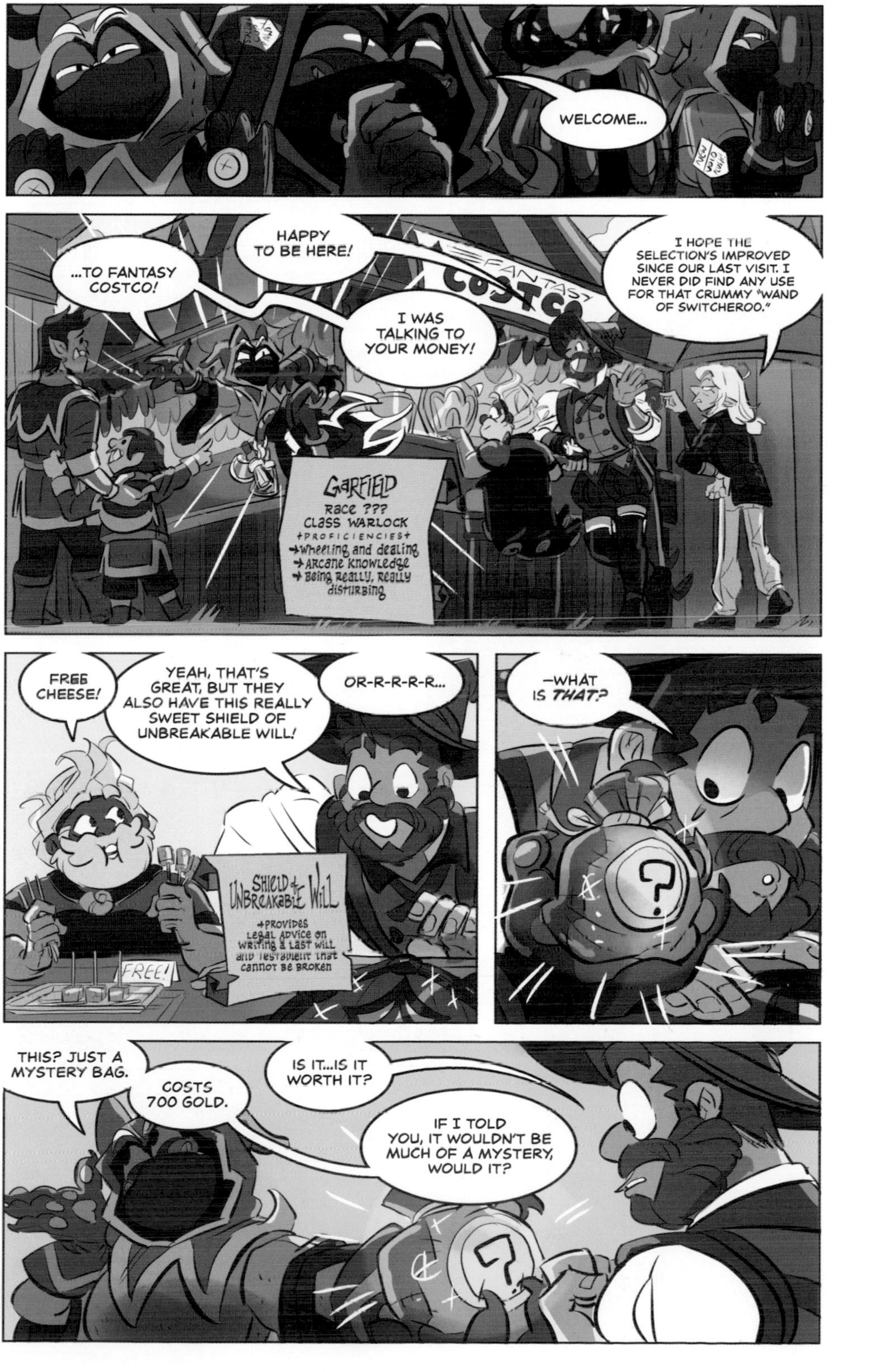
WELCOME...
...TO FANTASY COSTCO!
HAPPY TO BE HERE!
I WAS TALKING TO YOUR MONEY!
I HOPE THE SELECTION'S IMPROVED SINCE OUR LAST VISIT. I NEVER DID FIND ANY USE FOR THAT CRUMMY "WAND OF SWITCHEROO."
FANTASY COSTCO
GARFIELD
Race ???
Class Warlock
+PROFICIENCIES+
→Wheeling and dealing
→Arcane knowledge
→Being really, really disturbing
FREE CHEESE!
YEAH, THAT'S GREAT, BUT THEY ALSO HAVE THIS REALLY SWEET SHIELD OF UNBREAKABLE WILL!
OR-R-R-R-R...
SHIELD of UNBREAKABLE WILL
+Provides legal advice on writing a last will and testament that cannot be broken
FREE!
—WHAT IS *THAT?*
THIS? JUST A MYSTERY BAG.
COSTS 700 GOLD.
IS IT...IS IT WORTH IT?
IF I TOLD YOU, IT WOULDN'T BE MUCH OF A MYSTERY, WOULD IT?

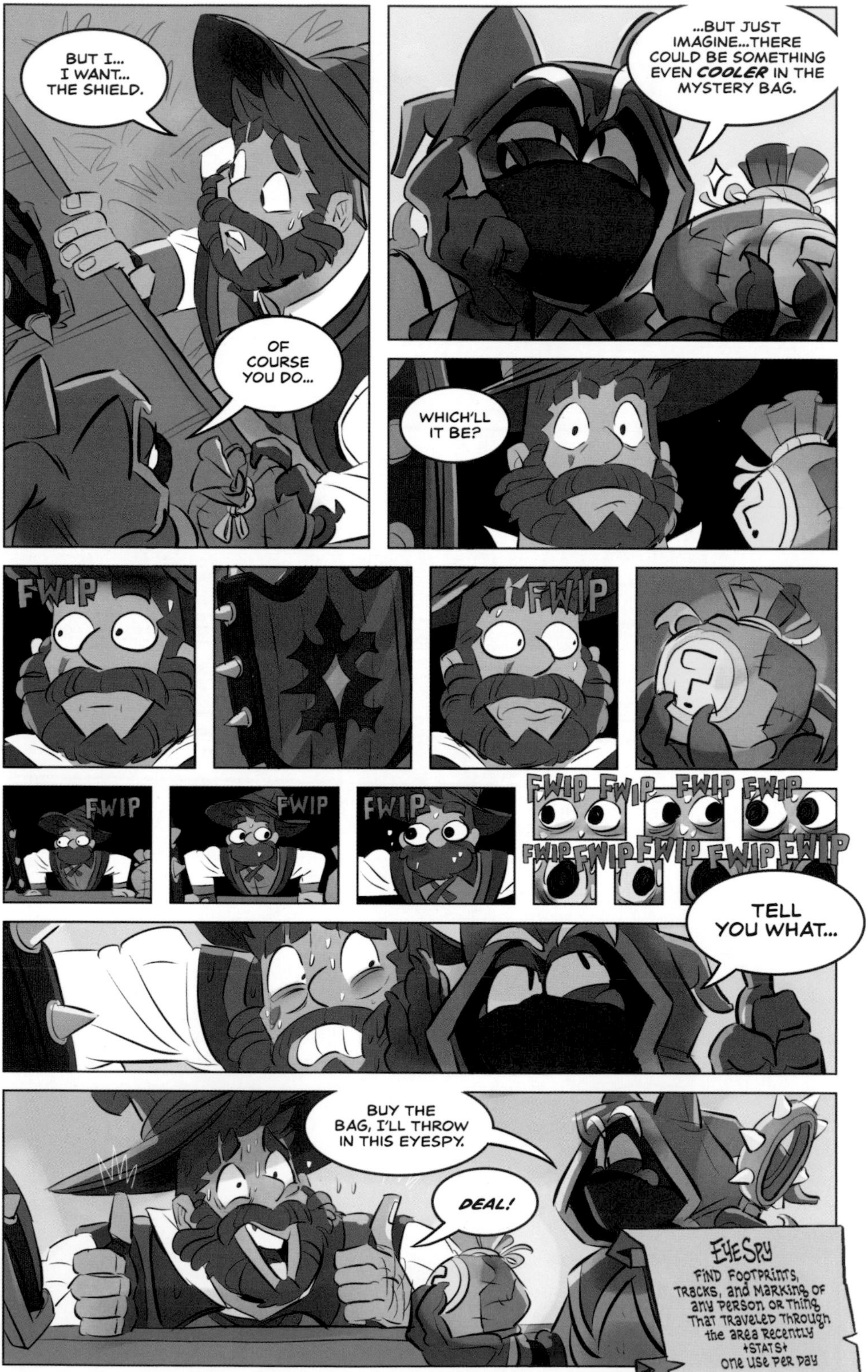
BUT I...
I WANT...
THE SHIELD.
OF COURSE YOU DO...
...BUT JUST IMAGINE...THERE COULD BE SOMETHING EVEN COOLER IN THE MYSTERY BAG.
WHICH'LL IT BE?
FWIP
FWIP
FWIP
FWIP
FWIP
FWIP FWIP FWIP FWIP
FWIP FWIP FWIP FWIP FWIP
TELL YOU WHAT...
BUY THE BAG, I'LL THROW IN THIS EYESPY.
DEAL!
EYESPY
FIND FOOTPRINTS, TRACKS, AND MARKINGS OF ANY PERSON OR THING THAT TRAVELED THROUGH THE AREA RECENTLY
+STATS+
ONE USE PER DAY

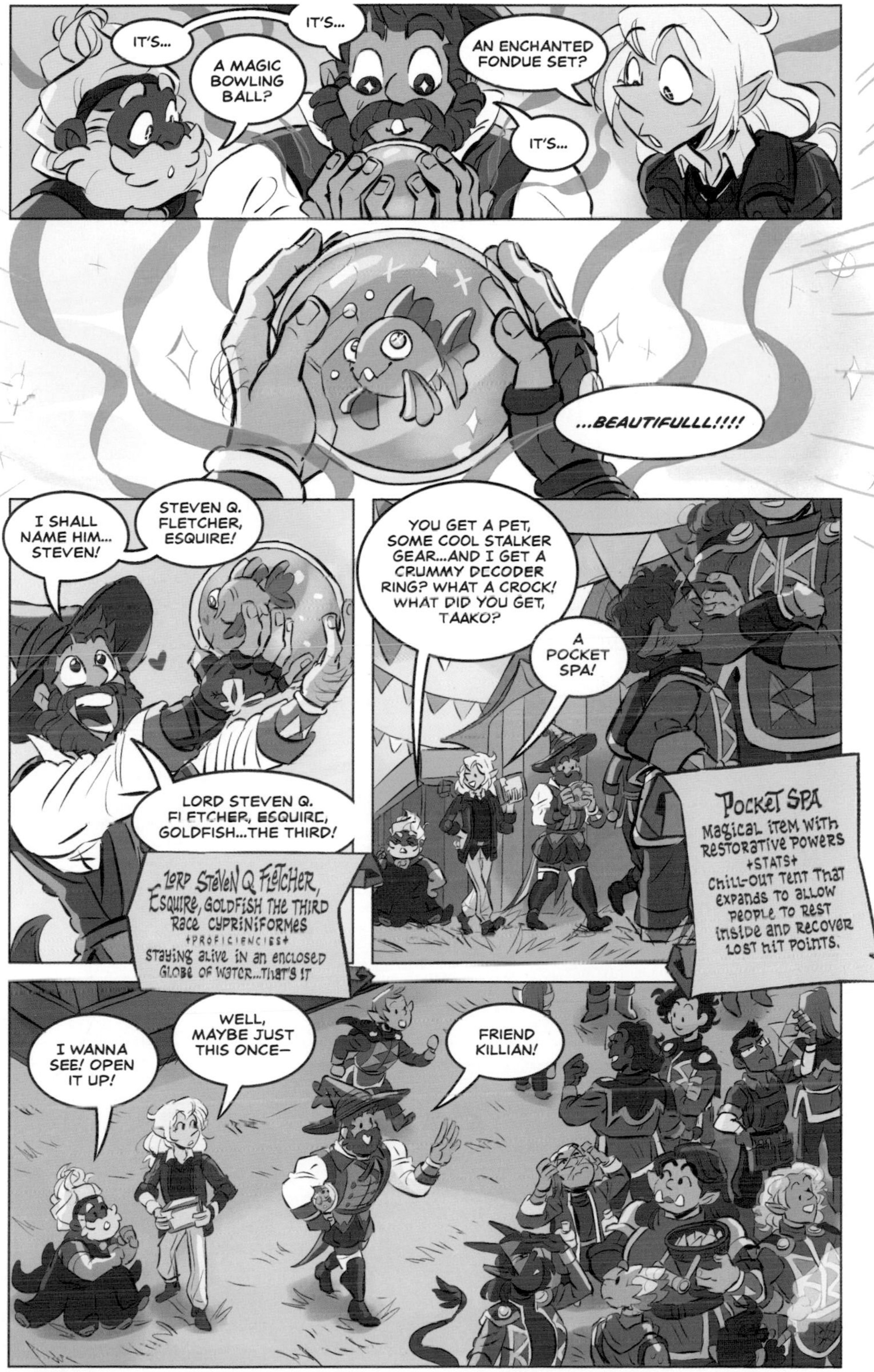

IT'S...
A MAGIC BOWLING BALL?
IT'S...
AN ENCHANTED FONDUE SET?
IT'S...
...BEAUTIFULLL!!!!
I SHALL NAME HIM... STEVEN!
STEVEN Q. FLETCHER, ESQUIRE!
LORD STEVEN Q. FLETCHER, ESQUIRE, GOLDFISH...THE THIRD!
LORD STEVEN Q FLETCHER, ESQUIRE, GOLDFISH THE THIRD
RACE CYPRINIFORMES
+PROFICIENCIES+
STAYING ALIVE IN AN ENCLOSED GLOBE OF WATER...THAT'S IT
YOU GET A PET, SOME COOL STALKER GEAR...AND I GET A CRUMMY DECODER RING? WHAT A CROCK! WHAT DID YOU GET, TAAKO?
A POCKET SPA!
POCKET SPA
MAGICAL ITEM WITH RESTORATIVE POWERS
+STATS+
CHILL-OUT TENT THAT EXPANDS TO ALLOW PEOPLE TO REST INSIDE AND RECOVER LOST HIT POINTS.
I WANNA SEE! OPEN IT UP!
WELL, MAYBE JUST THIS ONCE—
FRIEND KILLIAN!

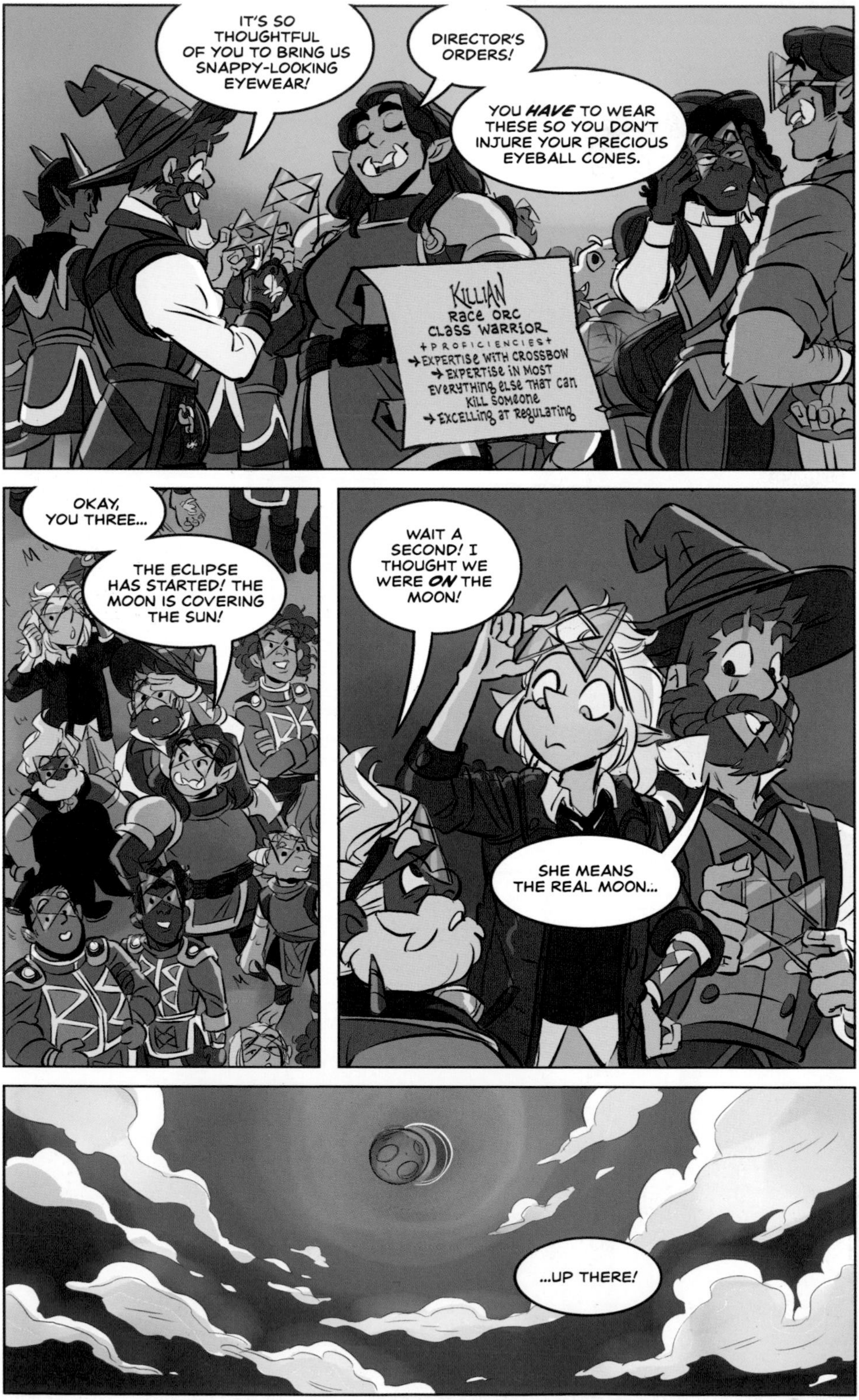
IT'S SO THOUGHTFUL OF YOU TO BRING US SNAPPY-LOOKING EYEWEAR!
DIRECTOR'S ORDERS!
YOU **HAVE** TO WEAR THESE SO YOU DON'T INJURE YOUR PRECIOUS EYEBALL CONES.
KILLIAN
Race ORC
CLASS WARRIOR
+PROFICIENCIES+
→EXPERTISE WITH CROSSBOW
→EXPERTISE IN MOST EVERYTHING ELSE THAT CAN KILL SOMEONE
→EXCELLING AT REGULATING
OKAY, YOU THREE...
THE ECLIPSE HAS STARTED! THE MOON IS COVERING THE SUN!
WAIT A SECOND! I THOUGHT WE WERE **ON** THE MOON!
SHE MEANS THE REAL MOON...
...UP THERE!

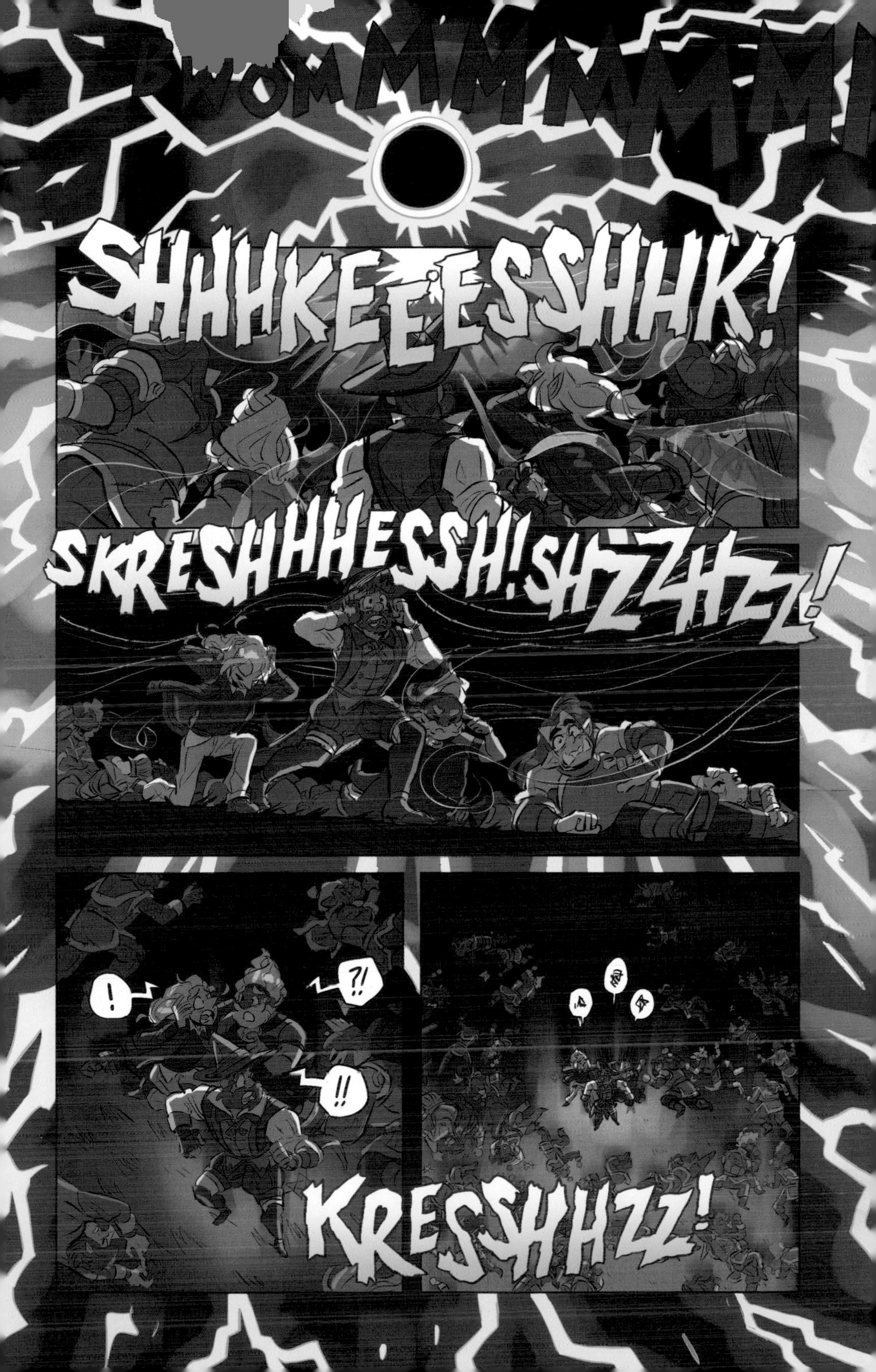
BWOMMMMMMMMM
SHHHKEEESSHHK!
SKRESHHHESSH! SHZZHZZ!
!
?!
!!
KRESSHZZ!

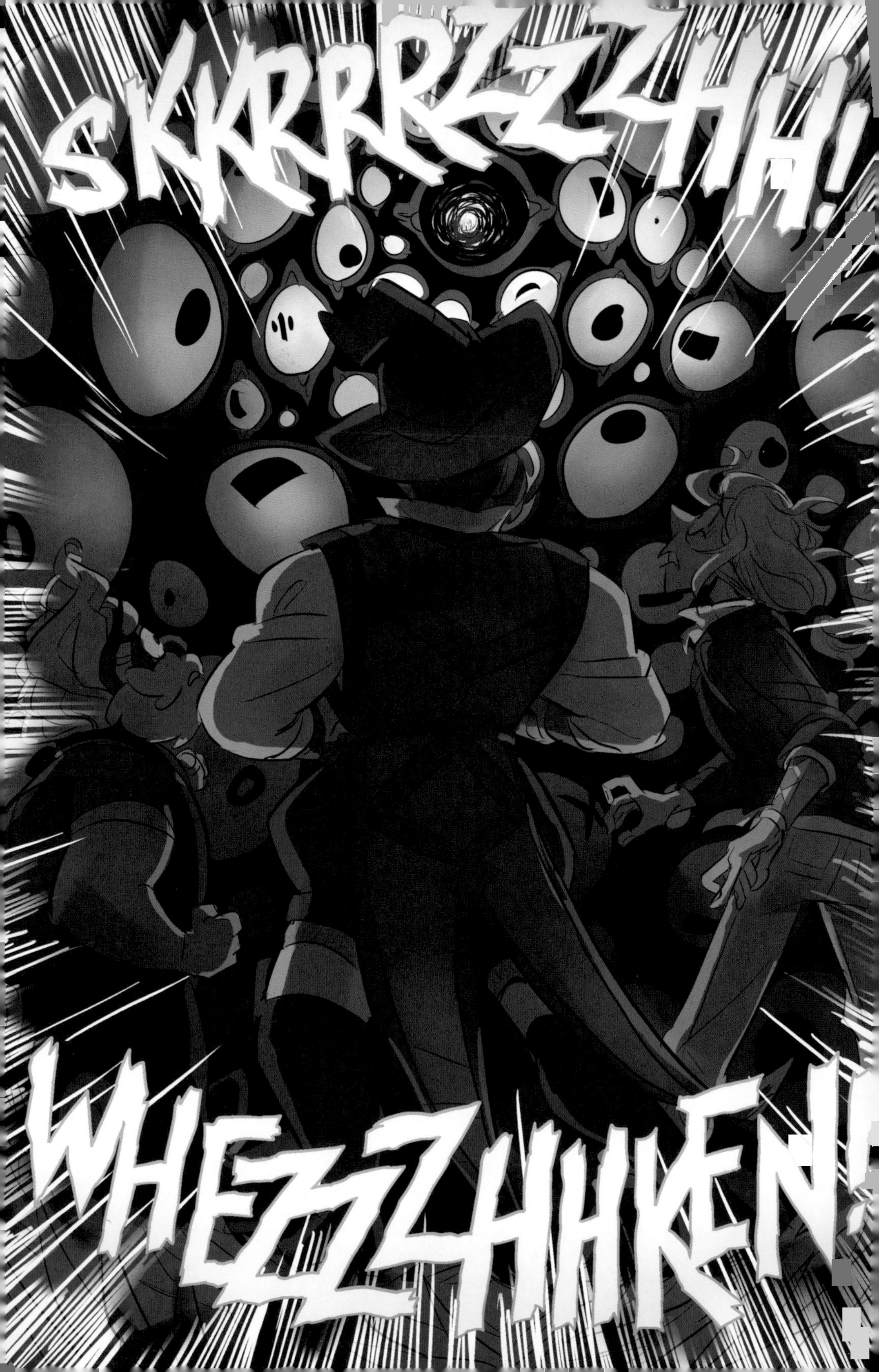
SKRRRZZZHH!
WHEZZZHHKEN!

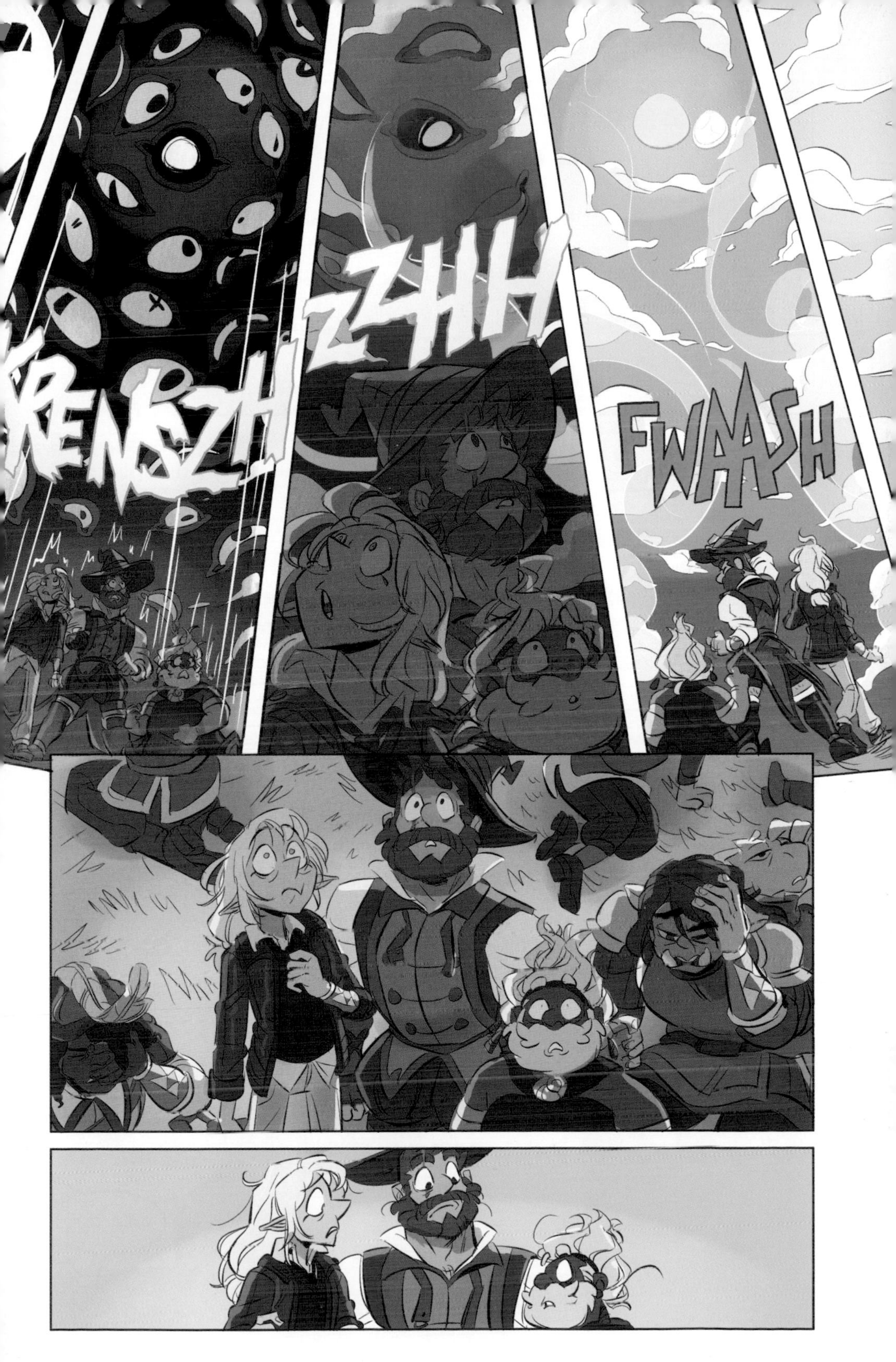
FRENSZH
ZZHH
FWAAASH

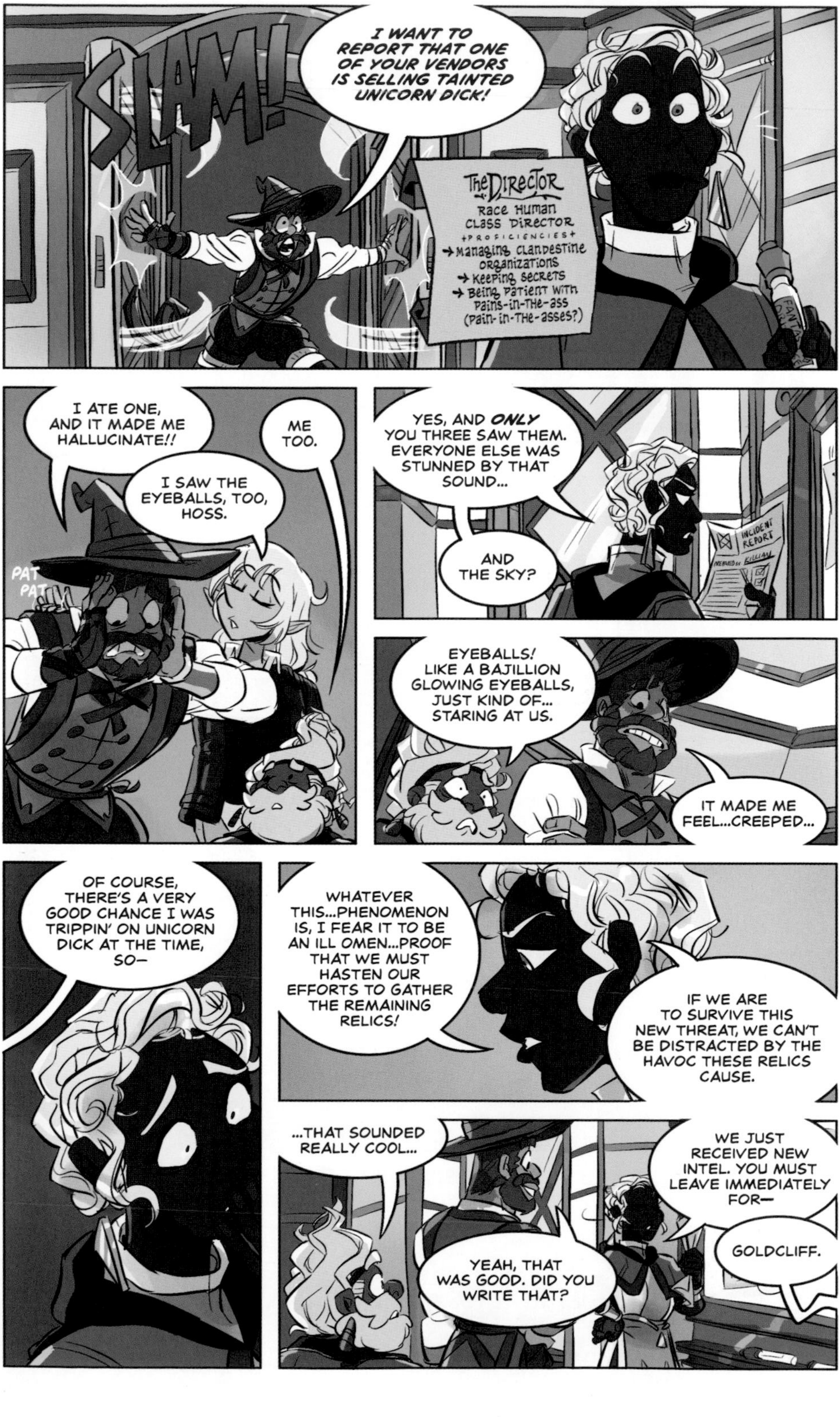
SLAM!
I WANT TO REPORT THAT ONE OF YOUR VENDORS IS SELLING TAINTED UNICORN DICK!
The Director
Race Human
Class Director
Proficiencies
→ Managing clandestine organizations
→ Keeping secrets
→ Being patient with pains-in-the-ass (pain-in-the-asses?)
I ATE ONE, AND IT MADE ME HALLUCINATE!!
ME TOO.
I SAW THE EYEBALLS, TOO, HOSS.
PAT PAT
YES, AND ONLY YOU THREE SAW THEM. EVERYONE ELSE WAS STUNNED BY THAT SOUND...
AND THE SKY?
INCIDENT REPORT
EYEBALLS! LIKE A BAJILLION GLOWING EYEBALLS, JUST KIND OF... STARING AT US.
IT MADE ME FEEL...CREEPED...
OF COURSE, THERE'S A VERY GOOD CHANCE I WAS TRIPPIN' ON UNICORN DICK AT THE TIME, SO—
WHATEVER THIS...PHENOMENON IS, I FEAR IT TO BE AN ILL OMEN...PROOF THAT WE MUST HASTEN OUR EFFORTS TO GATHER THE REMAINING RELICS!
IF WE ARE TO SURVIVE THIS NEW THREAT, WE CAN'T BE DISTRACTED BY THE HAVOC THESE RELICS CAUSE.
...THAT SOUNDED REALLY COOL...
YEAH, THAT WAS GOOD. DID YOU WRITE THAT?
WE JUST RECEIVED NEW INTEL. YOU MUST LEAVE IMMEDIATELY FOR—
GOLDCLIFF.

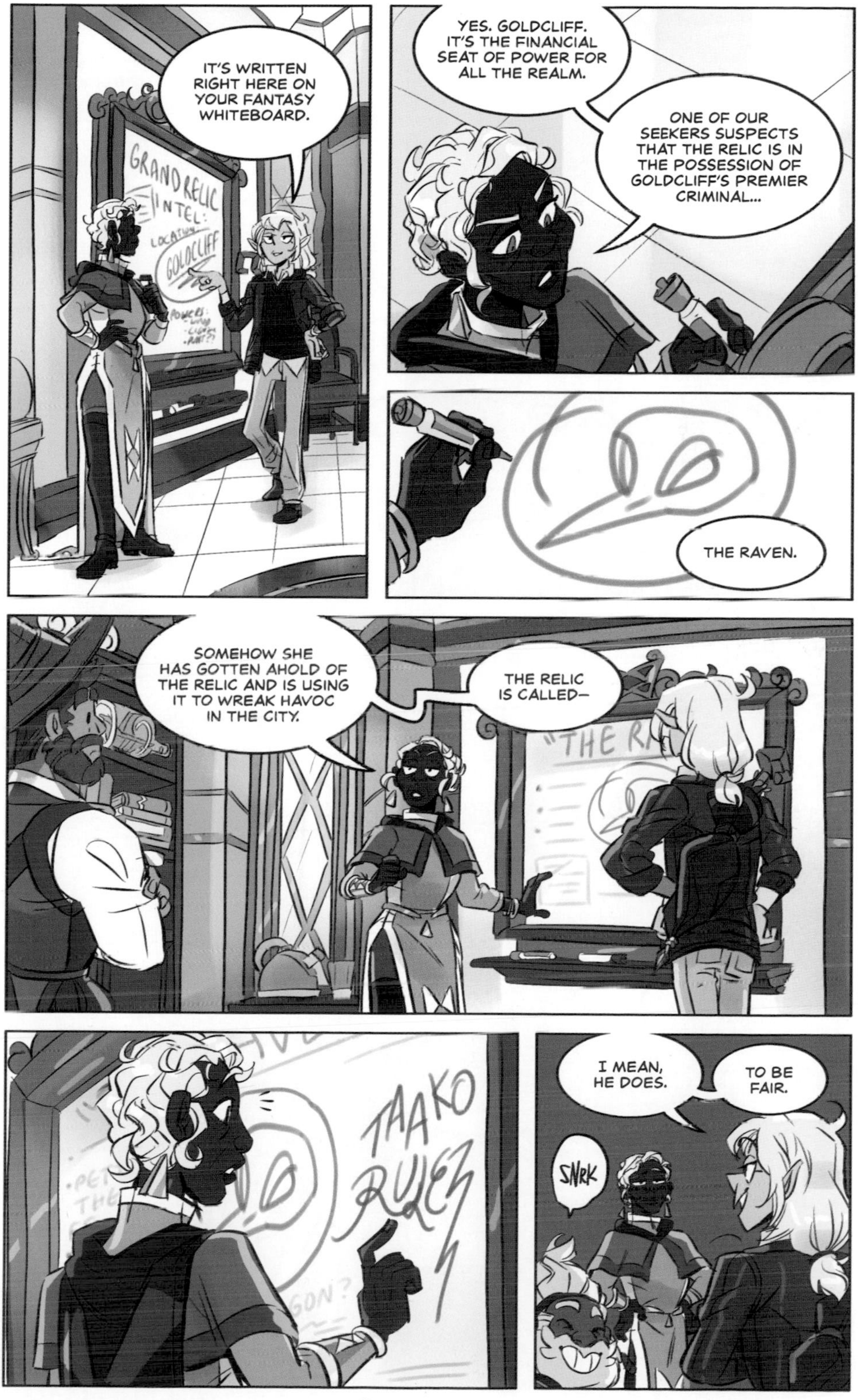
IT'S WRITTEN RIGHT HERE ON YOUR FANTASY WHITEBOARD.
GRAND RELIC INTEL:
LOCATION:
GOLDCLIFF
YES. GOLDCLIFF. IT'S THE FINANCIAL SEAT OF POWER FOR ALL THE REALM.
ONE OF OUR SEEKERS SUSPECTS THAT THE RELIC IS IN THE POSSESSION OF GOLDCLIFF'S PREMIER CRIMINAL...
THE RAVEN.
SOMEHOW SHE HAS GOTTEN AHOLD OF THE RELIC AND IS USING IT TO WREAK HAVOC IN THE CITY.
THE RELIC IS CALLED—
TAAKO RULEZ
I MEAN, HE DOES.
TO BE FAIR.
SNRK

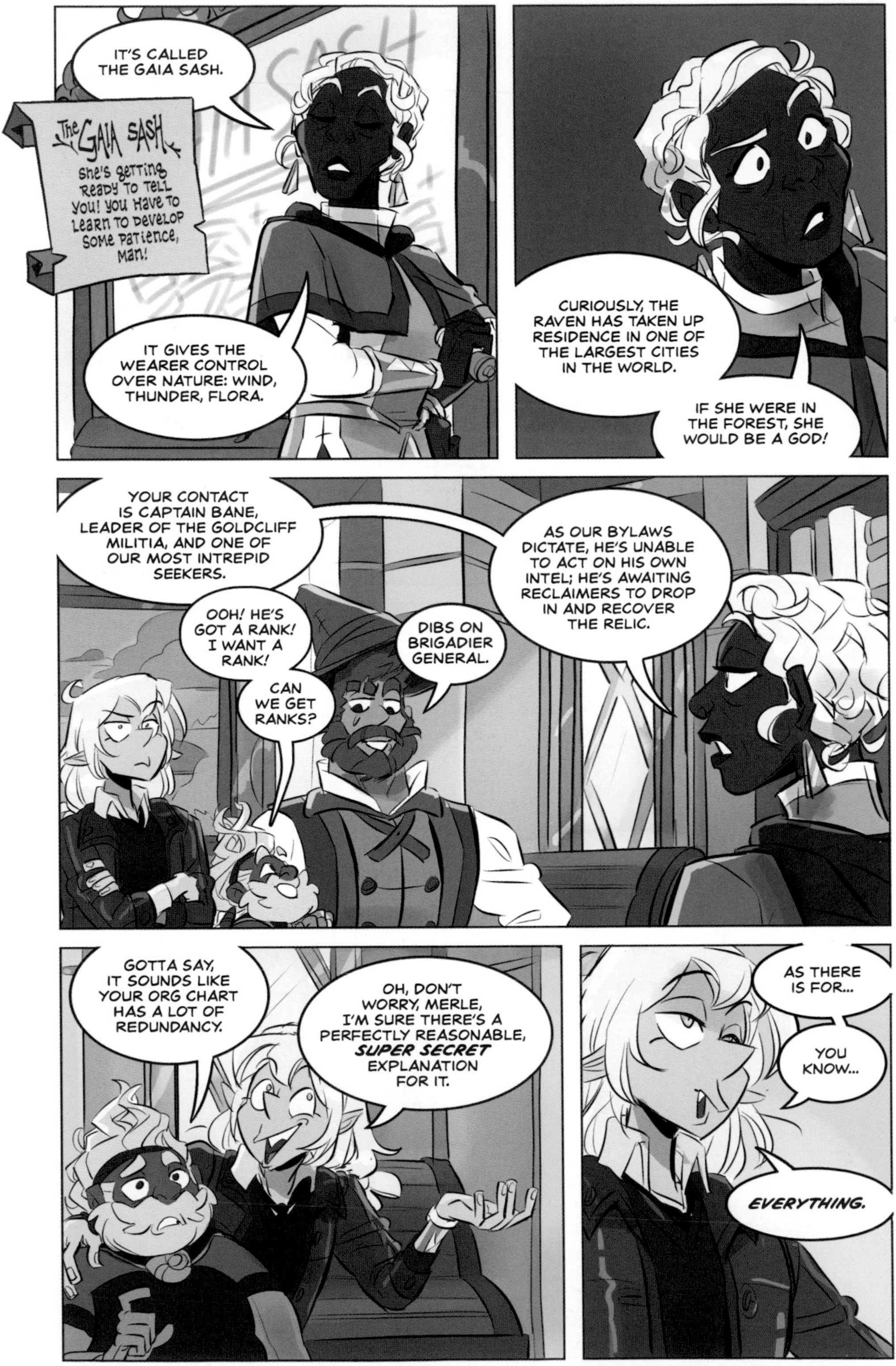
IT'S CALLED THE GAIA SASH.
The GAIA SASH
She's getting Ready to Tell You! You Have to Learn to Develop Some Patience, Man!
IT GIVES THE WEARER CONTROL OVER NATURE: WIND, THUNDER, FLORA.
CURIOUSLY, THE RAVEN HAS TAKEN UP RESIDENCE IN ONE OF THE LARGEST CITIES IN THE WORLD.
IF SHE WERE IN THE FOREST, SHE WOULD BE A GOD!
YOUR CONTACT IS CAPTAIN BANE, LEADER OF THE GOLDCLIFF MILITIA, AND ONE OF OUR MOST INTREPID SEEKERS.
OOH! HE'S GOT A RANK! I WANT A RANK!
CAN WE GET RANKS?
DIBS ON BRIGADIER GENERAL.
AS OUR BYLAWS DICTATE, HE'S UNABLE TO ACT ON HIS OWN INTEL; HE'S AWAITING RECLAIMERS TO DROP IN AND RECOVER THE RELIC.
GOTTA SAY, IT SOUNDS LIKE YOUR ORG CHART HAS A LOT OF REDUNDANCY.
OH, DON'T WORRY, MERLE, I'M SURE THERE'S A PERFECTLY REASONABLE, SUPER SECRET EXPLANATION FOR IT.
AS THERE IS FOR...
YOU KNOW...
EVERYTHING.

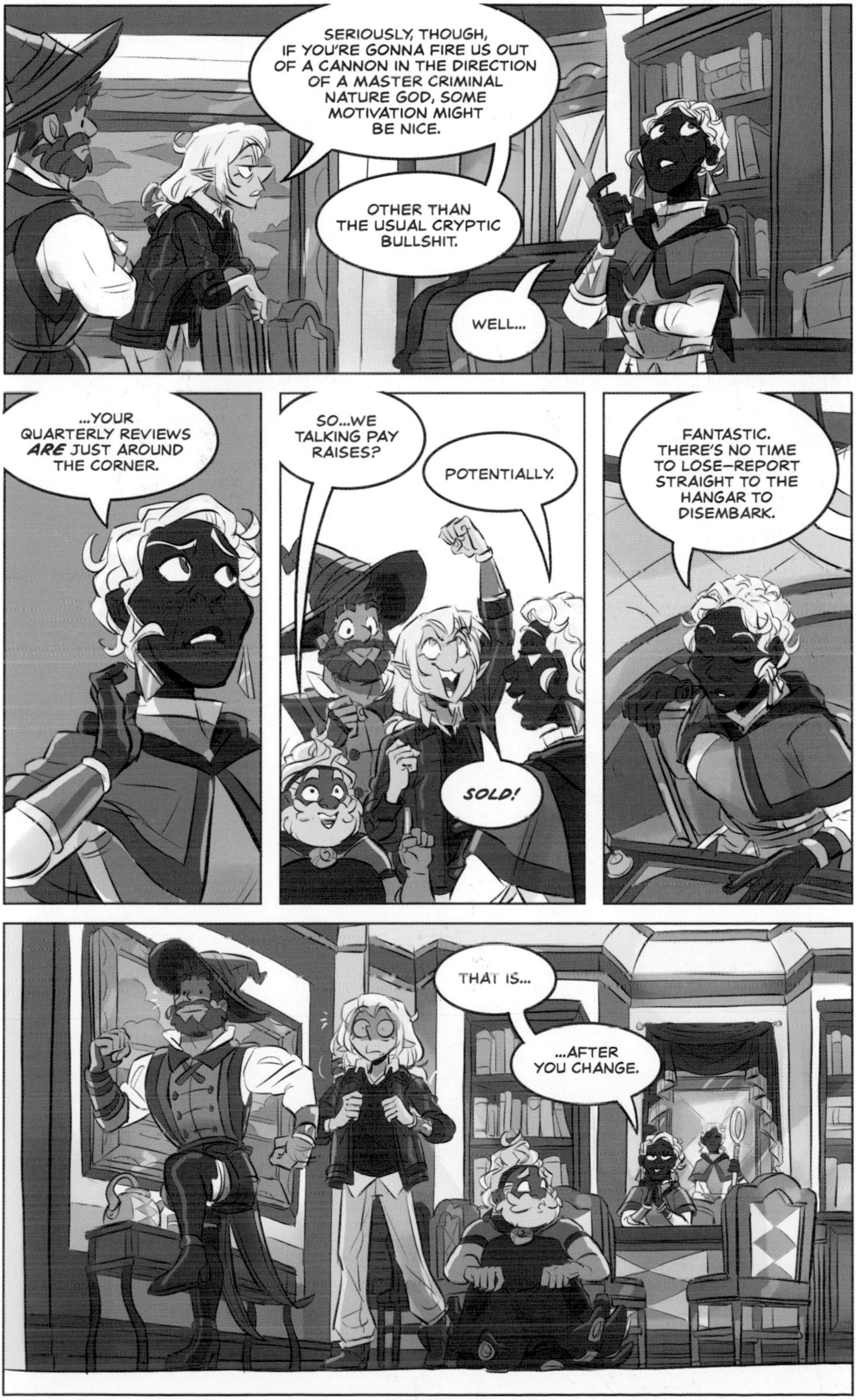
SERIOUSLY, THOUGH, IF YOU'RE GONNA FIRE US OUT OF A CANNON IN THE DIRECTION OF A MASTER CRIMINAL NATURE GOD, SOME MOTIVATION MIGHT BE NICE.
OTHER THAN THE USUAL CRYPTIC BULLSHIT.
WELL...
...YOUR QUARTERLY REVIEWS *ARE* JUST AROUND THE CORNER.
SO...WE TALKING PAY RAISES?
POTENTIALLY.
SOLD!
FANTASTIC. THERE'S NO TIME TO LOSE—REPORT STRAIGHT TO THE HANGAR TO DISEMBARK.
THAT IS...
...AFTER YOU CHANGE.

Chapter 2

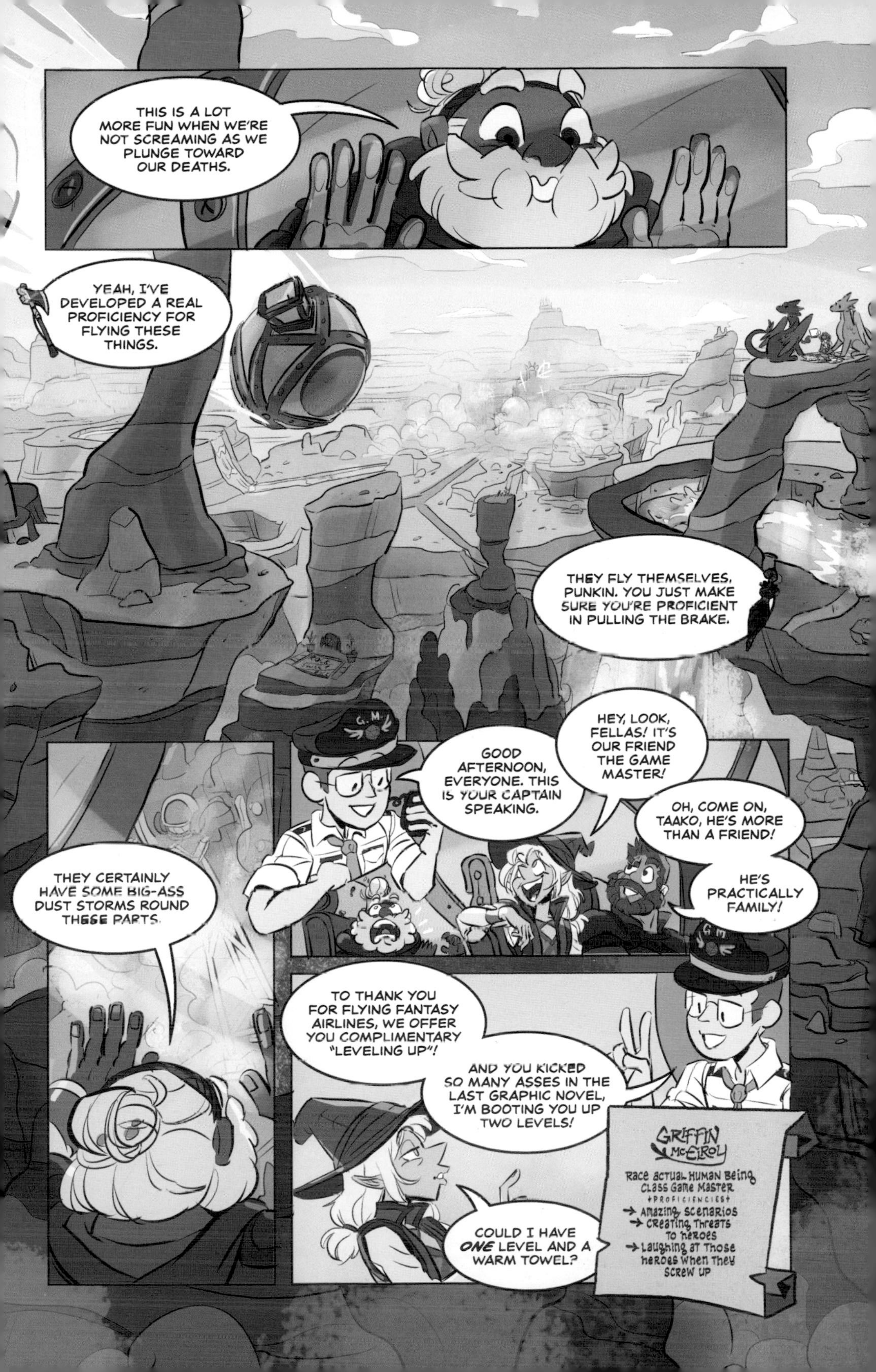
THIS IS A LOT MORE FUN WHEN WE'RE NOT SCREAMING AS WE PLUNGE TOWARD OUR DEATHS.
YEAH, I'VE DEVELOPED A REAL PROFICIENCY FOR FLYING THESE THINGS.
THEY FLY THEMSELVES, PUNKIN. YOU JUST MAKE SURE YOU'RE PROFICIENT IN PULLING THE BRAKE.
THEY CERTAINLY HAVE SOME BIG-ASS DUST STORMS ROUND THESE PARTS.
GOOD AFTERNOON, EVERYONE. THIS IS YOUR CAPTAIN SPEAKING.
HEY, LOOK, FELLAS! IT'S OUR FRIEND THE GAME MASTER!
OH, COME ON, TAAKO, HE'S MORE THAN A FRIEND!
HE'S PRACTICALLY FAMILY!
TO THANK YOU FOR FLYING FANTASY AIRLINES, WE OFFER YOU COMPLIMENTARY "LEVELING UP"!
AND YOU KICKED SO MANY ASSES IN THE LAST GRAPHIC NOVEL, I'M BOOTING YOU UP TWO LEVELS!
COULD I HAVE ONE LEVEL AND A WARM TOWEL?
GRIFFIN McELROY
Race actual Human Being
Class Game Master
PROFICIENCIES
→ Amazing scenarios
→ Creating threats to heroes
→ Laughing at those heroes when they screw up

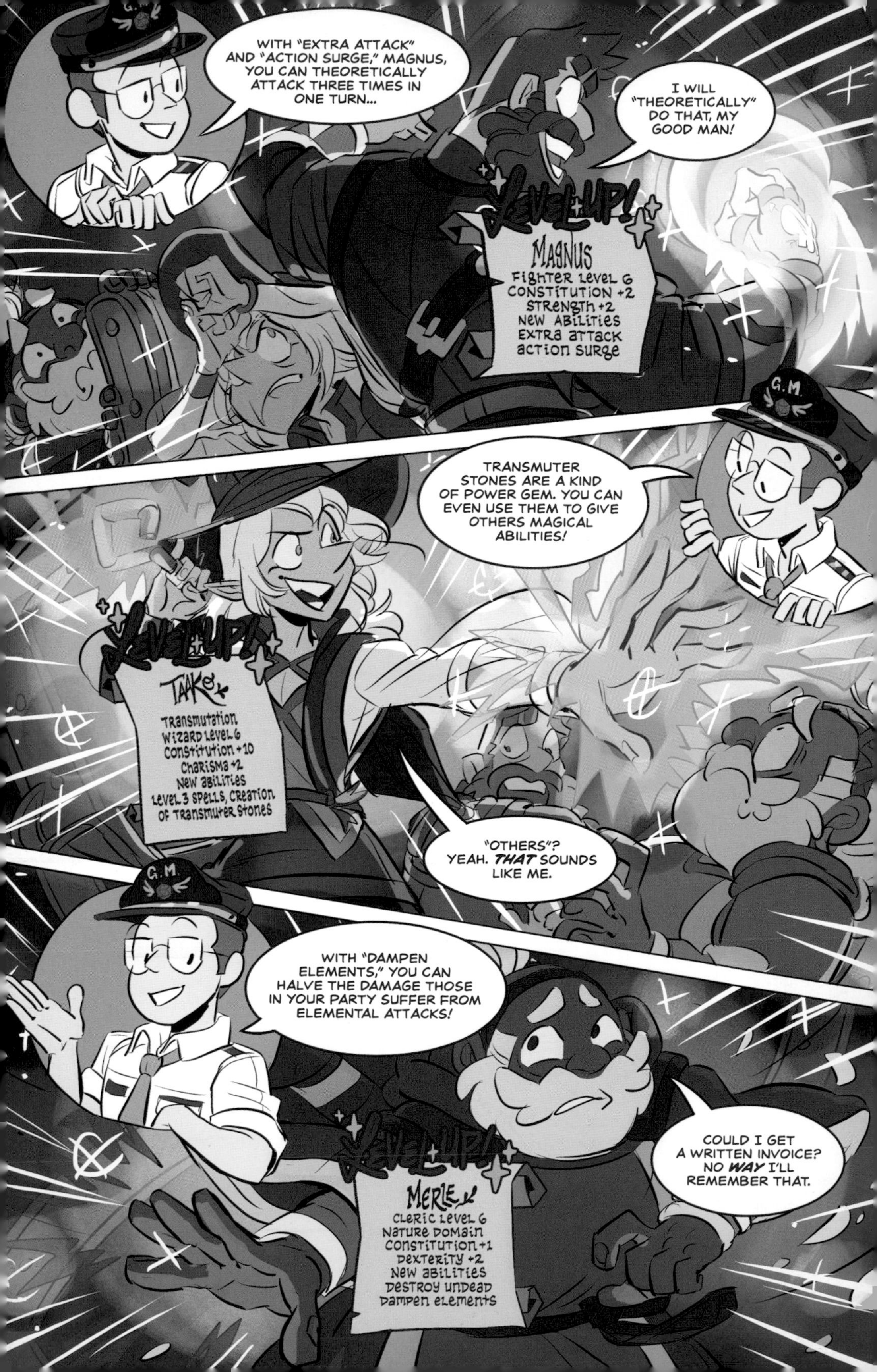
WITH "EXTRA ATTACK" AND "ACTION SURGE," MAGNUS, YOU CAN THEORETICALLY ATTACK THREE TIMES IN ONE TURN...
I WILL "THEORETICALLY" DO THAT, MY GOOD MAN!
LEVEL UP!
MAGNUS
FIGHTER LEVEL 6
CONSTITUTION +2
STRENGTH +2
NEW ABILITIES
EXTRA ATTACK
ACTION SURGE
TRANSMUTER STONES ARE A KIND OF POWER GEM. YOU CAN EVEN USE THEM TO GIVE OTHERS MAGICAL ABILITIES!
LEVEL UP!
TAAKO
TRANSMUTATION
WIZARD LEVEL 6
CONSTITUTION +10
CHARISMA +2
NEW ABILITIES
LEVEL 3 SPELLS, CREATION OF TRANSMUTER STONES
"OTHERS"? YEAH. *THAT* SOUNDS LIKE ME.
WITH "DAMPEN ELEMENTS," YOU CAN HALVE THE DAMAGE THOSE IN YOUR PARTY SUFFER FROM ELEMENTAL ATTACKS!
G.M.
LEVEL UP!
MERLE
CLERIC LEVEL 6
NATURE DOMAIN
CONSTITUTION +1
DEXTERITY +2
NEW ABILITIES
DESTROY UNDEAD
DAMPEN ELEMENTS
COULD I GET A WRITTEN INVOICE? NO *WAY* I'LL REMEMBER THAT.

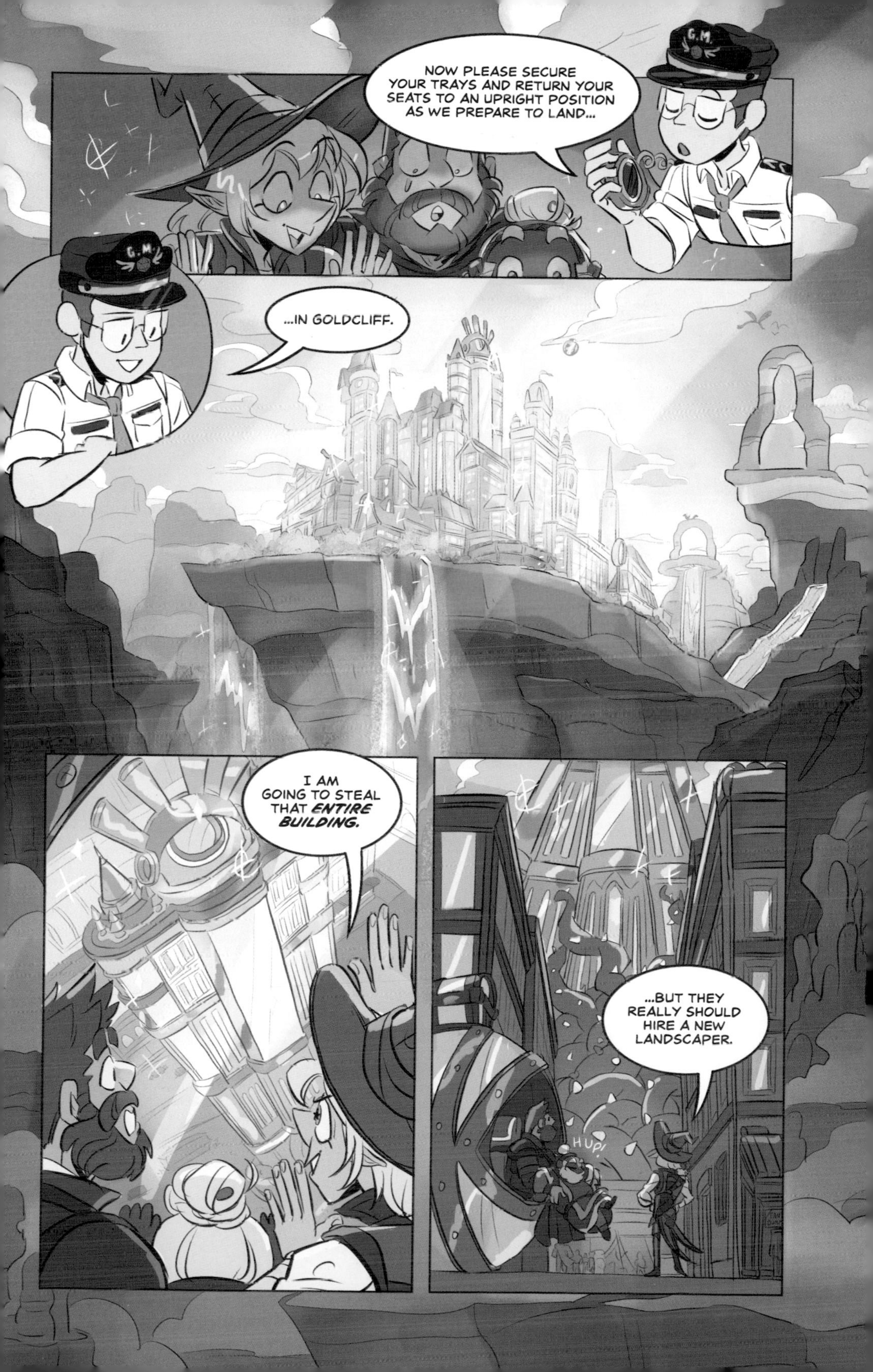
NOW PLEASE SECURE YOUR TRAYS AND RETURN YOUR SEATS TO AN UPRIGHT POSITION AS WE PREPARE TO LAND...
G.M.
G.M.
...IN GOLDCLIFF.
I AM GOING TO STEAL THAT *ENTIRE BUILDING.*
HUP!
...BUT THEY REALLY SHOULD HIRE A NEW LANDSCAPER.

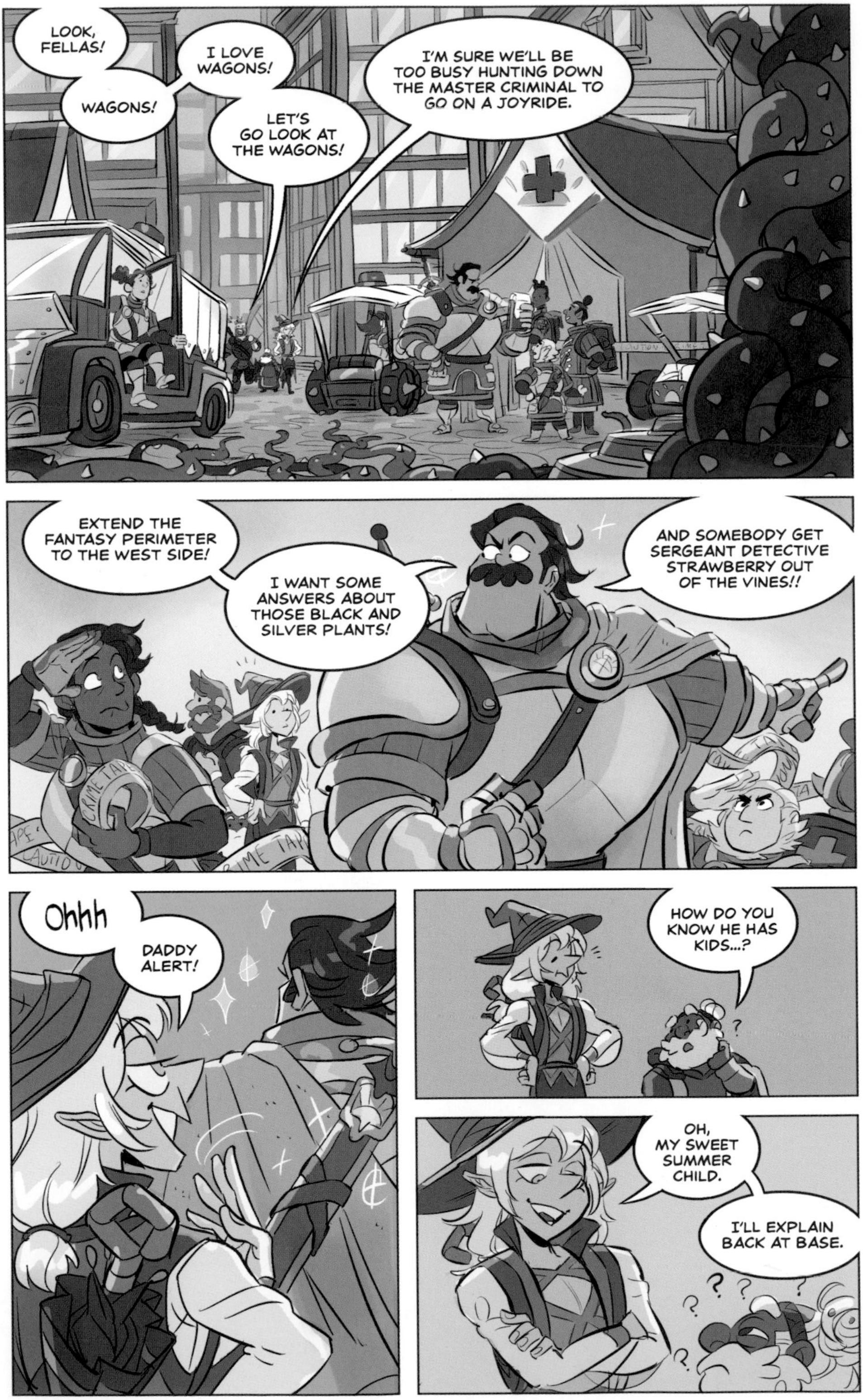
LOOK, FELLAS!
WAGONS!
I LOVE WAGONS!
LET'S GO LOOK AT THE WAGONS!
I'M SURE WE'LL BE TOO BUSY HUNTING DOWN THE MASTER CRIMINAL TO GO ON A JOYRIDE.
EXTEND THE FANTASY PERIMETER TO THE WEST SIDE!
I WANT SOME ANSWERS ABOUT THOSE BLACK AND SILVER PLANTS!
AND SOMEBODY GET SERGEANT DETECTIVE STRAWBERRY OUT OF THE VINES!!
Ohhh
DADDY ALERT!
HOW DO YOU KNOW HE HAS KIDS...?
OH, MY SWEET SUMMER CHILD.
I'LL EXPLAIN BACK AT BASE.

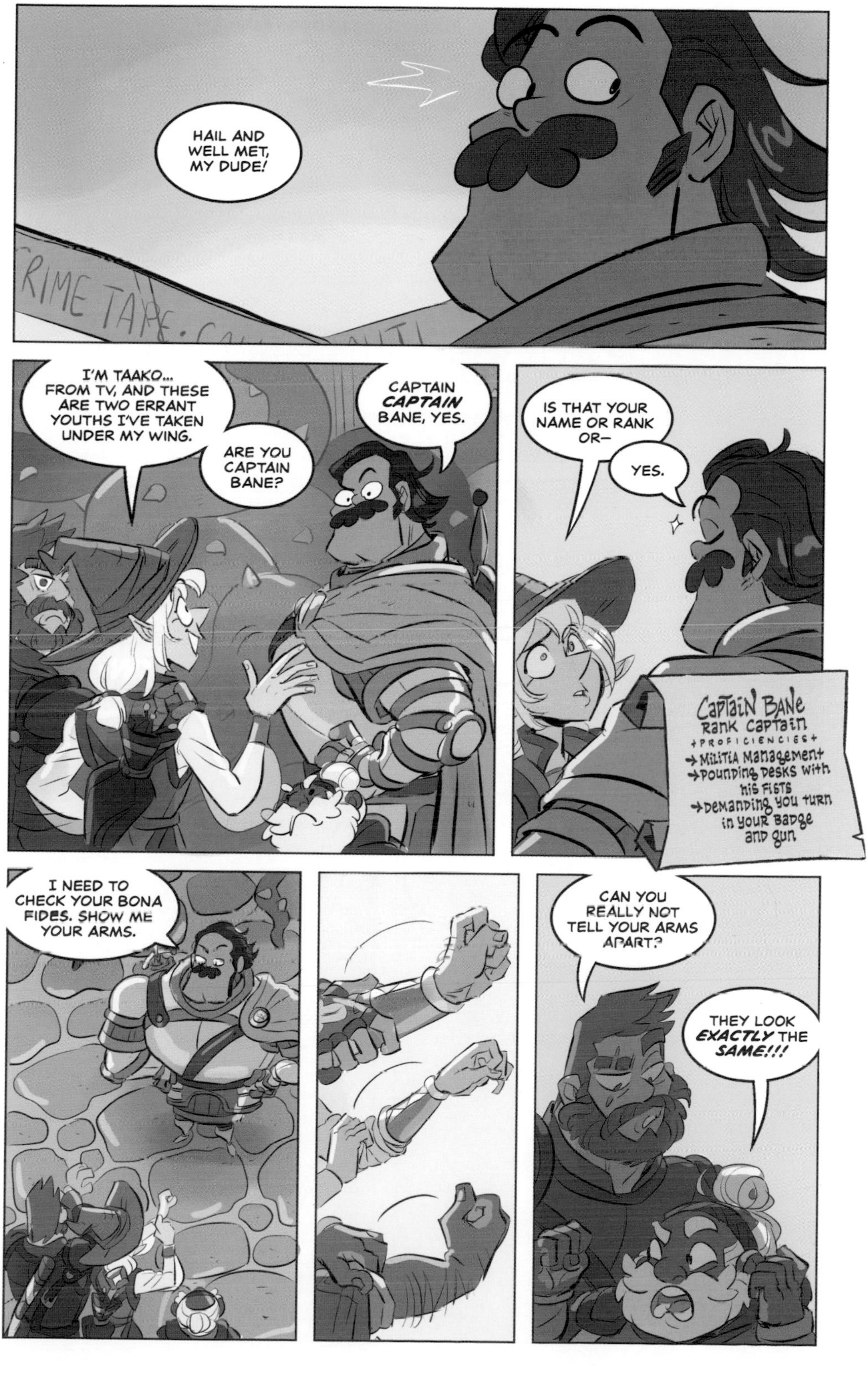
HAIL AND WELL MET, MY DUDE!
I'M TAAKO... FROM TV, AND THESE ARE TWO ERRANT YOUTHS I'VE TAKEN UNDER MY WING.
ARE YOU CAPTAIN BANE?
CAPTAIN *CAPTAIN* BANE, YES.
IS THAT YOUR NAME OR RANK OR—
YES.
CAPTAIN BANE
RANK CAPTAIN
PROFICIENCIES
→MILITIA MANAGEMENT
→POUNDING DESKS WITH HIS FISTS
→DEMANDING YOU TURN IN YOUR BADGE AND GUN
I NEED TO CHECK YOUR BONA FIDES. SHOW ME YOUR ARMS.
CAN YOU REALLY NOT TELL YOUR ARMS APART?
THEY LOOK *EXACTLY* THE *SAME!!!*

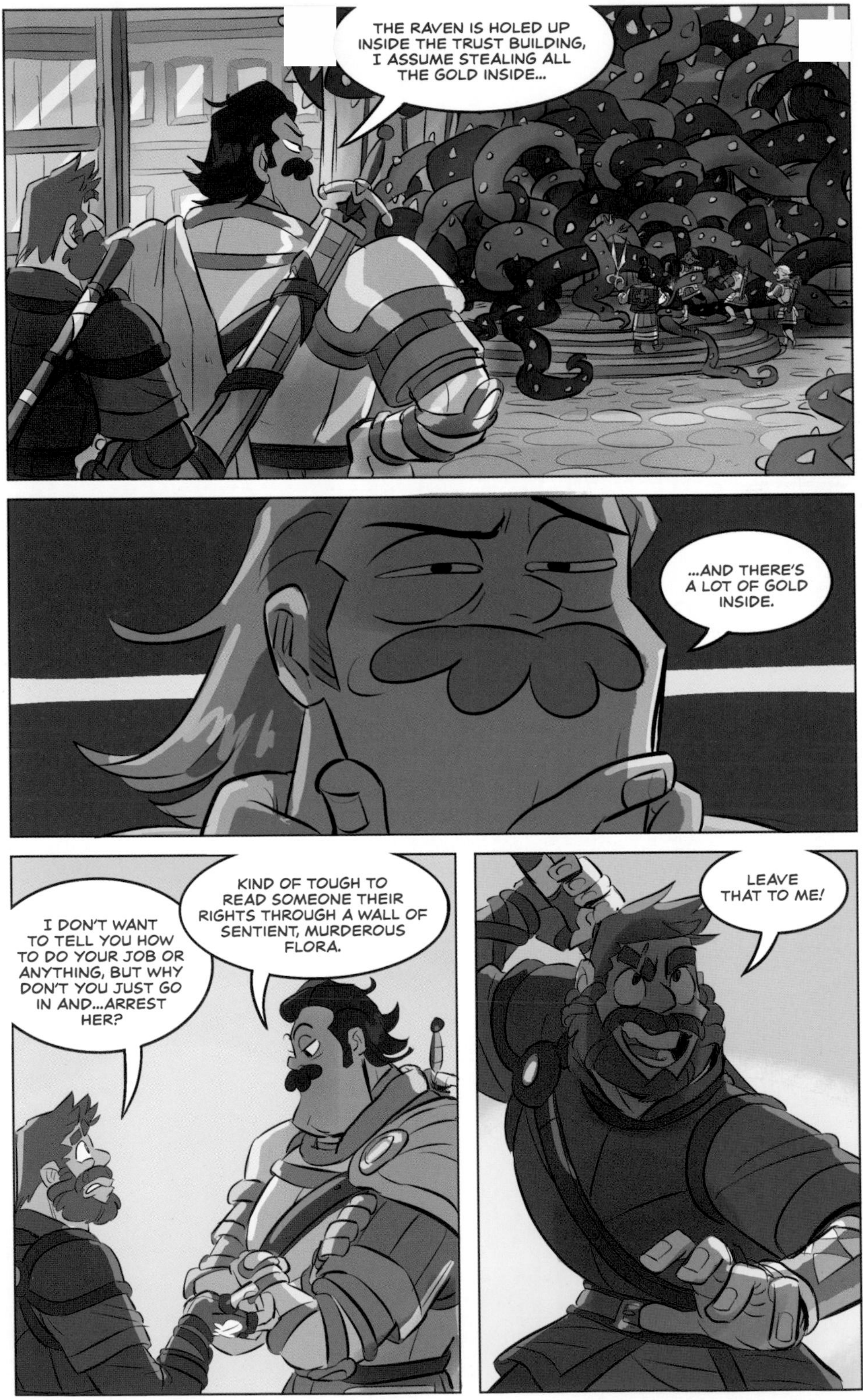
THE RAVEN IS HOLED UP INSIDE THE TRUST BUILDING, I ASSUME STEALING ALL THE GOLD INSIDE...
...AND THERE'S A LOT OF GOLD INSIDE.
I DON'T WANT TO TELL YOU HOW TO DO YOUR JOB OR ANYTHING, BUT WHY DON'T YOU JUST GO IN AND...ARREST HER?
KIND OF TOUGH TO READ SOMEONE THEIR RIGHTS THROUGH A WALL OF SENTIENT, MURDEROUS FLORA.
LEAVE THAT TO ME!

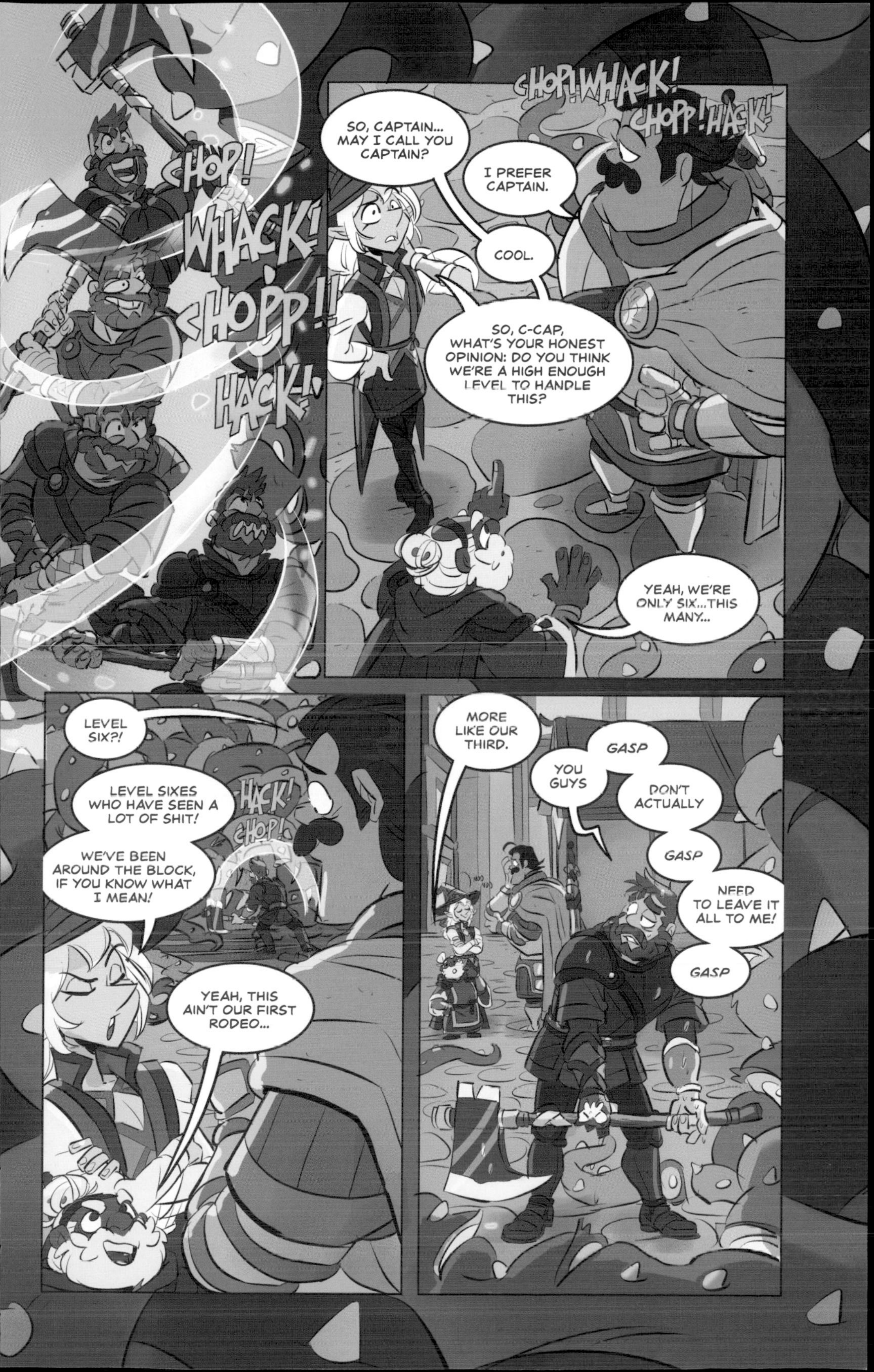
CHOP!
WHACK!
CHOPP!!
HACK!
CHOP! WHACK!
CHOPP! HACK!
SO, CAPTAIN... MAY I CALL YOU CAPTAIN?
I PREFER CAPTAIN.
COOL.
SO, C-CAP, WHAT'S YOUR HONEST OPINION: DO YOU THINK WE'RE A HIGH ENOUGH LEVEL TO HANDLE THIS?
YEAH, WE'RE ONLY SIX...THIS MANY...
LEVEL SIX?!
LEVEL SIXES WHO HAVE SEEN A LOT OF SHIT!
HACK!
CHOP!
WE'VE BEEN AROUND THE BLOCK, IF YOU KNOW WHAT I MEAN!
YEAH, THIS AIN'T OUR FIRST RODEO...
MORE LIKE OUR THIRD.
GASP
YOU GUYS
DON'T ACTUALLY
GASP
NEED TO LEAVE IT ALL TO ME!
GASP

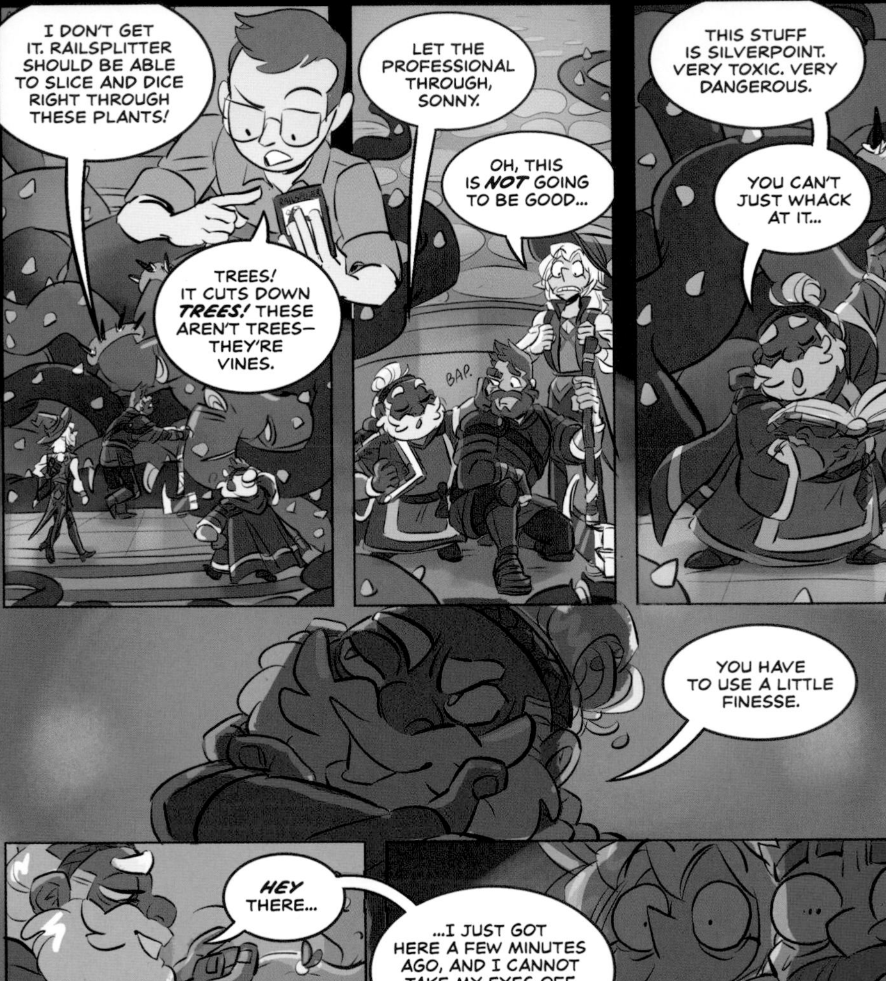

I DON'T GET IT. RAILSPLITTER SHOULD BE ABLE TO SLICE AND DICE RIGHT THROUGH THESE PLANTS!
TREES! IT CUTS DOWN TREES! THESE AREN'T TREES—THEY'RE VINES.
LET THE PROFESSIONAL THROUGH, SONNY.
OH, THIS IS NOT GOING TO BE GOOD...
BAP.
THIS STUFF IS SILVERPOINT. VERY TOXIC. VERY DANGEROUS.
YOU CAN'T JUST WHACK AT IT...
YOU HAVE TO USE A LITTLE FINESSE.
HEY THERE...
...I JUST GOT HERE A FEW MINUTES AGO, AND I CANNOT TAKE MY EYES OFF YOUR PISTILS AND STAMENS...
...AND THAT SWEET, SWEET POLLEN SAC!
HA
HA HA!
SIXTY FEET AWAY, AND ALL I COULD THINK WAS, "DO NOT BE CHOPPIN' ON THIS BABY!"
NO-NO-NO-NO-NO!!
WE'RE GONNA HAVE TO NAME THIS ARC "FIFTY SHADES OF GREEN."

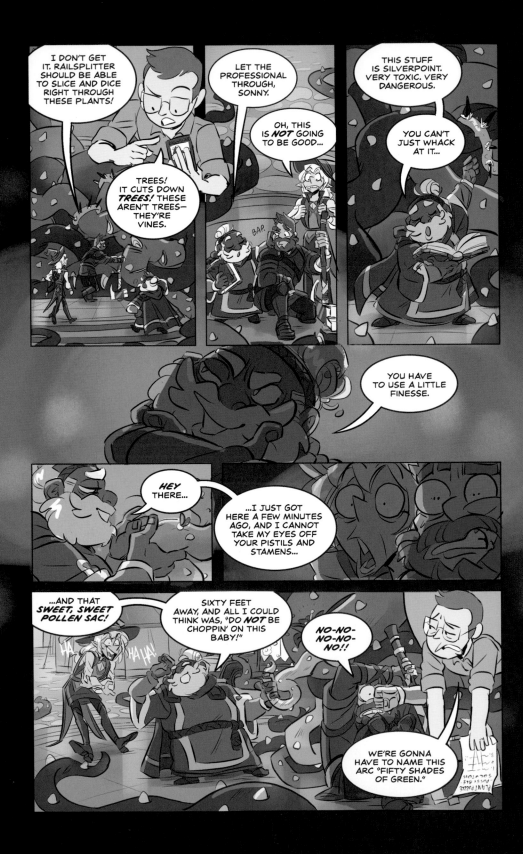

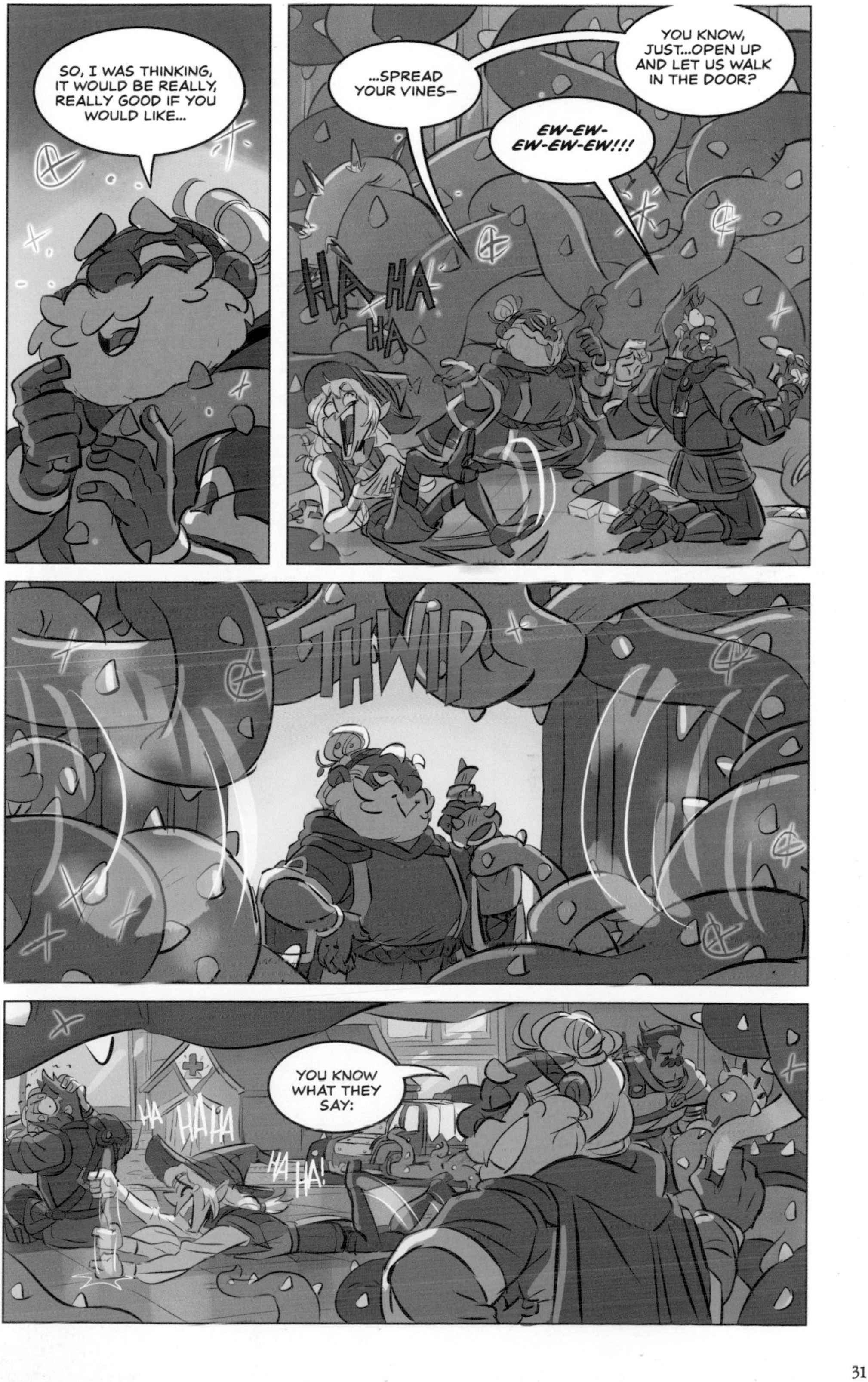
SO, I WAS THINKING, IT WOULD BE REALLY, REALLY GOOD IF YOU WOULD LIKE...
...SPREAD YOUR VINES—
YOU KNOW, JUST...OPEN UP AND LET US WALK IN THE DOOR?
EW-EW-EW-EW-EW!!!
HA HA HA
THWIP
YOU KNOW WHAT THEY SAY:
HA HAHA
HA HA!

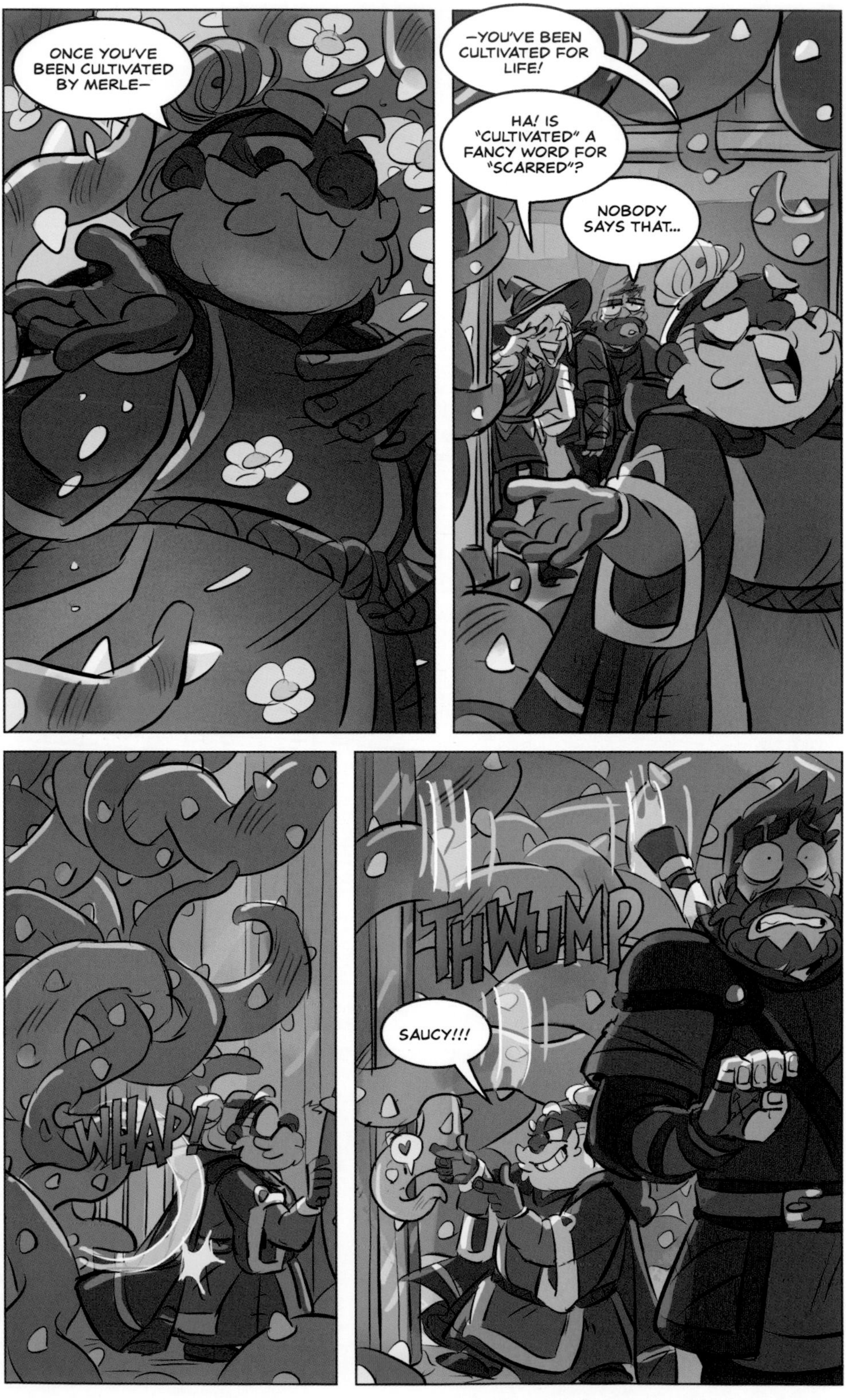
ONCE YOU'VE BEEN CULTIVATED BY MERLE—
—YOU'VE BEEN CULTIVATED FOR LIFE!
HA! IS "CULTIVATED" A FANCY WORD FOR "SCARRED"?
NOBODY SAYS THAT...
WHAP!
THWUMP
SAUCY!!!

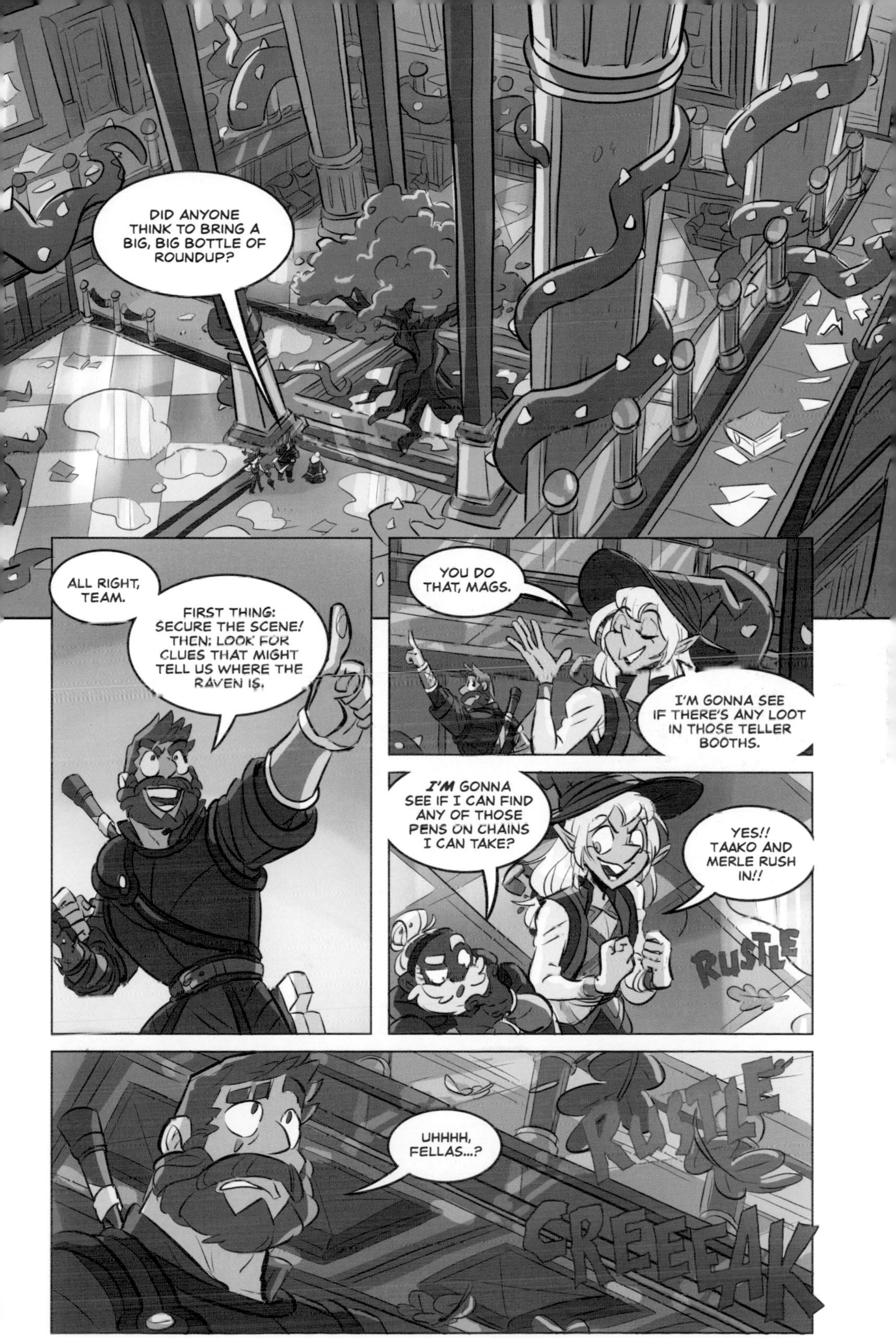
DID ANYONE THINK TO BRING A BIG, BIG BOTTLE OF ROUNDUP?
ALL RIGHT, TEAM.
FIRST THING: SECURE THE SCENE! THEN: LOOK FOR CLUES THAT MIGHT TELL US WHERE THE RAVEN IS.
YOU DO THAT, MAGS.
I'M GONNA SEE IF THERE'S ANY LOOT IN THOSE TELLER BOOTHS.
I'M GONNA SEE IF I CAN FIND ANY OF THOSE PENS ON CHAINS I CAN TAKE?
YES!! TAAKO AND MERLE RUSH IN!!
RUSTLE
UHHHH, FELLAS...?
RUSTLE
CREEEAK

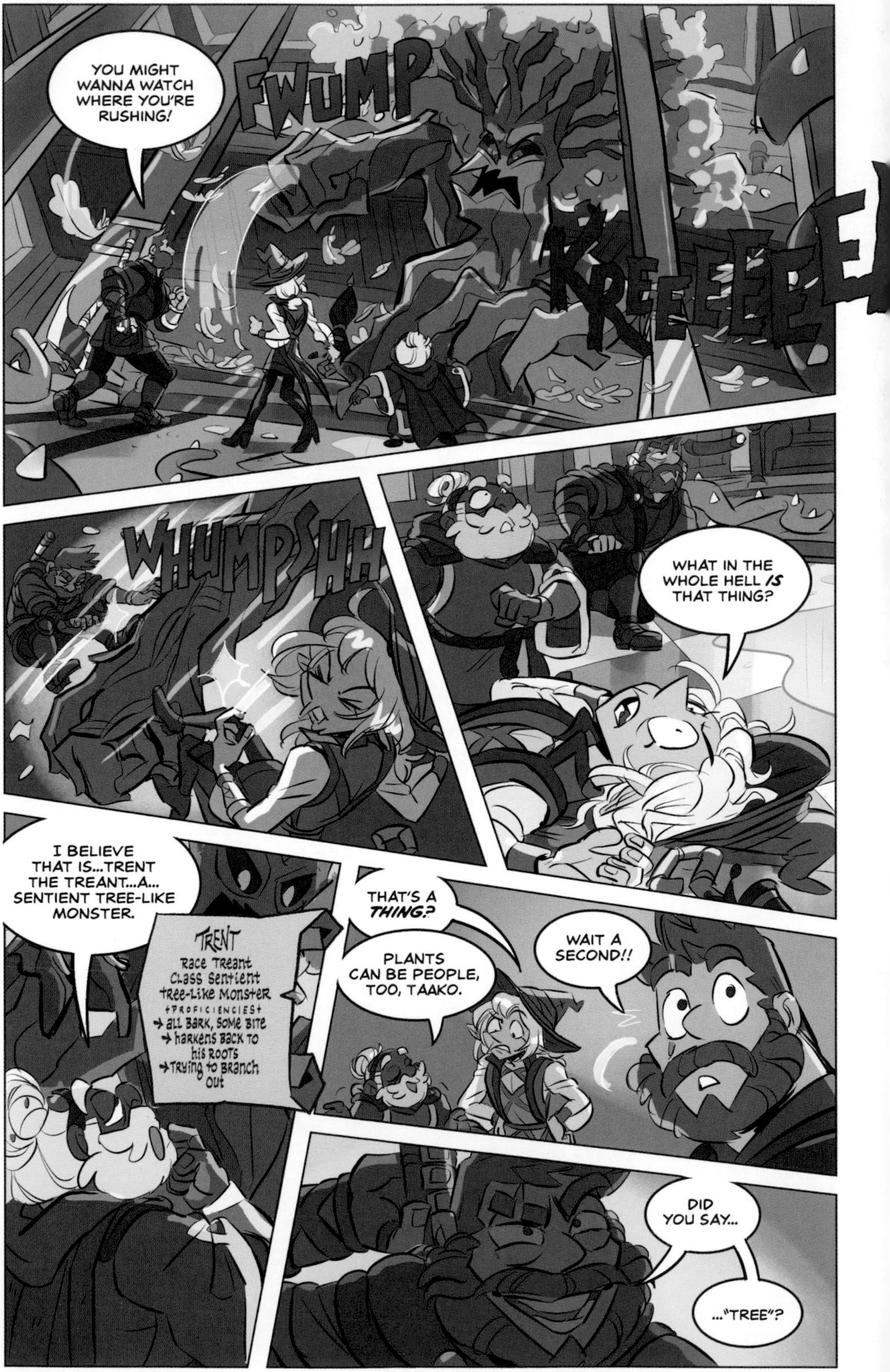
YOU MIGHT WANNA WATCH WHERE YOU'RE RUSHING!
FWUMP
KREEEEEE
WHUMPSHH
WHAT IN THE WHOLE HELL *IS* THAT THING?
I BELIEVE THAT IS...TRENT THE TREANT...A... SENTIENT TREE-LIKE MONSTER.
TRENT
Race Treant
Class Sentient tree-Like Monster
PROFICIENCIES
→ all Bark, Some Bite
→ harkens Back to his Roots
→ Trying to Branch out
THAT'S A ***THING?***
PLANTS CAN BE PEOPLE, TOO, TAAKO.
WAIT A SECOND!!
DID YOU SAY...
..."TREE"?

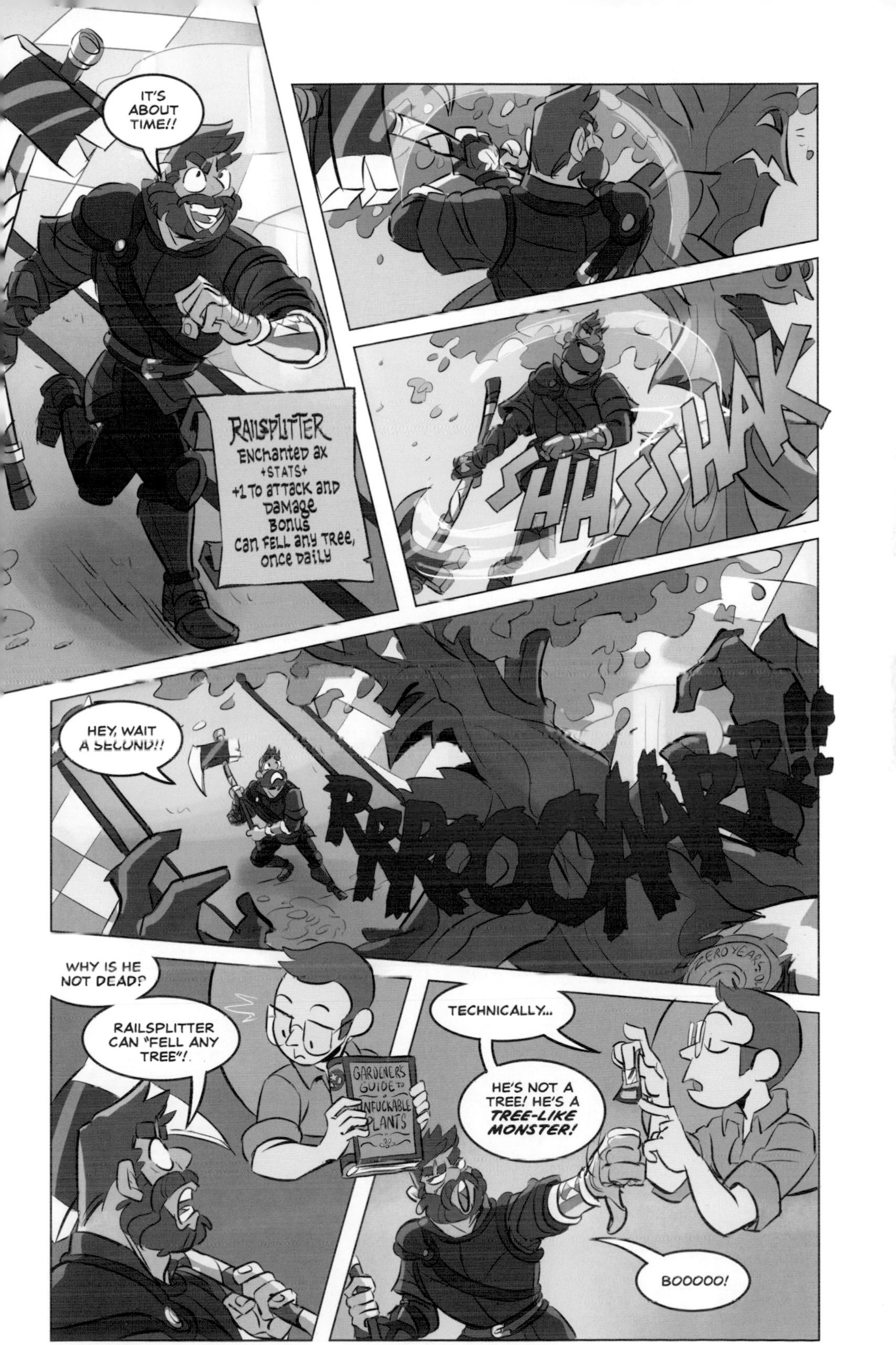
IT'S ABOUT TIME!!
RAILSPLITTER
Enchanted ax
+STATS+
+1 TO attack and Damage Bonus
can fell any tree, once daily
SHHSSHAK
HEY, WAIT A SECOND!!
RRRROOOOARR!!
WHY IS HE NOT DEAD?
RAILSPLITTER CAN "FELL ANY TREE"!
GARDENER'S GUIDE TO UNFUCKABLE PLANTS
TECHNICALLY...
HE'S NOT A TREE! HE'S A ***TREE-LIKE MONSTER!***
BOOOOO!

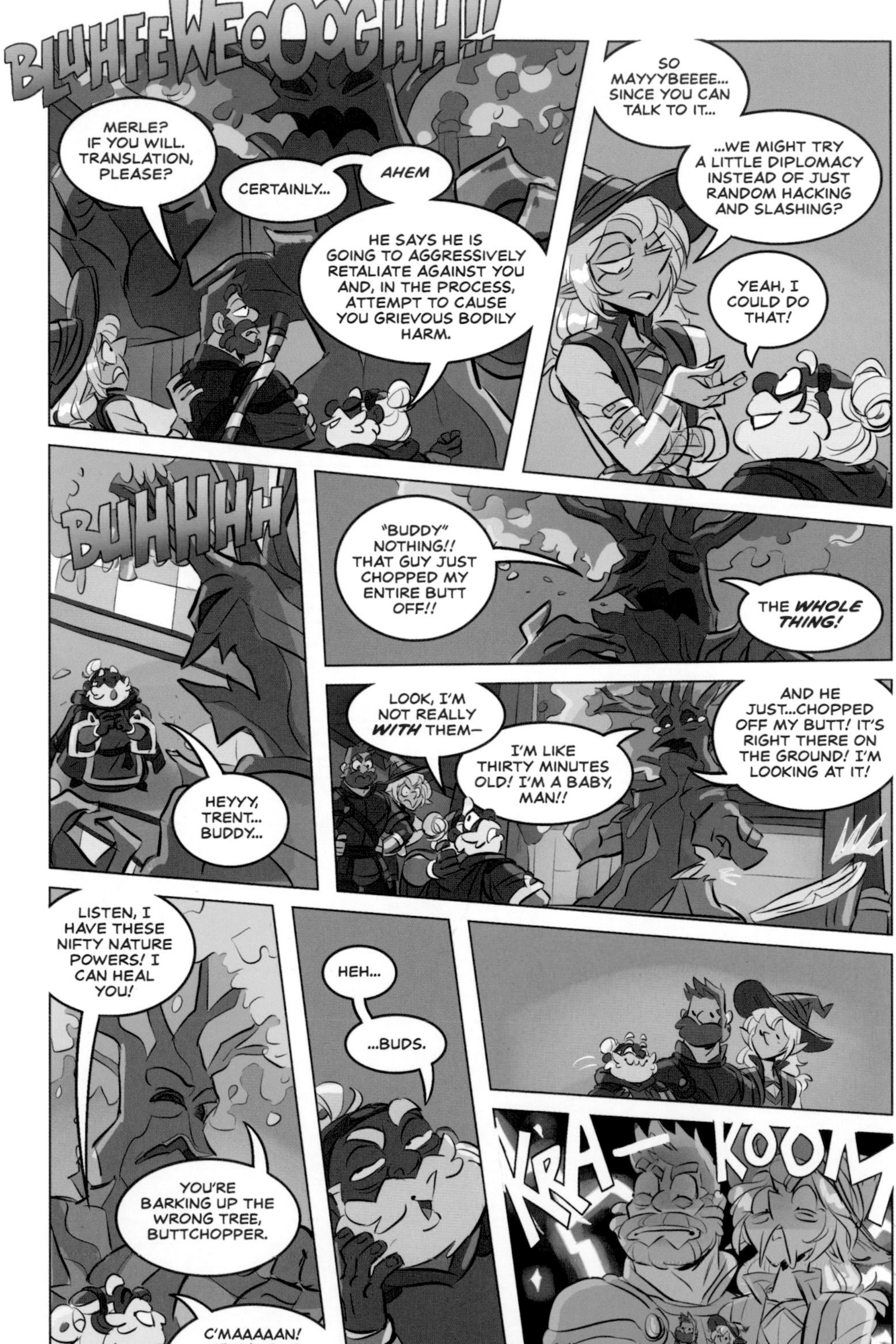
BLUHFEWEOOOGHH!!
MERLE? IF YOU WILL. TRANSLATION, PLEASE?
CERTAINLY...
AHEM
HE SAYS HE IS GOING TO AGGRESSIVELY RETALIATE AGAINST YOU AND, IN THE PROCESS, ATTEMPT TO CAUSE YOU GRIEVOUS BODILY HARM.
SO MAYYYBEEEE... SINCE YOU CAN TALK TO IT...
...WE MIGHT TRY A LITTLE DIPLOMACY INSTEAD OF JUST RANDOM HACKING AND SLASHING?
YEAH, I COULD DO THAT!
BUHHHH
HEYYY, TRENT... BUDDY...
"BUDDY" NOTHING!! THAT GUY JUST CHOPPED MY ENTIRE BUTT OFF!!
THE *WHOLE THING!*
LOOK, I'M NOT REALLY *WITH* THEM—
I'M LIKE THIRTY MINUTES OLD! I'M A BABY, MAN!!
AND HE JUST...CHOPPED OFF MY BUTT! IT'S RIGHT THERE ON THE GROUND! I'M LOOKING AT IT!
LISTEN, I HAVE THESE NIFTY NATURE POWERS! I CAN HEAL YOU!
YOU'RE BARKING UP THE WRONG TREE, BUTTCHOPPER.
C'MAAAAAN! WE HAVE TO STOP THIS SILLY CONFLICT AND JUST BE BUDS!
HEH...
...BUDS.
KRA— KOOM

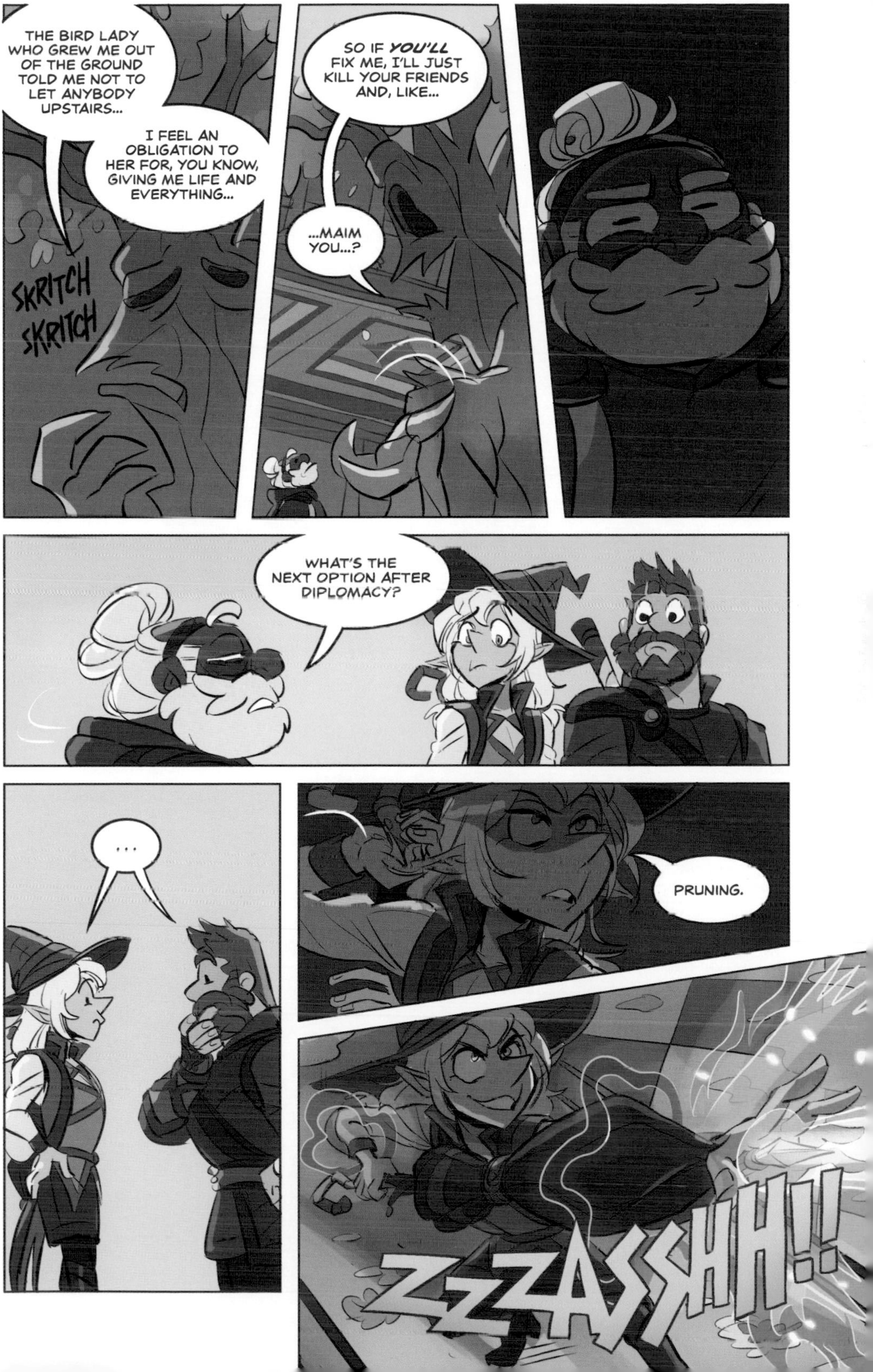
THE BIRD LADY WHO GREW ME OUT OF THE GROUND TOLD ME NOT TO LET ANYBODY UPSTAIRS...
I FEEL AN OBLIGATION TO HER FOR, YOU KNOW, GIVING ME LIFE AND EVERYTHING...
SKRITCH SKRITCH
SO IF YOU'LL FIX ME, I'LL JUST KILL YOUR FRIENDS AND, LIKE...
...MAIM YOU...?
WHAT'S THE NEXT OPTION AFTER DIPLOMACY?
...
PRUNING.
ZZZASSHH!!

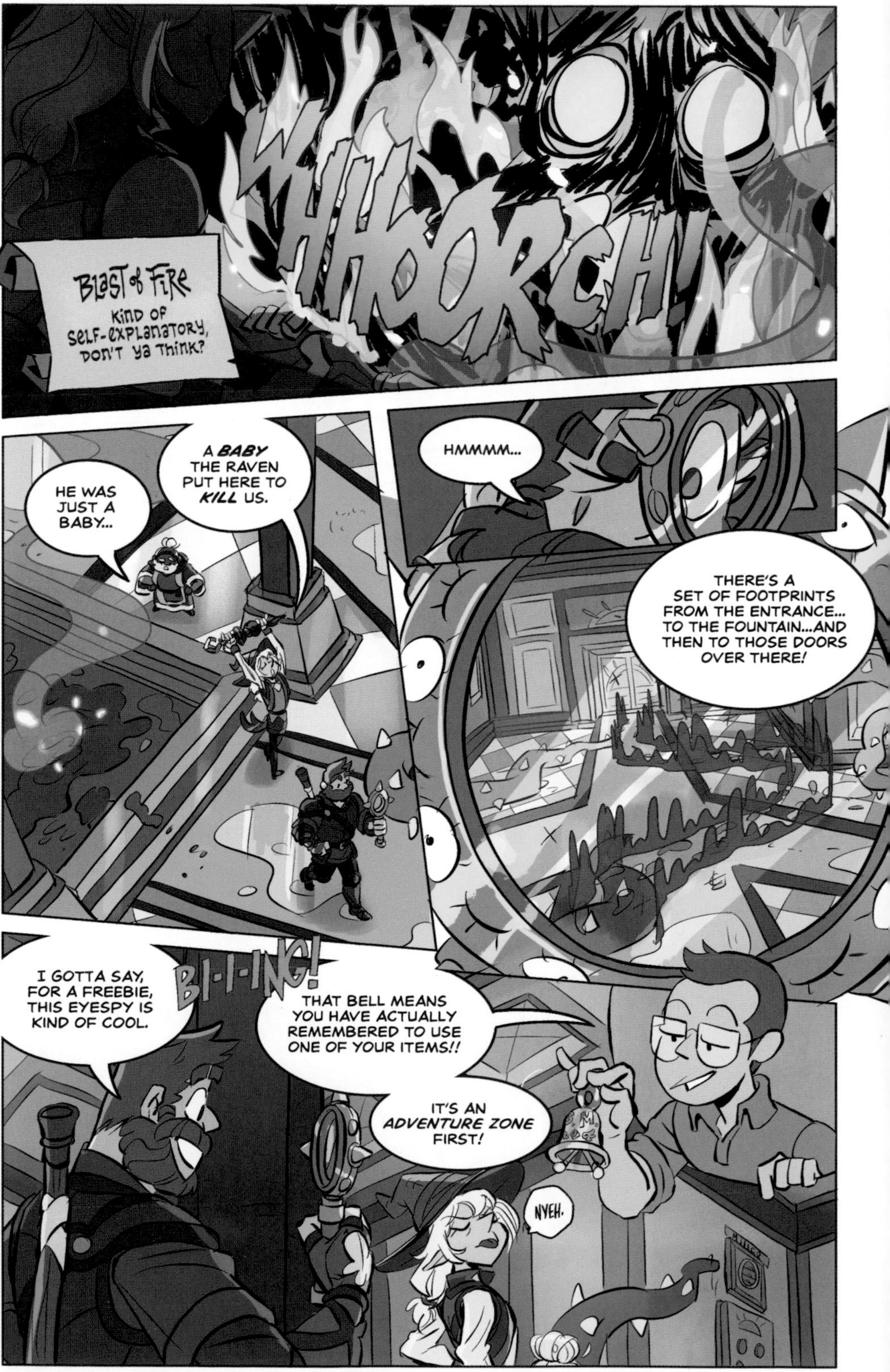
WHHOORCH!
BLAST of FIRE
Kind of self-explanatory, don't ya think?
HE WAS JUST A BABY...
A BABY THE RAVEN PUT HERE TO KILL US.
HMMMM...
THERE'S A SET OF FOOTPRINTS FROM THE ENTRANCE... TO THE FOUNTAIN...AND THEN TO THOSE DOORS OVER THERE!
I GOTTA SAY, FOR A FREEBIE, THIS EYESPY IS KIND OF COOL.
BI-I-ING!
THAT BELL MEANS YOU HAVE ACTUALLY REMEMBERED TO USE ONE OF YOUR ITEMS!!
IT'S AN ADVENTURE ZONE FIRST!
NYEH.

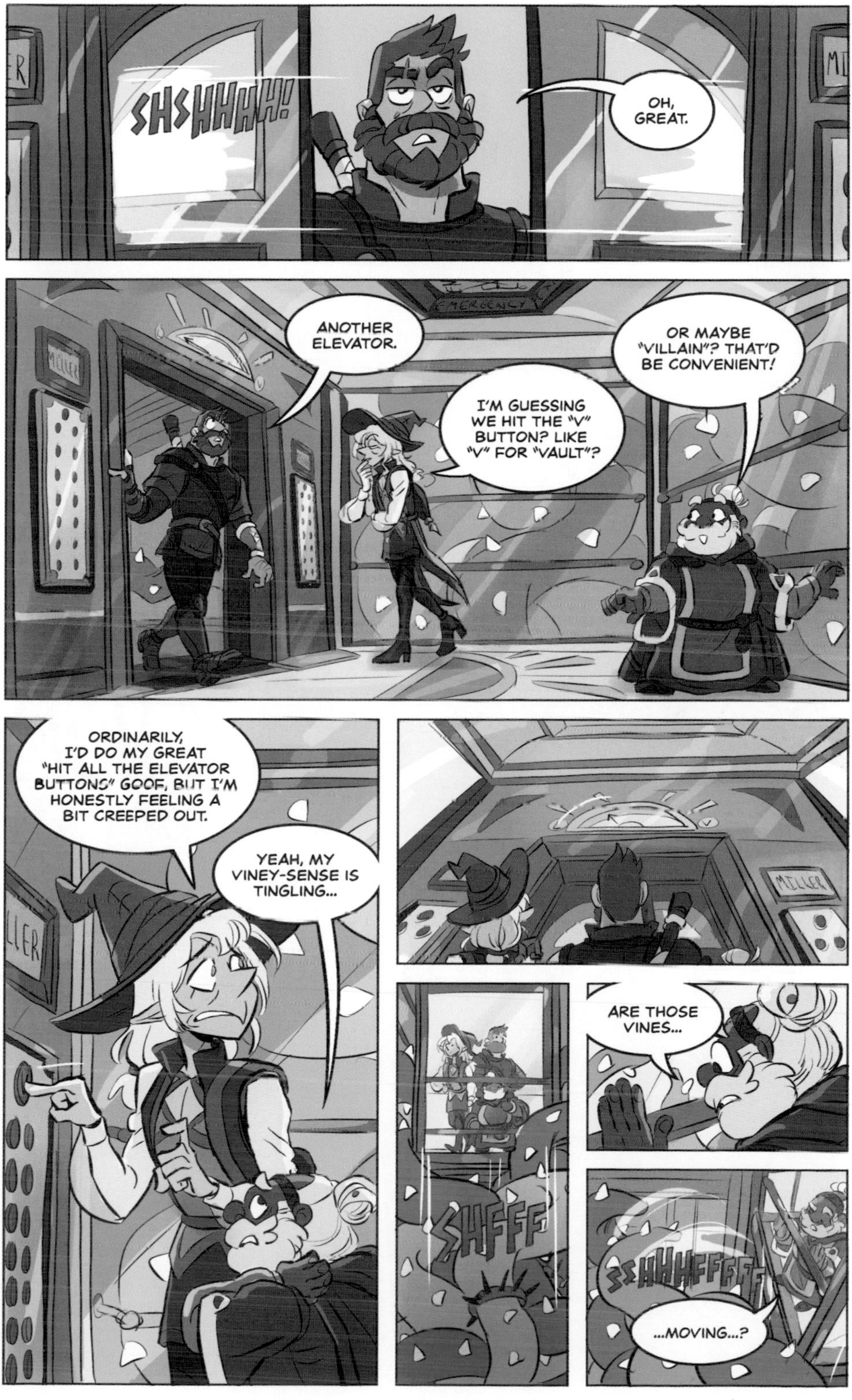
SHSHHHH!
OH, GREAT.
ANOTHER ELEVATOR.
I'M GUESSING WE HIT THE "V" BUTTON? LIKE "V" FOR "VAULT"?
OR MAYBE "VILLAIN"? THAT'D BE CONVENIENT!
ORDINARILY, I'D DO MY GREAT "HIT ALL THE ELEVATOR BUTTONS" GOOF, BUT I'M HONESTLY FEELING A BIT CREEPED OUT.
YEAH, MY VINEY-SENSE IS TINGLING...
ARE THOSE VINES...
SHFFF
SSHHHFFFFF
...MOVING...?

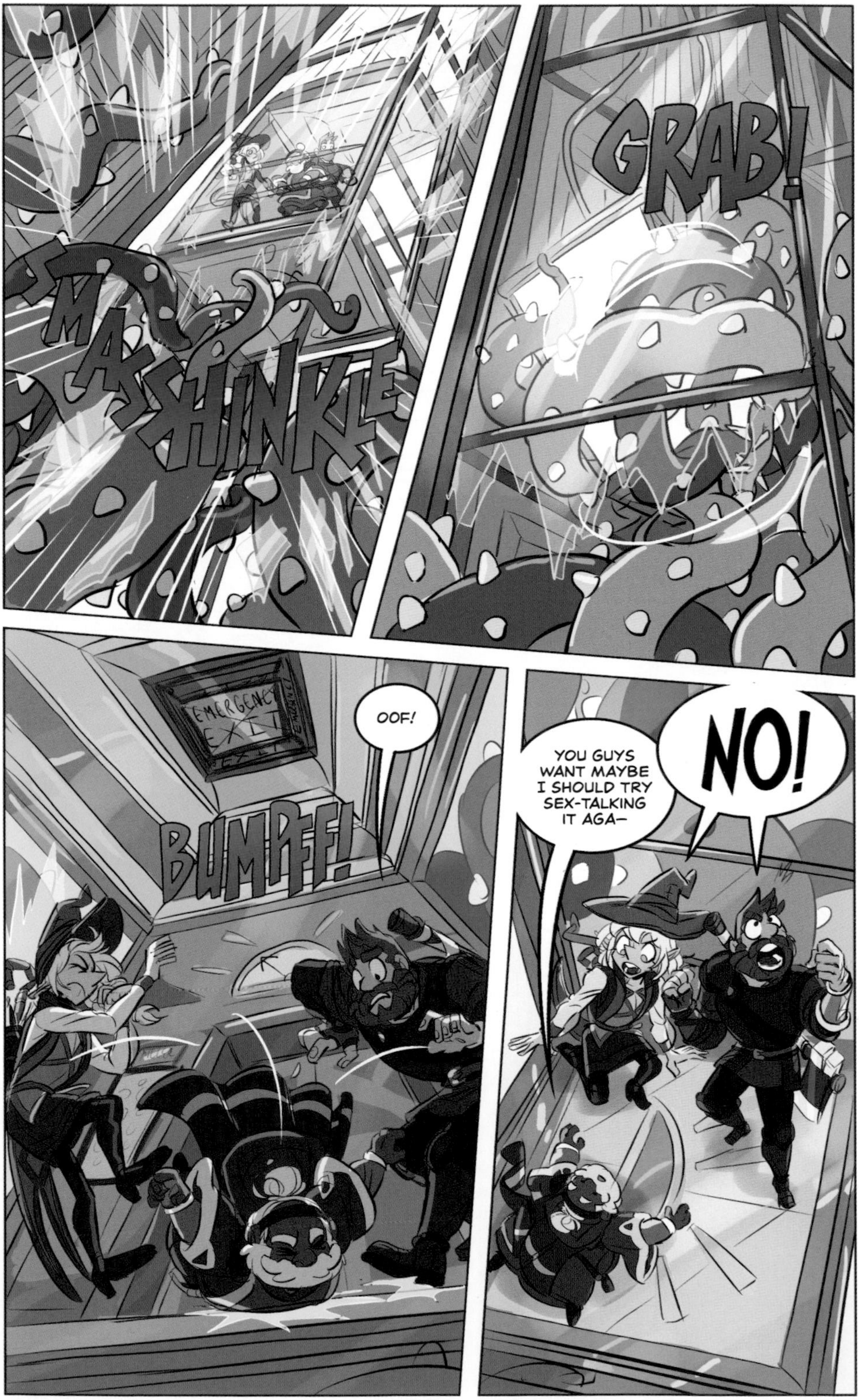
SMASHINKLE
GRAB!
EMERGENCY EXIT
OOF!
BUMPFF!
YOU GUYS WANT MAYBE I SHOULD TRY SEX-TALKING IT AGA—
NO!

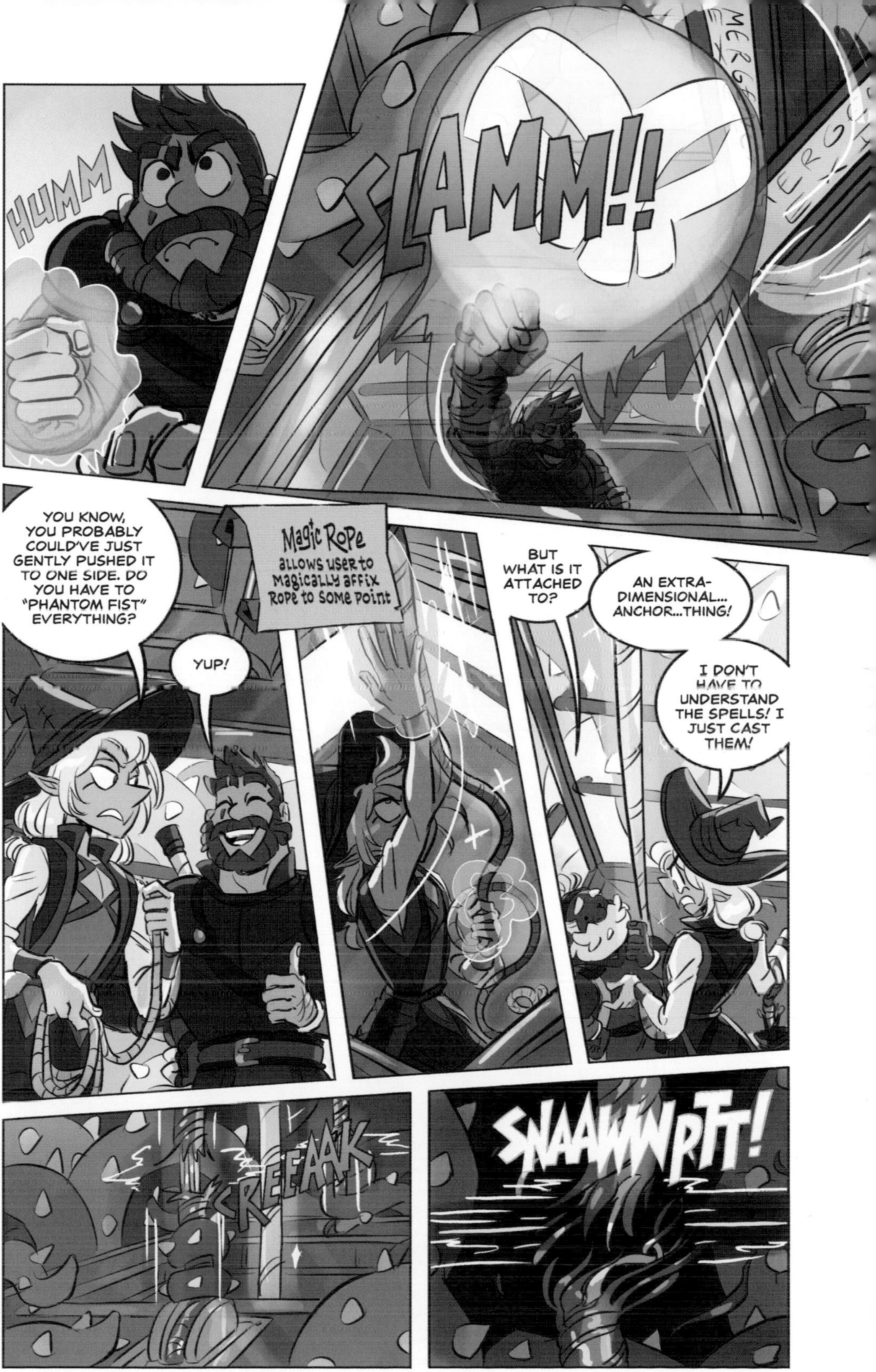
HUMM
SLAMM!!
MERGE
YOU KNOW, YOU PROBABLY COULD'VE JUST GENTLY PUSHED IT TO ONE SIDE. DO YOU HAVE TO "PHANTOM FIST" EVERYTHING?
YUP!
Magic Rope
allows user to magically affix Rope to some point
BUT WHAT IS IT ATTACHED TO?
AN EXTRA-DIMENSIONAL... ANCHOR...THING!
I DON'T HAVE TO UNDERSTAND THE SPELLS! I JUST CAST THEM!
CREEAAK
SNAAWWPFT!

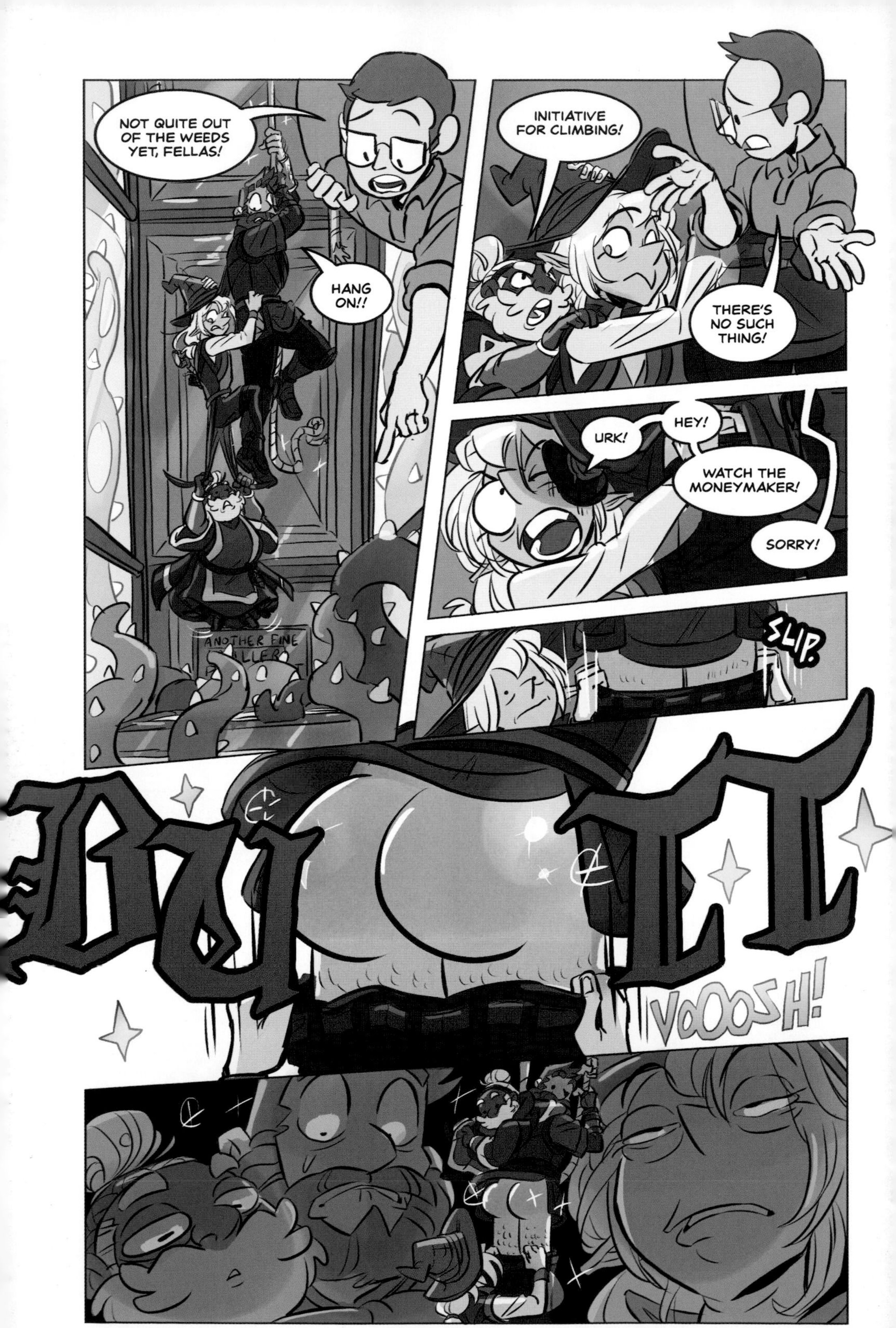
NOT QUITE OUT OF THE WEEDS YET, FELLAS!
HANG ON!!
ANOTHER FINE
INITIATIVE FOR CLIMBING!
THERE'S NO SUCH THING!
URK!
HEY!
WATCH THE MONEYMAKER!
SORRY!
SLIP.
BUTT
VOOOSH!

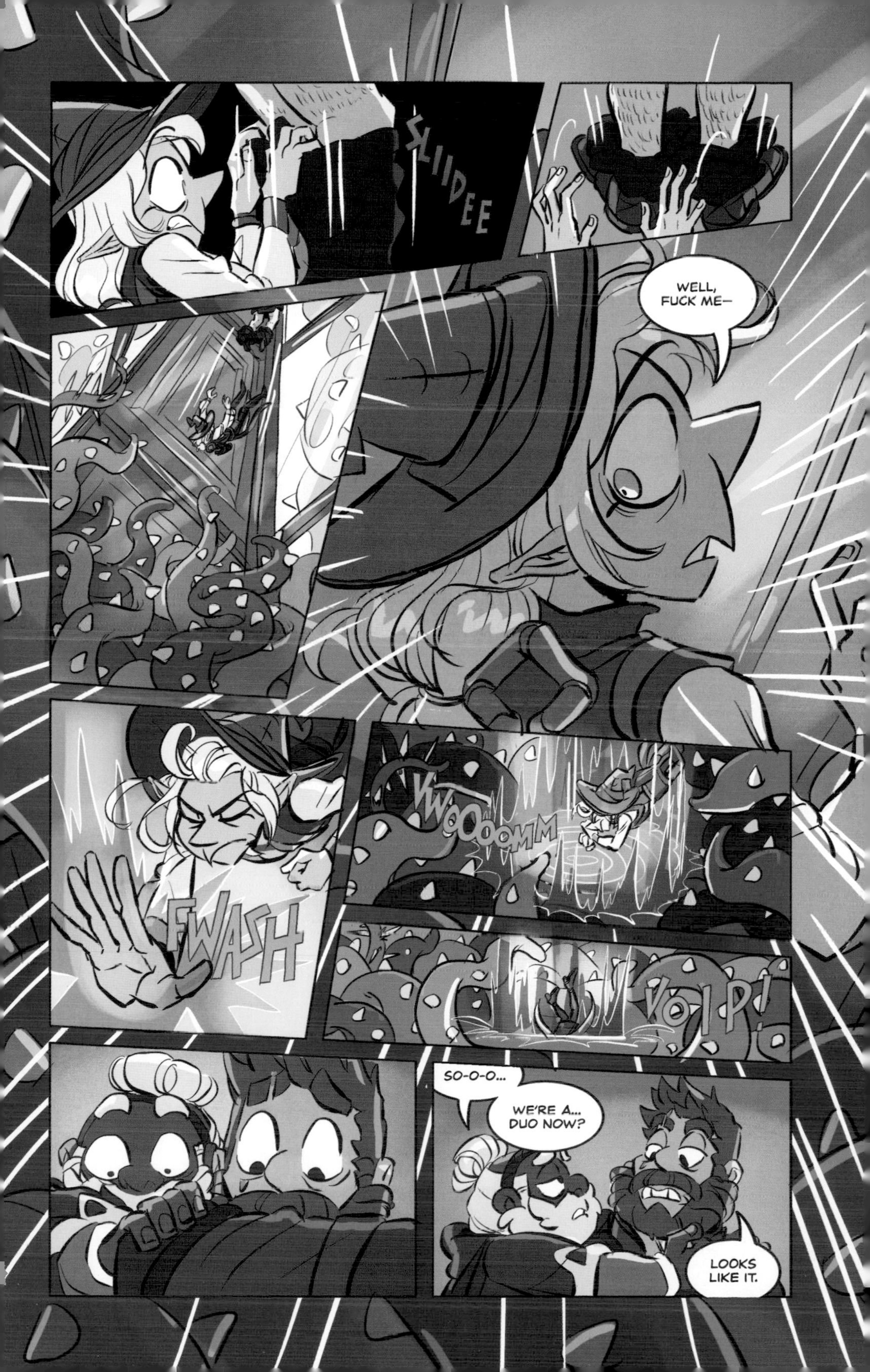
SLIIDEE
WELL, FUCK ME—
FWASH
VWOOOOMM
VOIP!
SO-O-O...
WE'RE A... DUO NOW?
LOOKS LIKE IT.

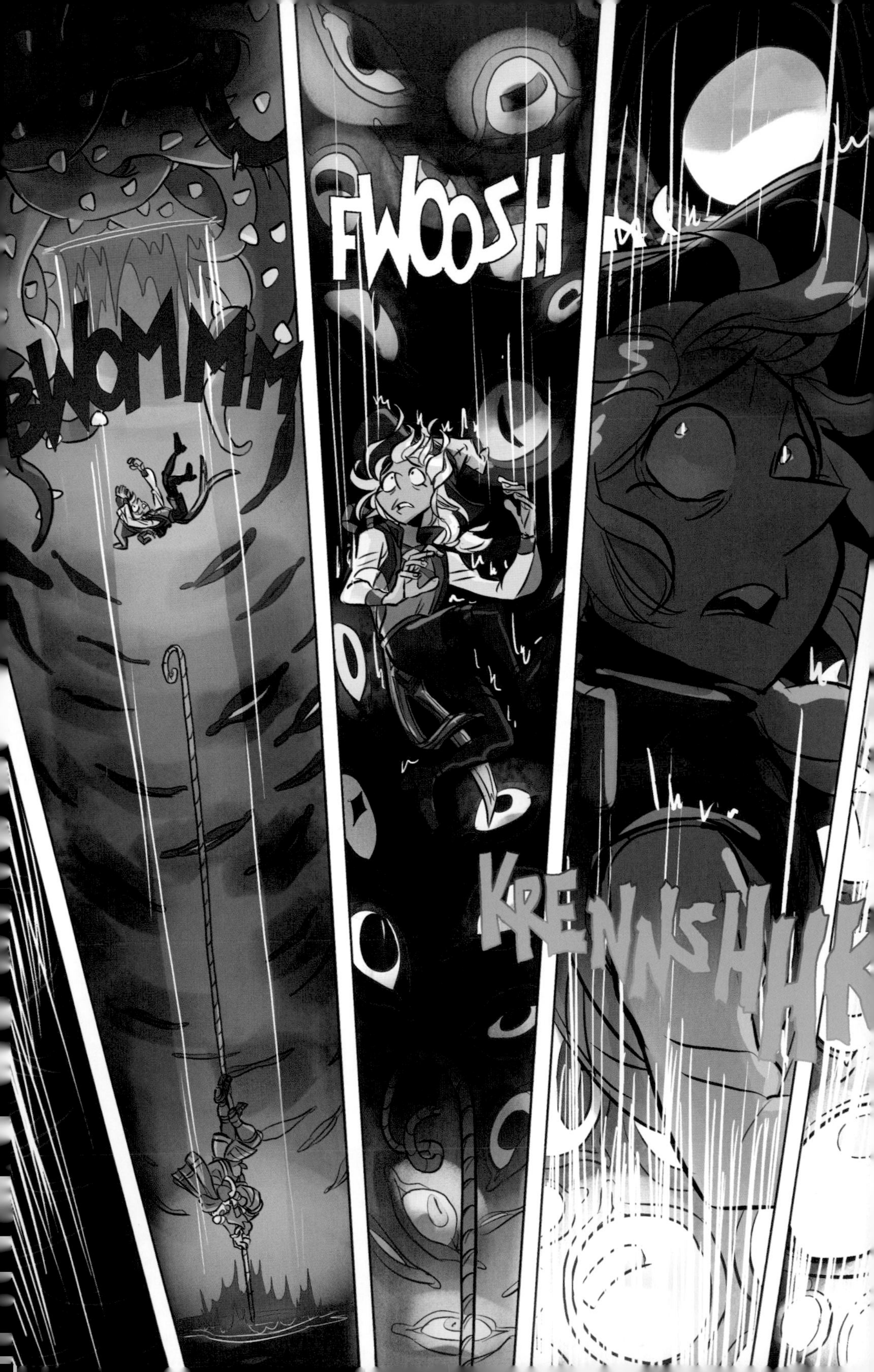
BWOMMM
FWOOSH
KRENNSHHK

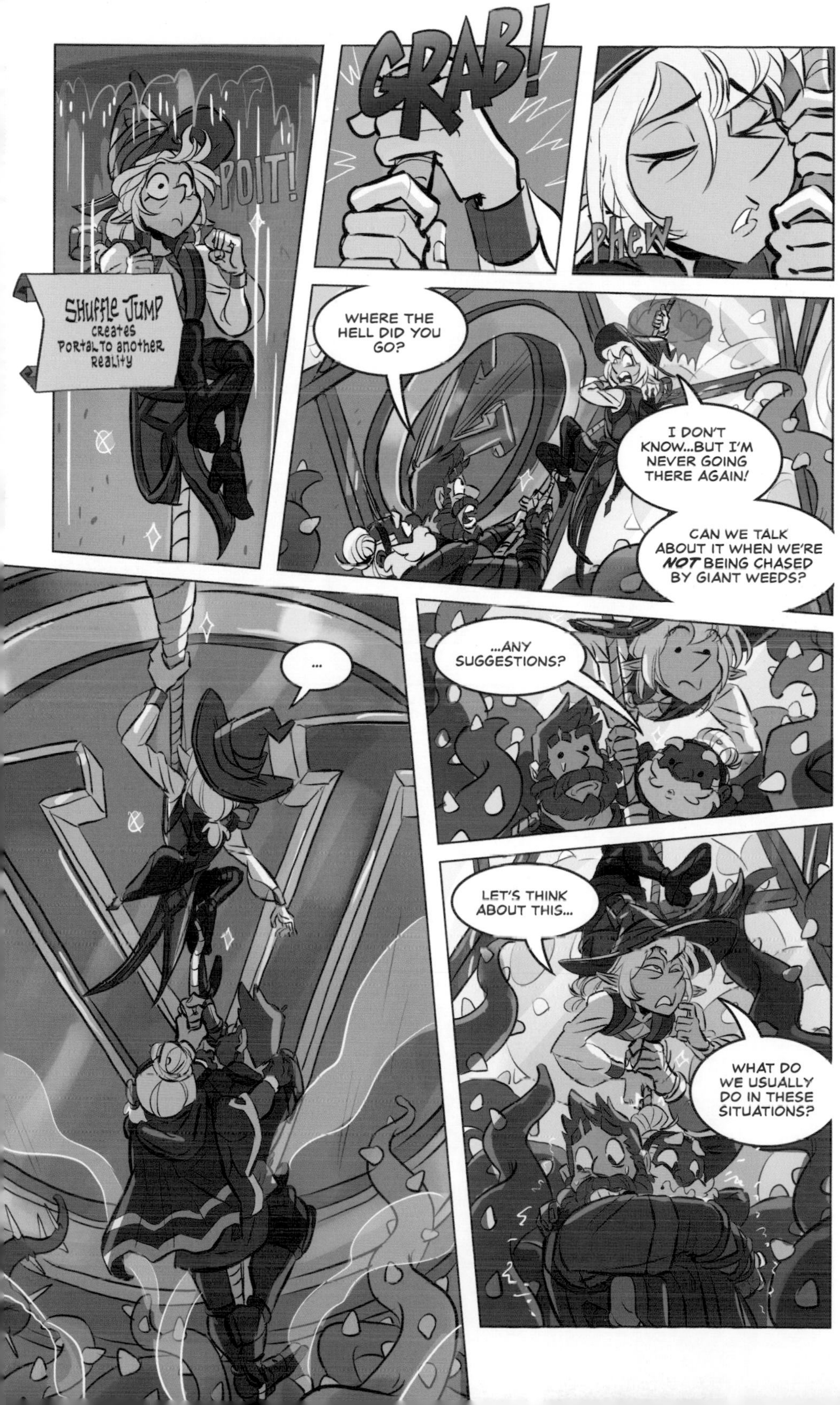

POIT!
GRAB!
PHEW
SHUFFLE JUMP creates portal to another reality
WHERE THE HELL DID YOU GO?
I DON'T KNOW...BUT I'M NEVER GOING THERE AGAIN!
CAN WE TALK ABOUT IT WHEN WE'RE NOT BEING CHASED BY GIANT WEEDS?
...
...ANY SUGGESTIONS?
LET'S THINK ABOUT THIS...
WHAT DO WE USUALLY DO IN THESE SITUATIONS?

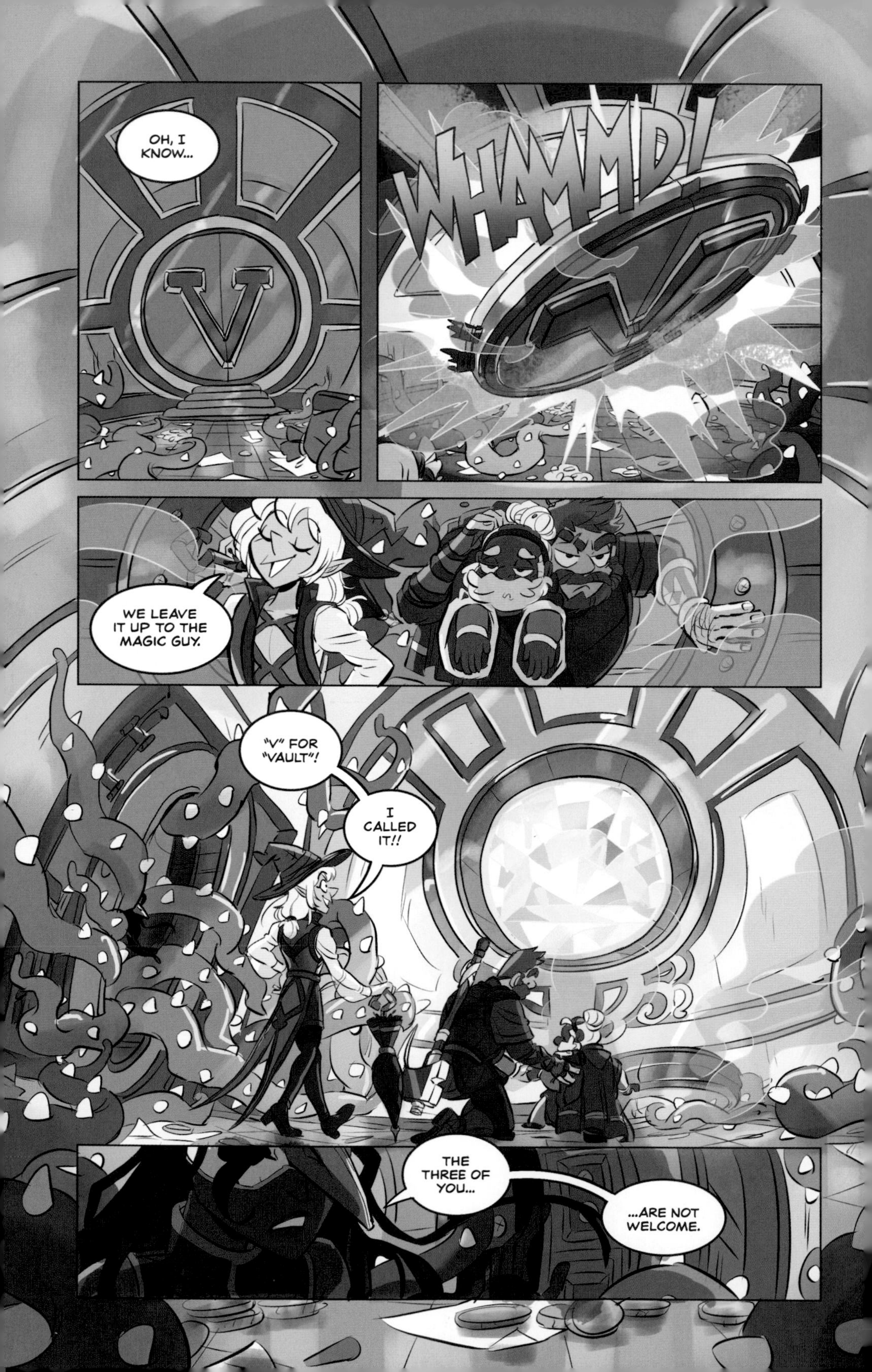
OH, I KNOW...
WHAMMD!
WE LEAVE IT UP TO THE MAGIC GUY.
"V" FOR "VAULT"!
I CALLED IT!!
THE THREE OF YOU...
...ARE NOT WELCOME.

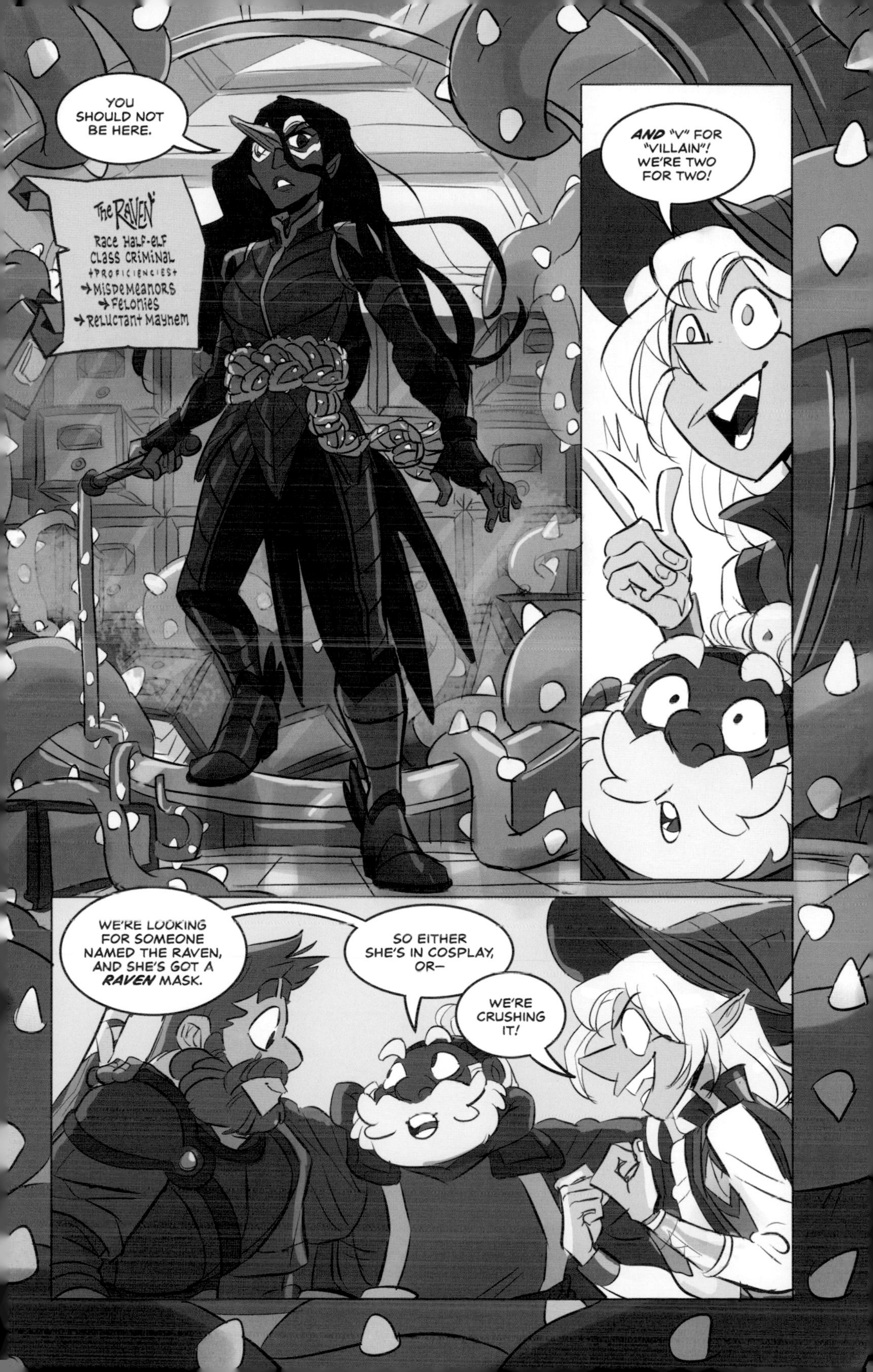
YOU SHOULD NOT BE HERE.
THE RAVEN
RACE HALF-ELF
CLASS CRIMINAL
PROFICIENCIES
→MISDEMEANORS
→FELONIES
→RELUCTANT MAYHEM
AND "V" FOR "VILLAIN"! WE'RE TWO FOR TWO!
WE'RE LOOKING FOR SOMEONE NAMED THE RAVEN, AND SHE'S GOT A RAVEN MASK.
SO EITHER SHE'S IN COSPLAY, OR—
WE'RE CRUSHING IT!

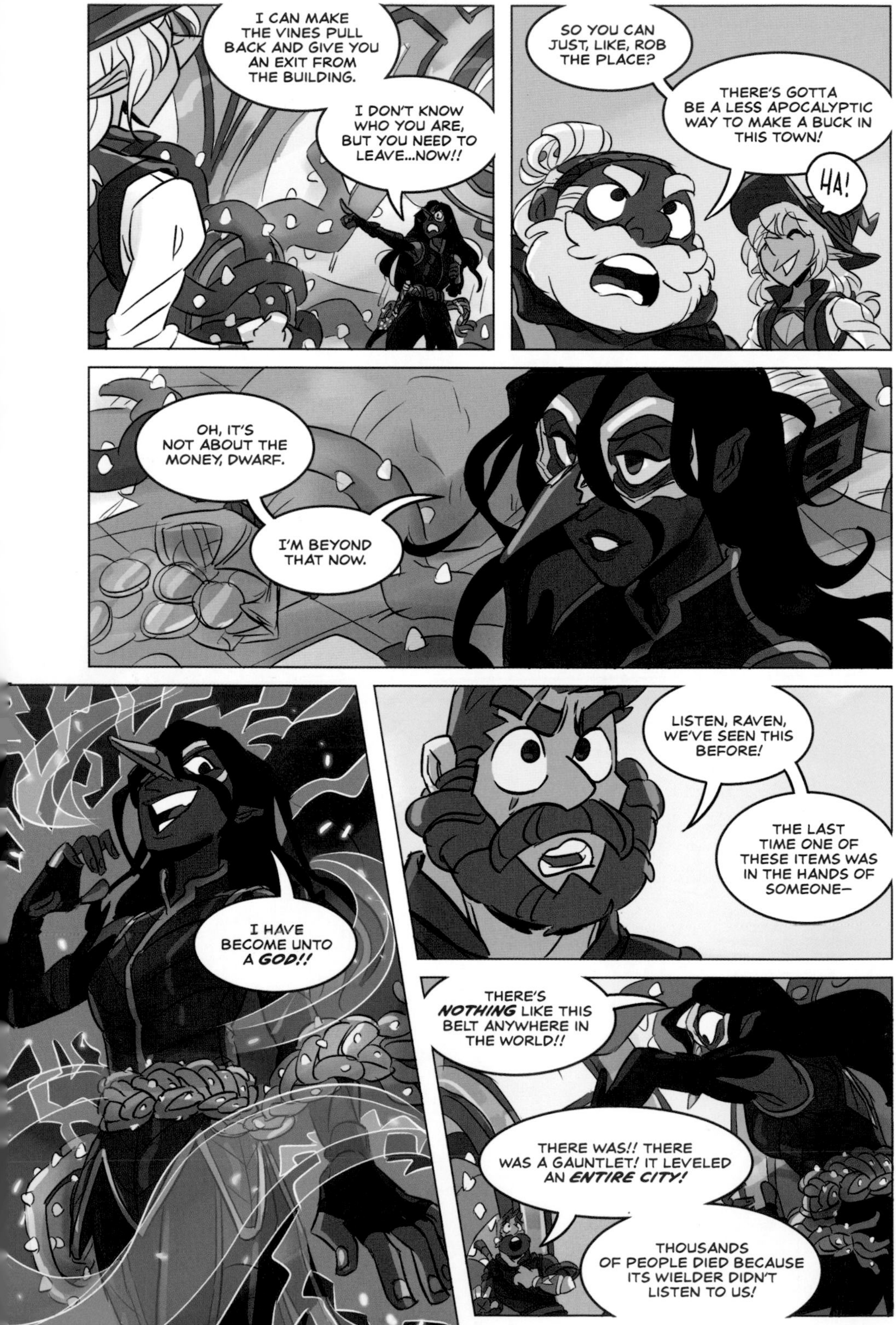
I CAN MAKE THE VINES PULL BACK AND GIVE YOU AN EXIT FROM THE BUILDING.
I DON'T KNOW WHO YOU ARE, BUT YOU NEED TO LEAVE...NOW!!
SO YOU CAN JUST, LIKE, ROB THE PLACE?
THERE'S GOTTA BE A LESS APOCALYPTIC WAY TO MAKE A BUCK IN THIS TOWN!
HA!
OH, IT'S NOT ABOUT THE MONEY, DWARF.
I'M BEYOND THAT NOW.
I HAVE BECOME UNTO A *GOD!!*
LISTEN, RAVEN, WE'VE SEEN THIS BEFORE!
THE LAST TIME ONE OF THESE ITEMS WAS IN THE HANDS OF SOMEONE–
THERE'S ***NOTHING*** LIKE THIS BELT ANYWHERE IN THE WORLD!!
THERE WAS!! THERE WAS A GAUNTLET! IT LEVELED AN ***ENTIRE CITY!***
THOUSANDS OF PEOPLE DIED BECAUSE ITS WIELDER DIDN'T LISTEN TO US!

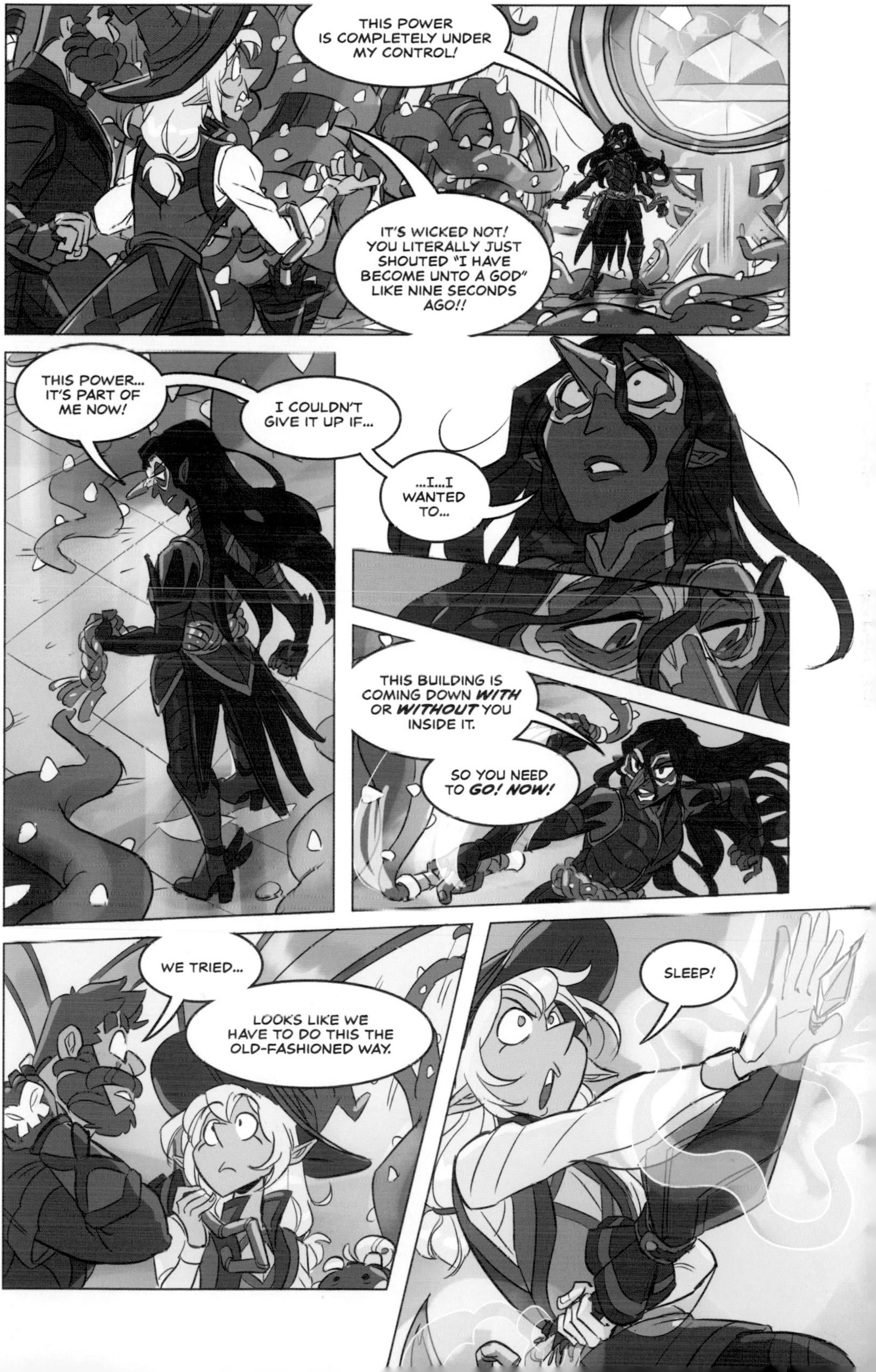
THIS POWER IS COMPLETELY UNDER MY CONTROL!
IT'S WICKED NOT! YOU LITERALLY JUST SHOUTED "I HAVE BECOME UNTO A GOD" LIKE NINE SECONDS AGO!!
THIS POWER... IT'S PART OF ME NOW!
I COULDN'T GIVE IT UP IF...
...I...I WANTED TO...
THIS BUILDING IS COMING DOWN *WITH* OR *WITHOUT* YOU INSIDE IT.
SO YOU NEED TO *GO! NOW!*
WE TRIED...
LOOKS LIKE WE HAVE TO DO THIS THE OLD-FASHIONED WAY.
SLEEP!

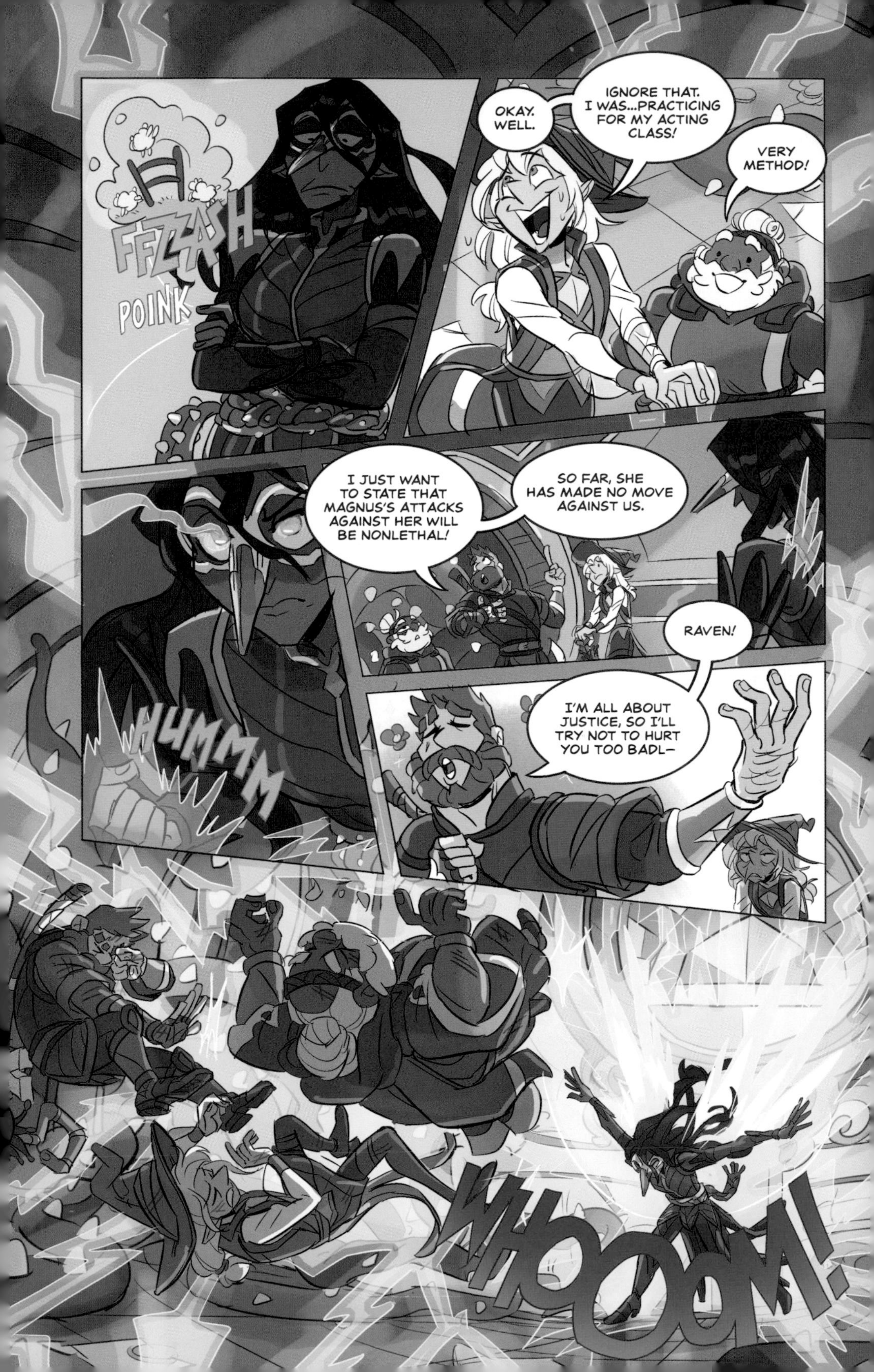
FFZZASH
POINK
OKAY. WELL.
IGNORE THAT. I WAS...PRACTICING FOR MY ACTING CLASS!
VERY METHOD!
I JUST WANT TO STATE THAT MAGNUS'S ATTACKS AGAINST HER WILL BE NONLETHAL!
SO FAR, SHE HAS MADE NO MOVE AGAINST US.
HUMMMM
RAVEN!
I'M ALL ABOUT JUSTICE, SO I'LL TRY NOT TO HURT YOU TOO BADL—
WHOOOM!

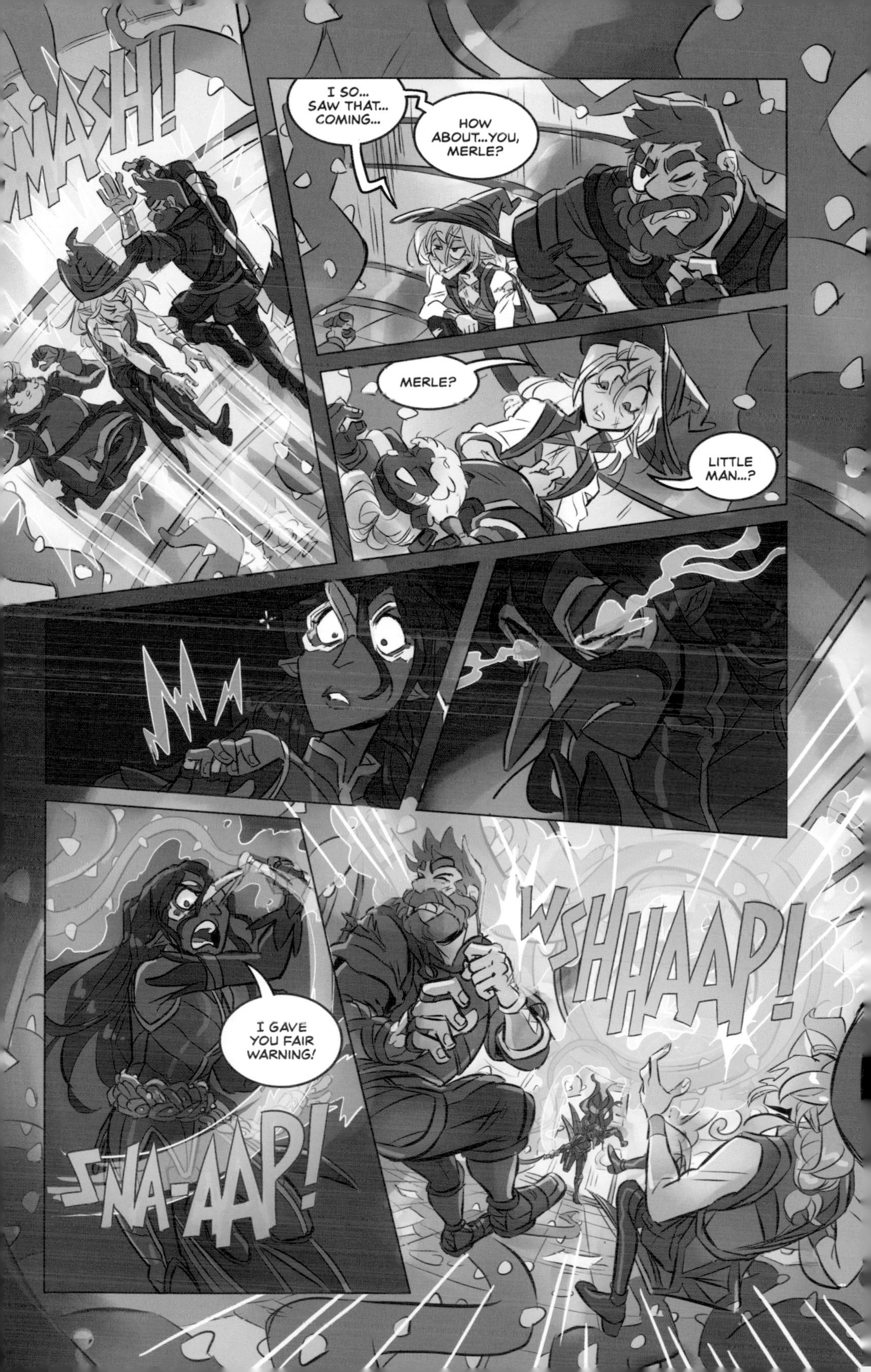
WASH!
I SO... SAW THAT... COMING...
HOW ABOUT...YOU, MERLE?
MERLE?
LITTLE MAN...?
I GAVE YOU FAIR WARNING!
WSHHAAP!
SNA-AAP!

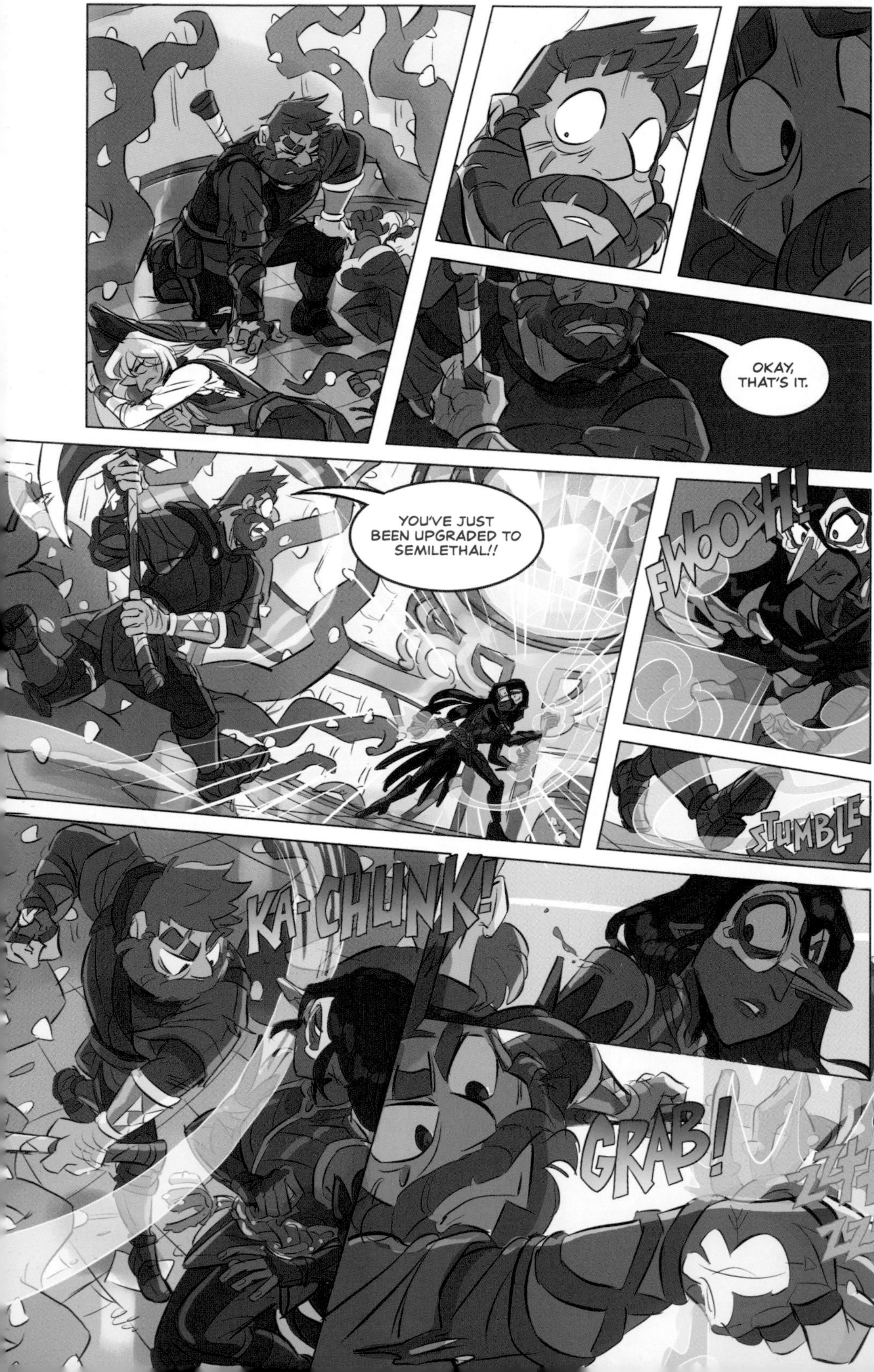
OKAY, THAT'S IT.
YOU'VE JUST BEEN UPGRADED TO SEMILETHAL!!
FWOOSH!
STUMBLE
KA-CHUNK!
GRAB!

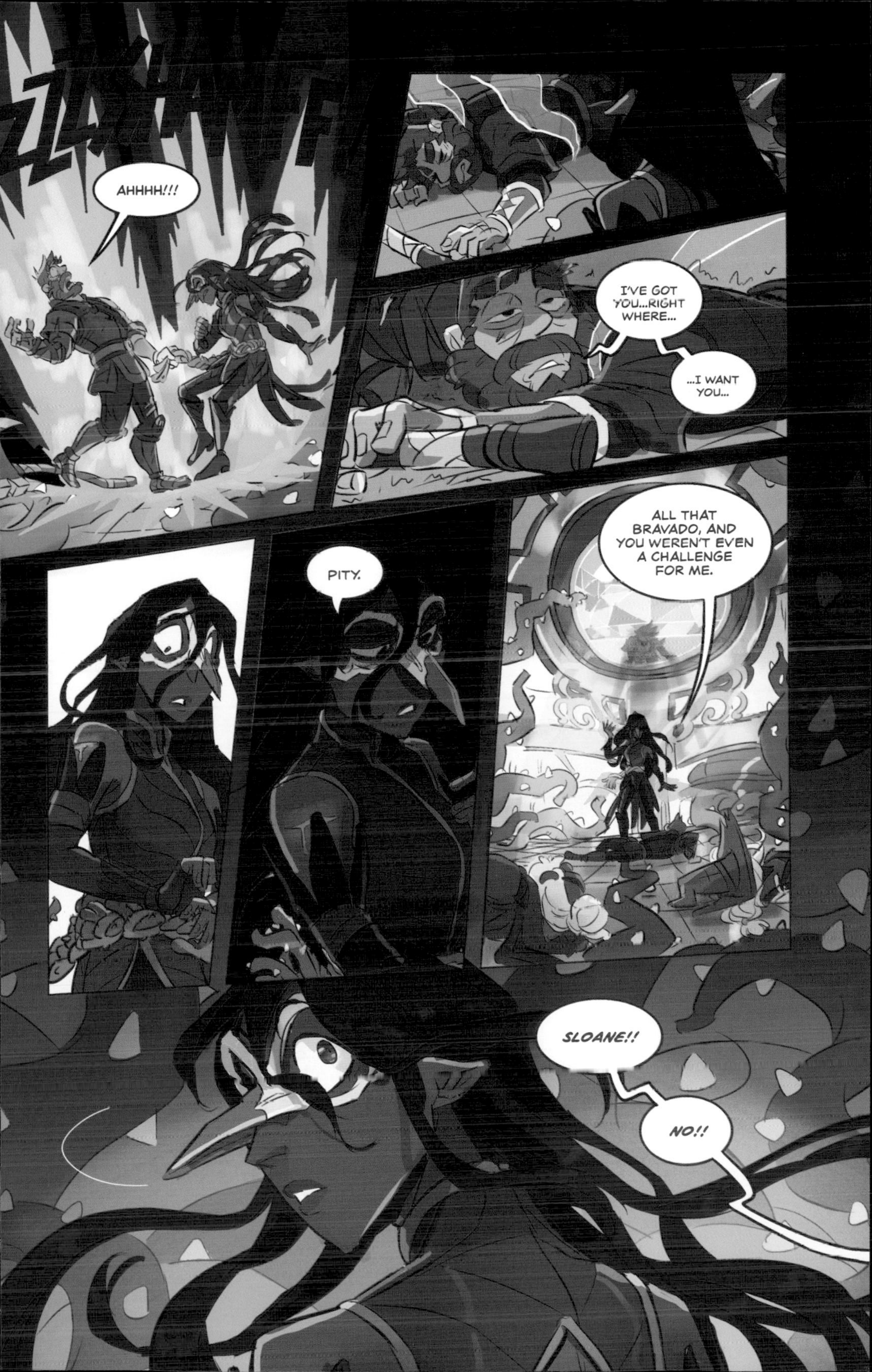
ZZAKT
AHHHH!!!
I'VE GOT YOU...RIGHT WHERE...
...I WANT YOU...
PITY.
ALL THAT BRAVADO, AND YOU WEREN'T EVEN A CHALLENGE FOR ME.
SLOANE!!
NO!!

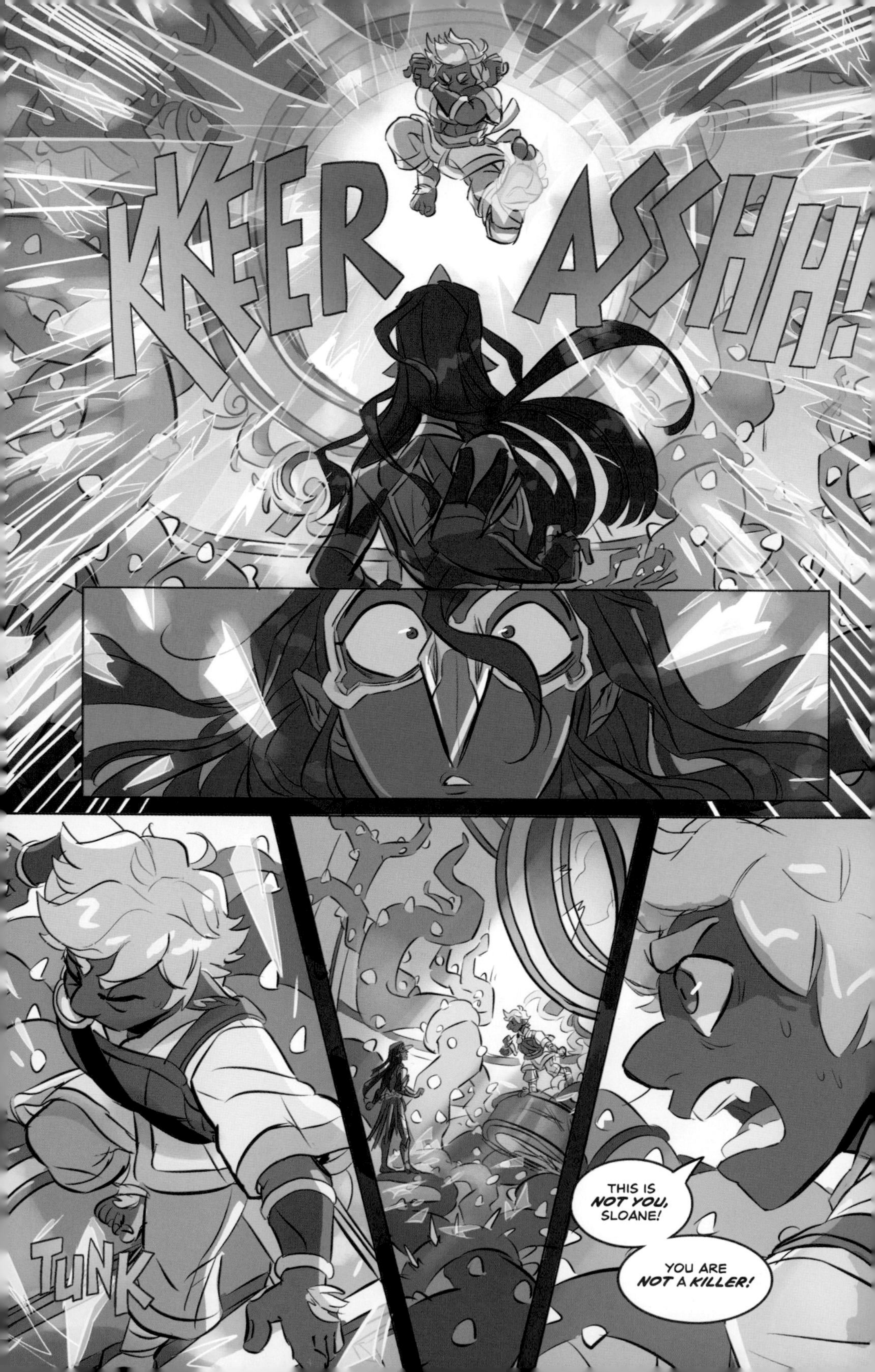
KKEER ASSHH!
TUNK
THIS IS NOT YOU, SLOANE!
YOU ARE NOT A KILLER!

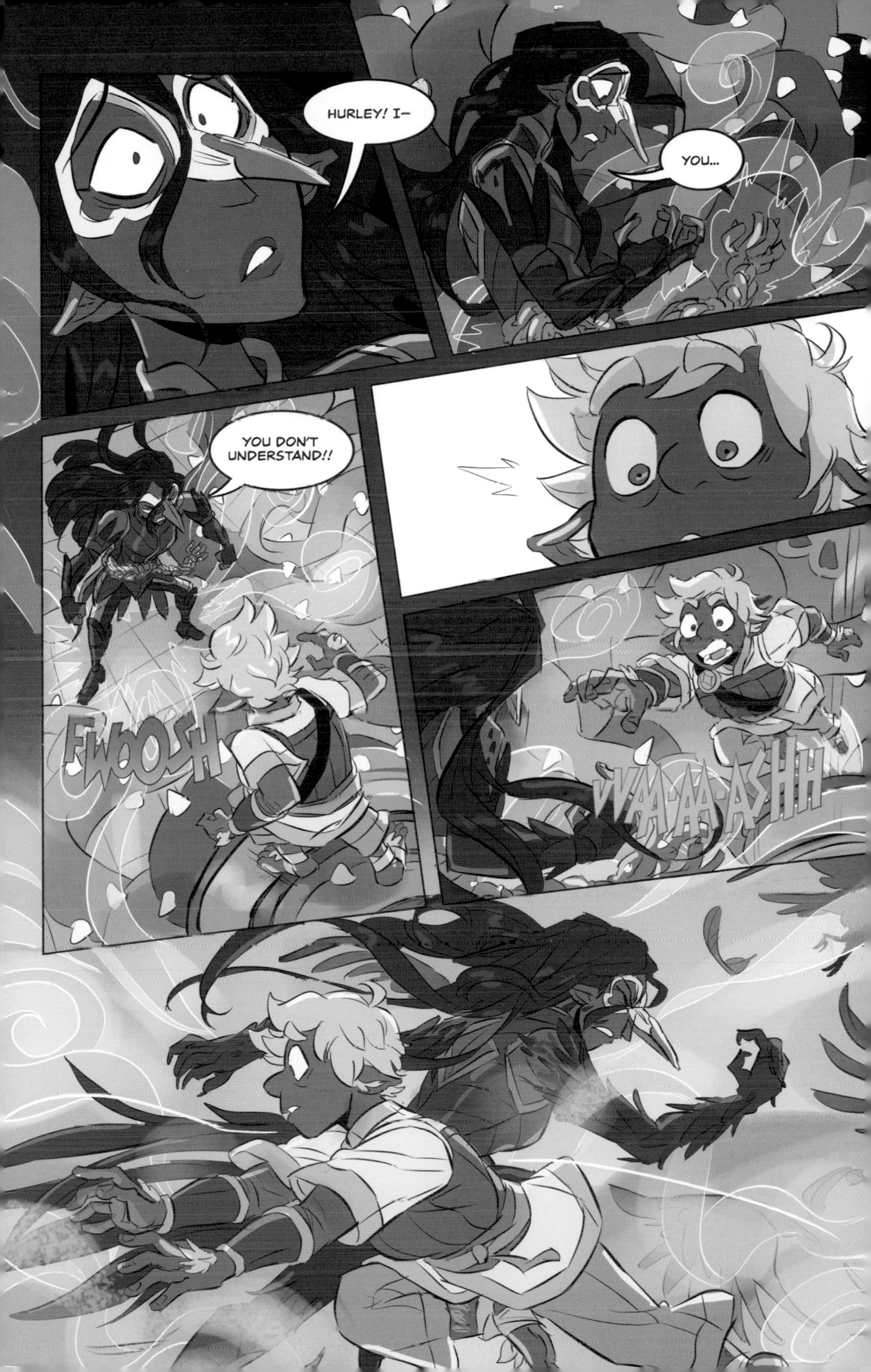
HURLEY! I—
YOU...
YOU DON'T UNDERSTAND!!
FWOOSH
WAAA-ASHH

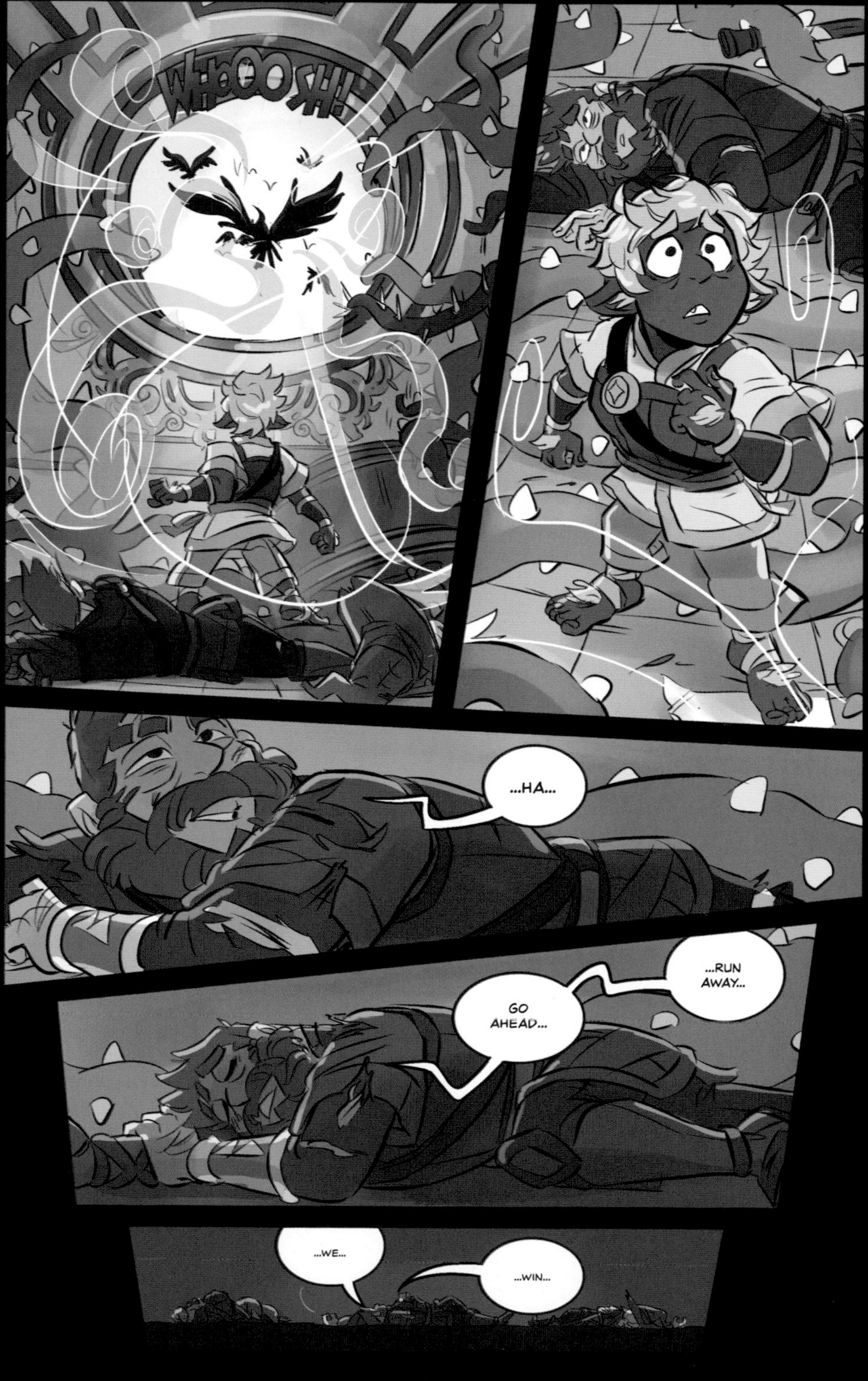
WHOOSH!!
...HA...
...RUN AWAY...
GO AHEAD...
...WE...
...WIN...

Chapter 3

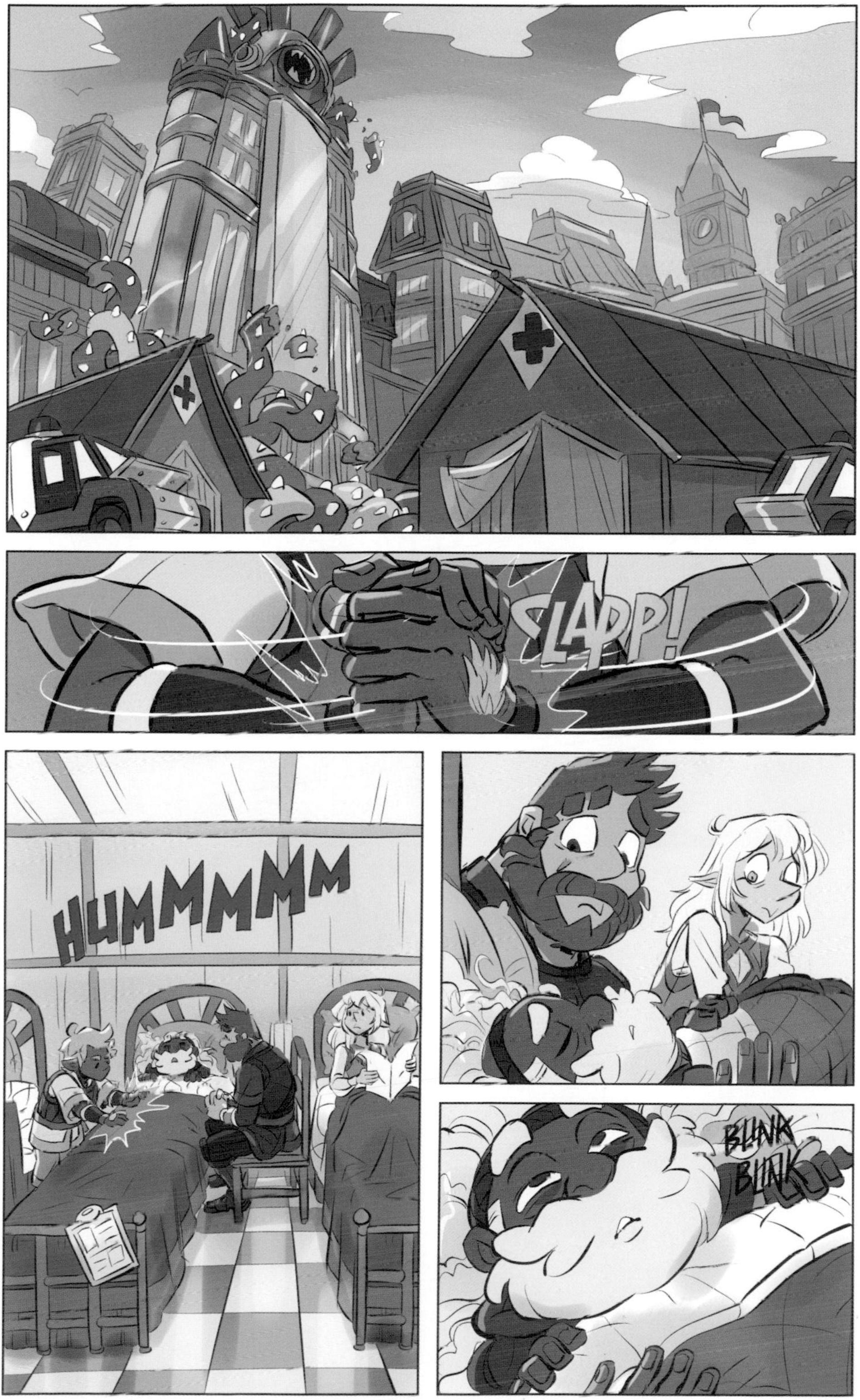
SLAPP!
HUMMMMMM
BLINK
BLINK

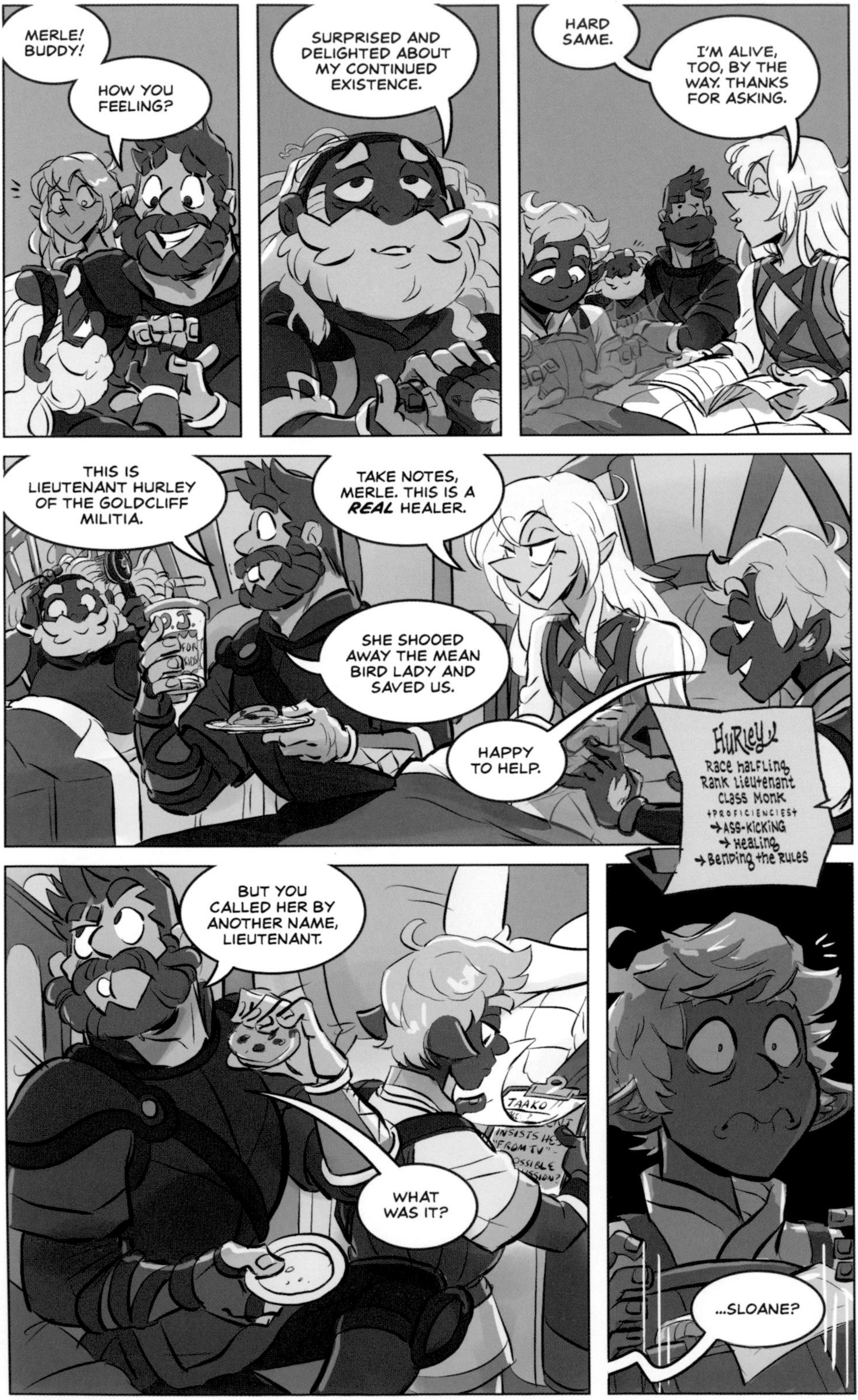
MERLE! BUDDY!
HOW YOU FEELING?
SURPRISED AND DELIGHTED ABOUT MY CONTINUED EXISTENCE.
HARD SAME.
I'M ALIVE, TOO, BY THE WAY. THANKS FOR ASKING.
THIS IS LIEUTENANT HURLEY OF THE GOLDCLIFF MILITIA.
TAKE NOTES, MERLE. THIS IS A *REAL* HEALER.
SHE SHOOED AWAY THE MEAN BIRD LADY AND SAVED US.
HAPPY TO HELP.
HURLEY
Race halfling
Rank Lieutenant
Class Monk
PROFICIENCIES
→ ASS-KICKING
→ Healing
→ Bending the Rules
BUT YOU CALLED HER BY ANOTHER NAME, LIEUTENANT.
WHAT WAS IT?
TAAKO
...SLOANE?

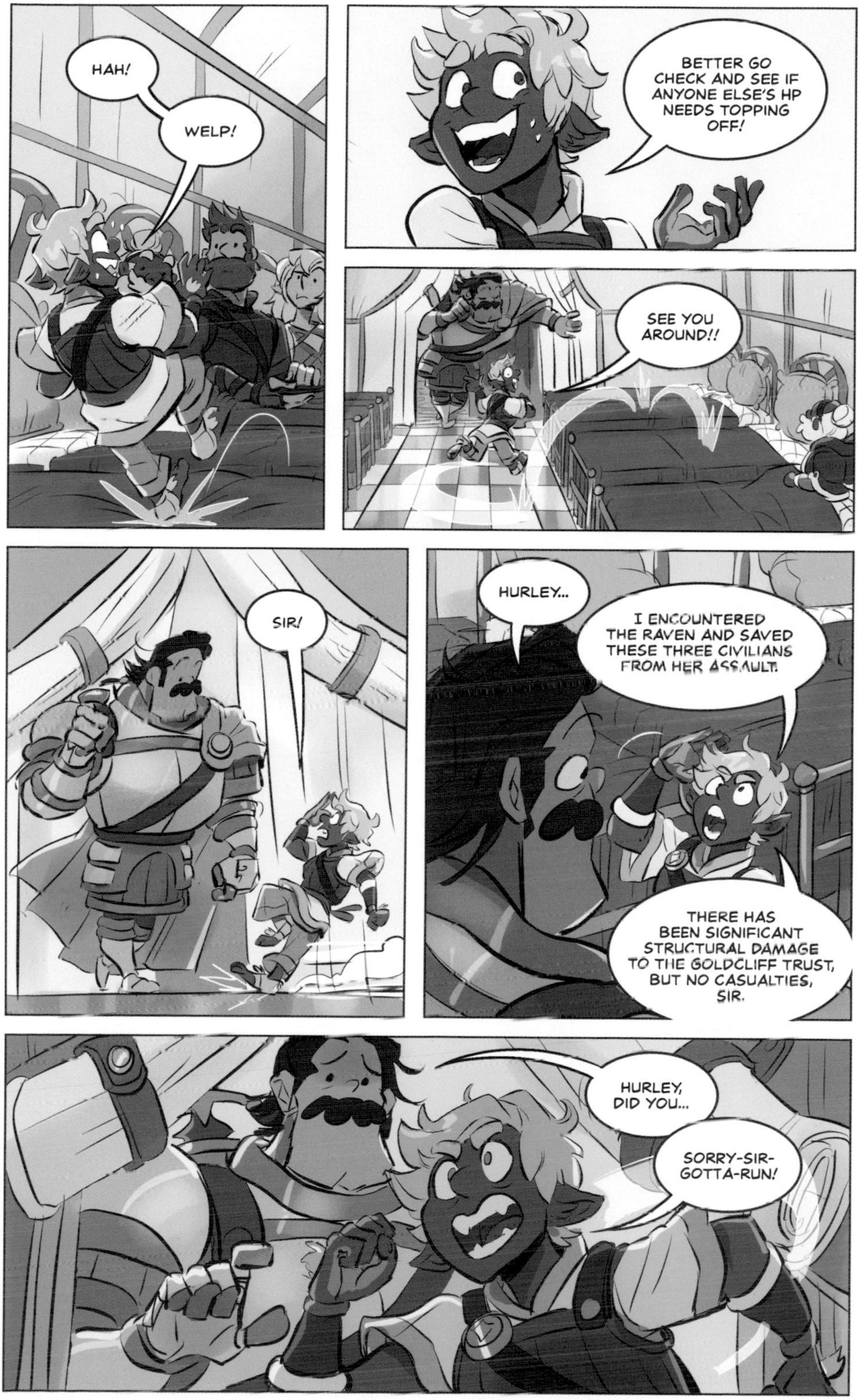
HAH!
WELP!
BETTER GO CHECK AND SEE IF ANYONE ELSE'S HP NEEDS TOPPING OFF!
SEE YOU AROUND!!
SIR!
HURLEY...
I ENCOUNTERED THE RAVEN AND SAVED THESE THREE CIVILIANS FROM HER ASSAULT.
THERE HAS BEEN SIGNIFICANT STRUCTURAL DAMAGE TO THE GOLDCLIFF TRUST, BUT NO CASUALTIES, SIR.
HURLEY, DID YOU...
SORRY-SIR-GOTTA-RUN!

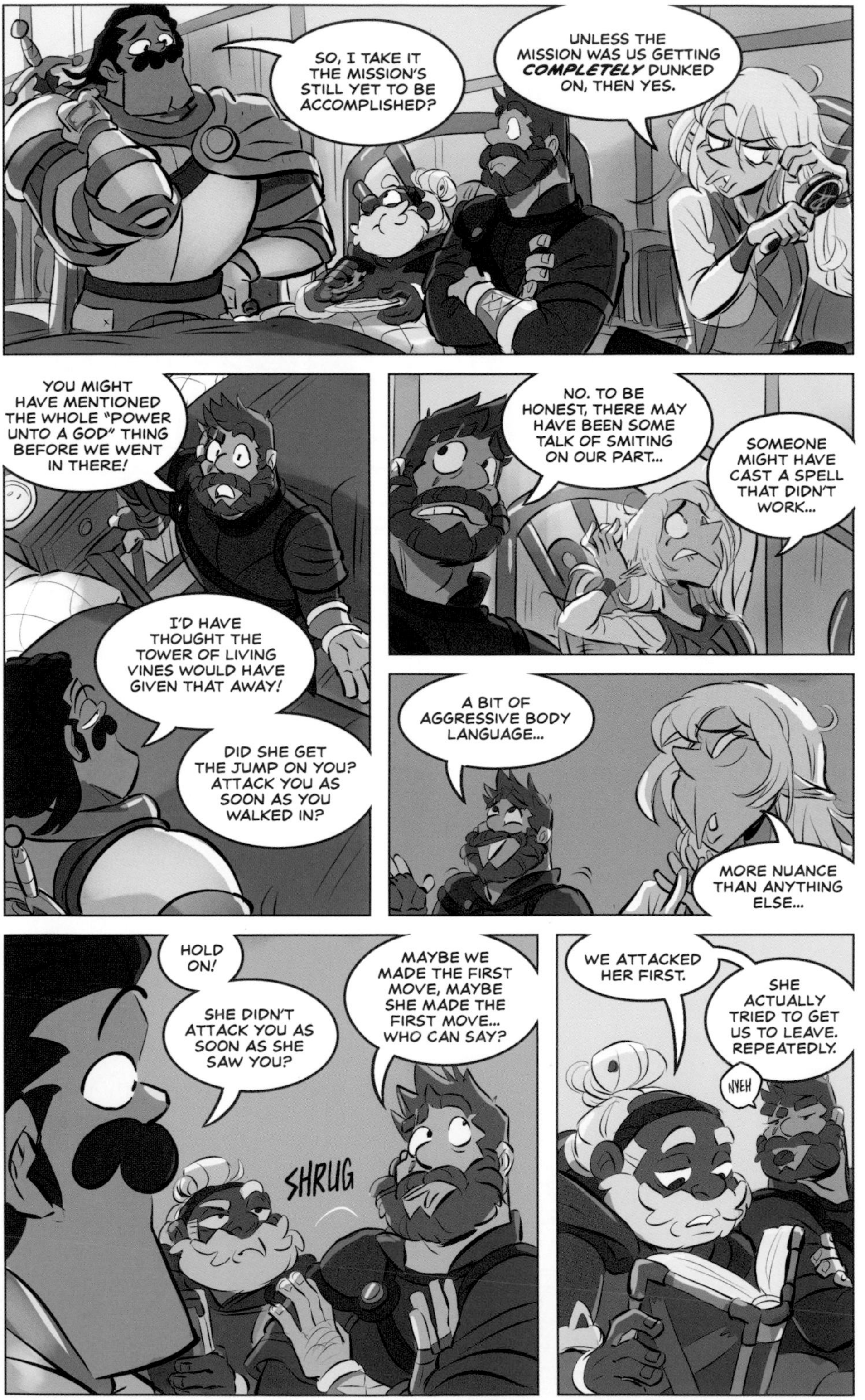
SO, I TAKE IT THE MISSION'S STILL YET TO BE ACCOMPLISHED?
UNLESS THE MISSION WAS US GETTING *COMPLETELY* DUNKED ON, THEN YES.
YOU MIGHT HAVE MENTIONED THE WHOLE "POWER UNTO A GOD" THING BEFORE WE WENT IN THERE!
I'D HAVE THOUGHT THE TOWER OF LIVING VINES WOULD HAVE GIVEN THAT AWAY!
DID SHE GET THE JUMP ON YOU? ATTACK YOU AS SOON AS YOU WALKED IN?
NO. TO BE HONEST, THERE MAY HAVE BEEN SOME TALK OF SMITING ON OUR PART...
SOMEONE MIGHT HAVE CAST A SPELL THAT DIDN'T WORK...
A BIT OF AGGRESSIVE BODY LANGUAGE...
MORE NUANCE THAN ANYTHING ELSE...
HOLD ON!
SHE DIDN'T ATTACK YOU AS SOON AS SHE SAW YOU?
MAYBE WE MADE THE FIRST MOVE, MAYBE SHE MADE THE FIRST MOVE... WHO CAN SAY?
SHRUG
WE ATTACKED HER FIRST.
SHE ACTUALLY TRIED TO GET US TO LEAVE. REPEATEDLY.
NYEH

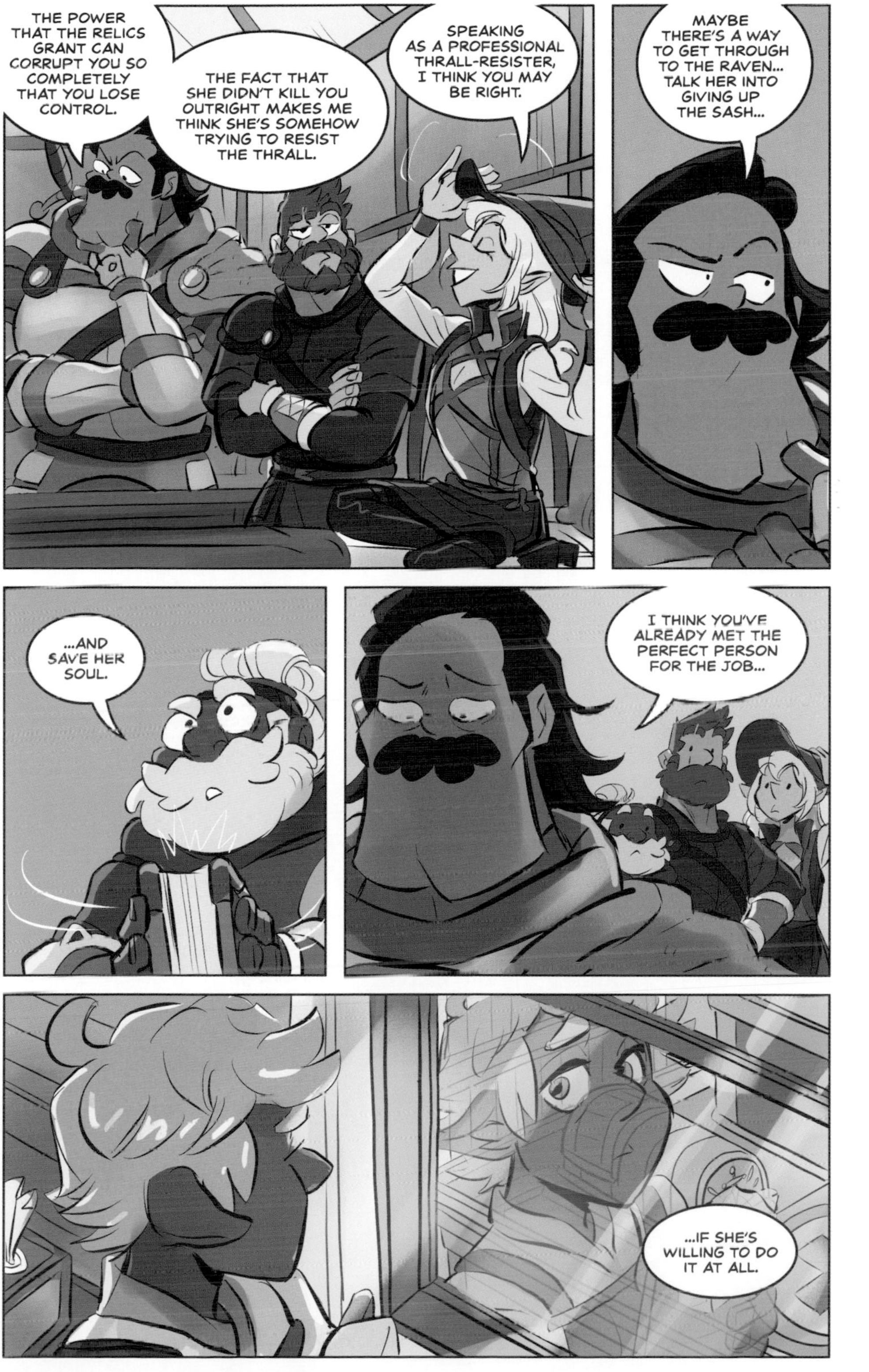
THE POWER THAT THE RELICS GRANT CAN CORRUPT YOU SO COMPLETELY THAT YOU LOSE CONTROL.
THE FACT THAT SHE DIDN'T KILL YOU OUTRIGHT MAKES ME THINK SHE'S SOMEHOW TRYING TO RESIST THE THRALL.
SPEAKING AS A PROFESSIONAL THRALL-RESISTER, I THINK YOU MAY BE RIGHT.
MAYBE THERE'S A WAY TO GET THROUGH TO THE RAVEN... TALK HER INTO GIVING UP THE SASH...
...AND SAVE HER SOUL.
I THINK YOU'VE ALREADY MET THE PERFECT PERSON FOR THE JOB...
...IF SHE'S WILLING TO DO IT AT ALL.

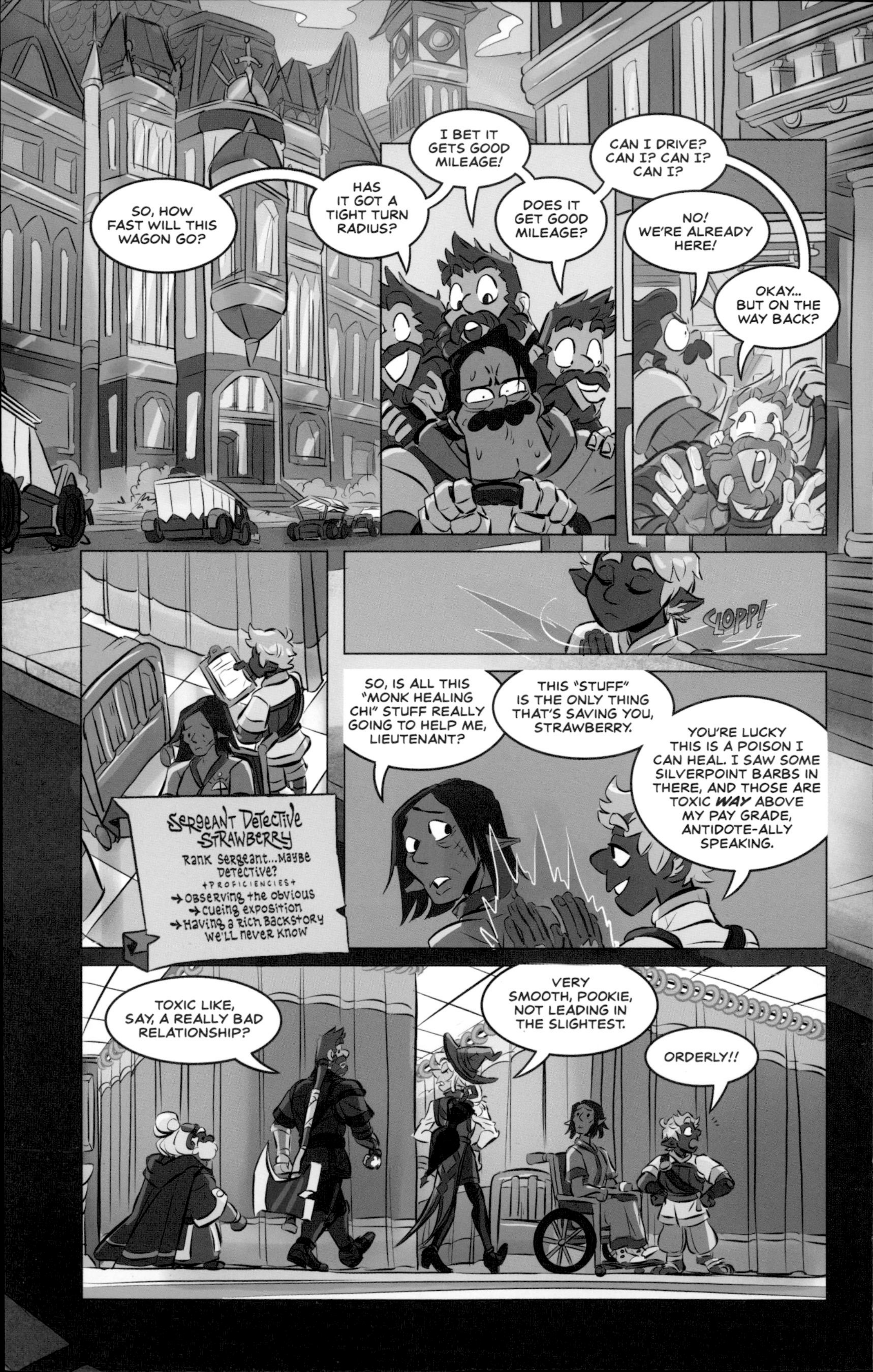
SO, HOW FAST WILL THIS WAGON GO?
HAS IT GOT A TIGHT TURN RADIUS?
I BET IT GETS GOOD MILEAGE!
DOES IT GET GOOD MILEAGE?
CAN I DRIVE? CAN I? CAN I? CAN I?
NO! WE'RE ALREADY HERE!
OKAY... BUT ON THE WAY BACK?
CLOPP!
SERGEANT DETECTIVE STRAWBERRY
RANK SERGEANT...MAYBE DETECTIVE?
+PROFICIENCIES+
→OBSERVING THE OBVIOUS
→CUEING EXPOSITION
→HAVING A RICH BACKSTORY WE'LL NEVER KNOW
SO, IS ALL THIS "MONK HEALING CHI" STUFF REALLY GOING TO HELP ME, LIEUTENANT?
THIS "STUFF" IS THE ONLY THING THAT'S SAVING YOU, STRAWBERRY.
YOU'RE LUCKY THIS IS A POISON I CAN HEAL. I SAW SOME SILVERPOINT BARBS IN THERE, AND THOSE ARE TOXIC WAY ABOVE MY PAY GRADE, ANTIDOTE-ALLY SPEAKING.
TOXIC LIKE, SAY, A REALLY BAD RELATIONSHIP?
VERY SMOOTH, POOKIE, NOT LEADING IN THE SLIGHTEST.
ORDERLY!!

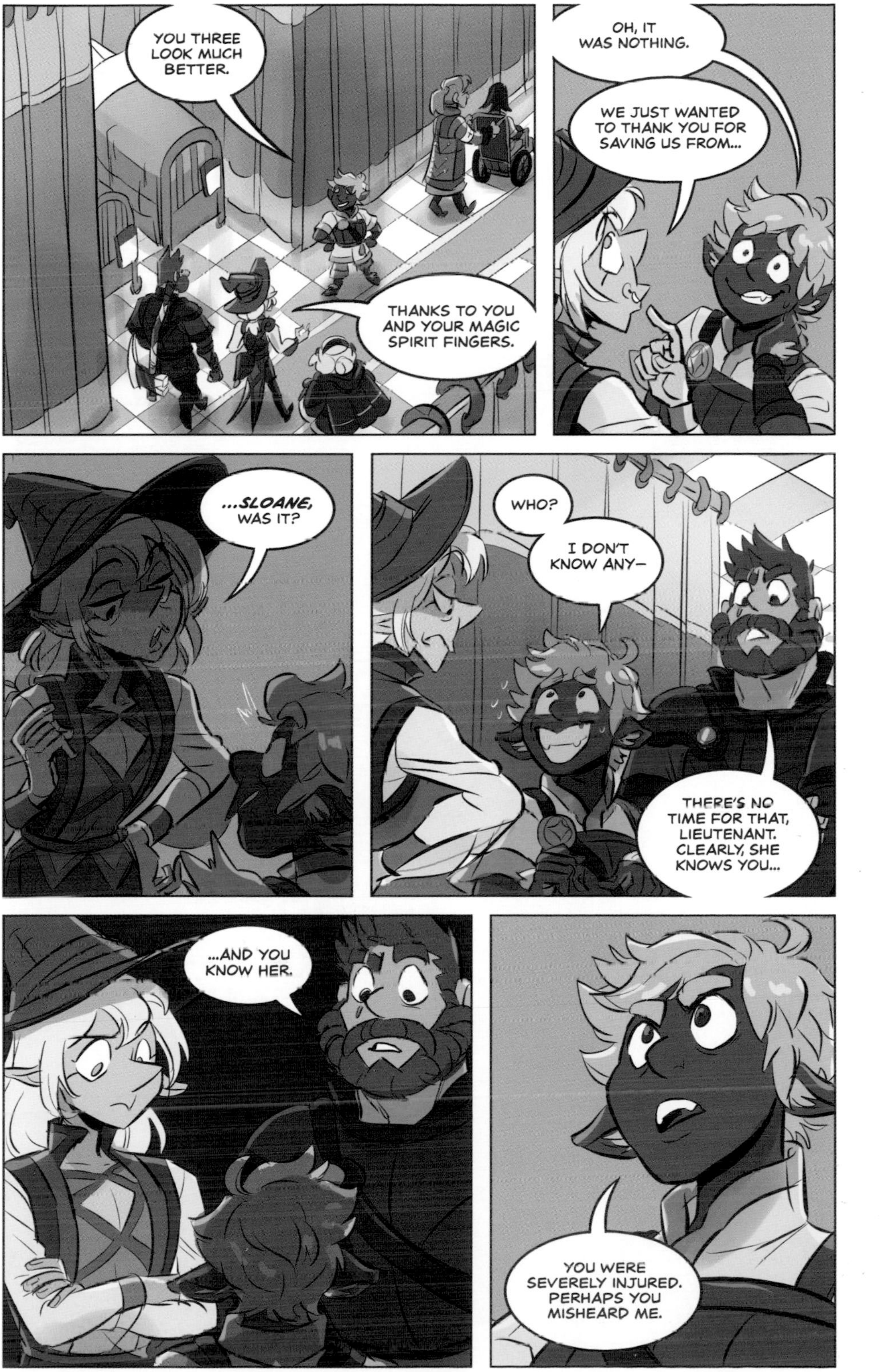
YOU THREE LOOK MUCH BETTER.
THANKS TO YOU AND YOUR MAGIC SPIRIT FINGERS.
OH, IT WAS NOTHING.
WE JUST WANTED TO THANK YOU FOR SAVING US FROM...
...SLOANE, WAS IT?
WHO?
I DON'T KNOW ANY—
THERE'S NO TIME FOR THAT, LIEUTENANT. CLEARLY, SHE KNOWS YOU...
...AND YOU KNOW HER.
YOU WERE SEVERELY INJURED. PERHAPS YOU MISHEARD ME.

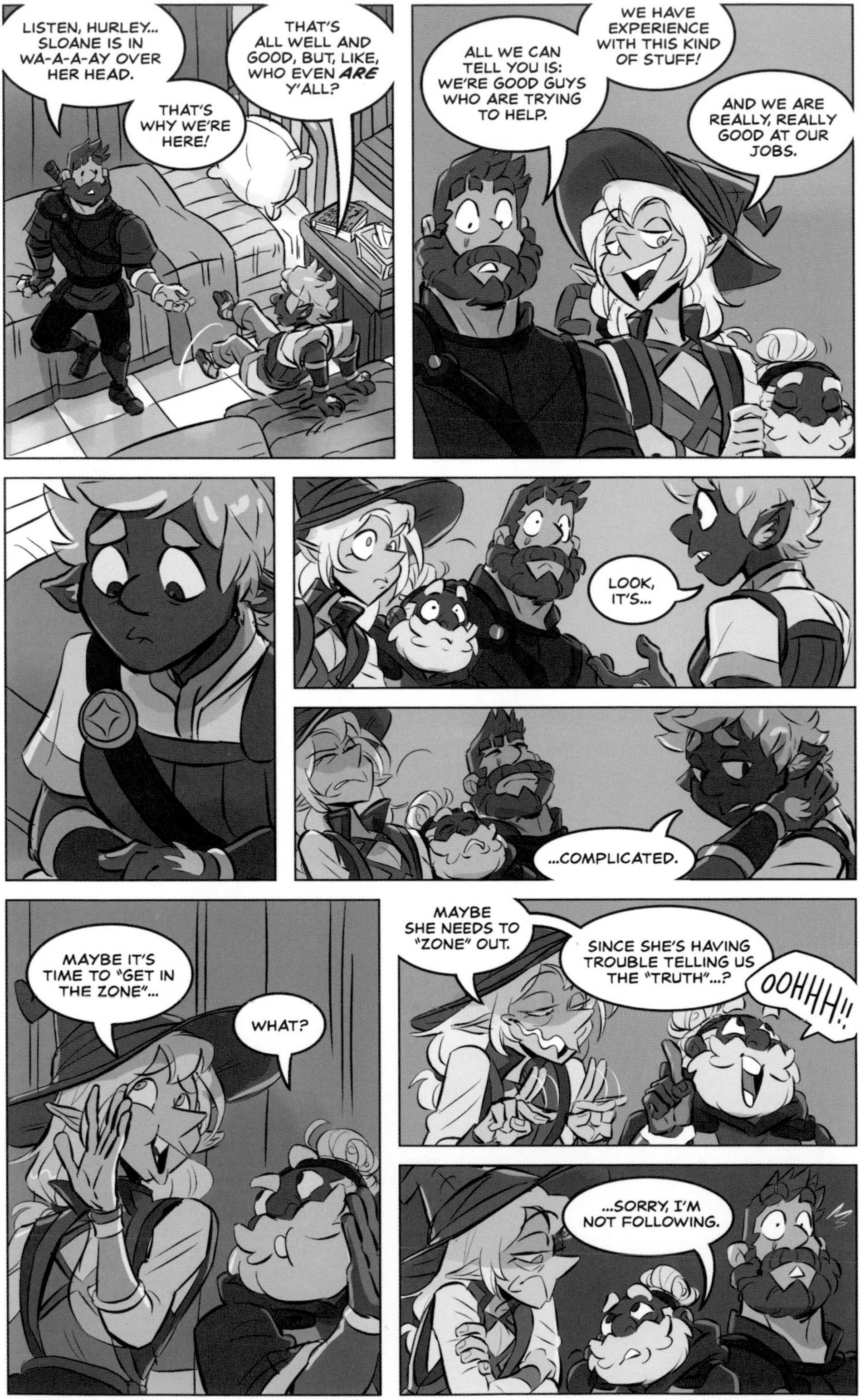
LISTEN, HURLEY... SLOANE IS IN WA-A-A-AY OVER HER HEAD.
THAT'S WHY WE'RE HERE!
THAT'S ALL WELL AND GOOD, BUT, LIKE, WHO EVEN ARE Y'ALL?
ALL WE CAN TELL YOU IS: WE'RE GOOD GUYS WHO ARE TRYING TO HELP.
WE HAVE EXPERIENCE WITH THIS KIND OF STUFF!
AND WE ARE REALLY, REALLY GOOD AT OUR JOBS.
LOOK, IT'S...
...COMPLICATED.
MAYBE IT'S TIME TO "GET IN THE ZONE"...
WHAT?
MAYBE SHE NEEDS TO "ZONE" OUT.
SINCE SHE'S HAVING TROUBLE TELLING US THE "TRUTH"...?
OOHHH!!
...SORRY, I'M NOT FOLLOWING.

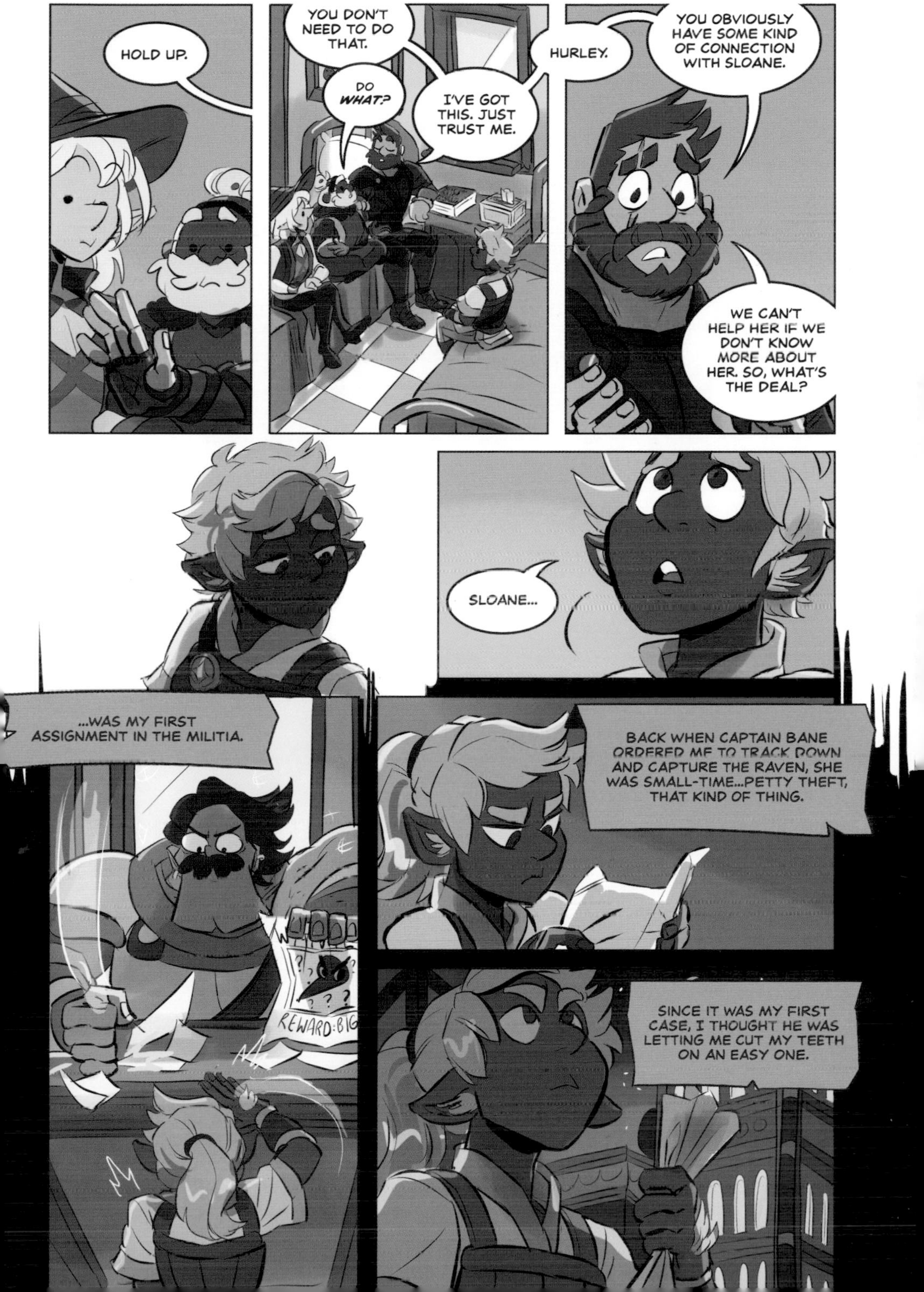
HOLD UP.
YOU DON'T NEED TO DO THAT.
DO WHAT?
I'VE GOT THIS. JUST TRUST ME.
HURLEY.
YOU OBVIOUSLY HAVE SOME KIND OF CONNECTION WITH SLOANE.
WE CAN'T HELP HER IF WE DON'T KNOW MORE ABOUT HER. SO, WHAT'S THE DEAL?
SLOANE...
...WAS MY FIRST ASSIGNMENT IN THE MILITIA.
REWARD: BIG
BACK WHEN CAPTAIN BANE ORDERED ME TO TRACK DOWN AND CAPTURE THE RAVEN, SHE WAS SMALL-TIME...PETTY THEFT, THAT KIND OF THING.
SINCE IT WAS MY FIRST CASE, I THOUGHT HE WAS LETTING ME CUT MY TEETH ON AN EASY ONE.

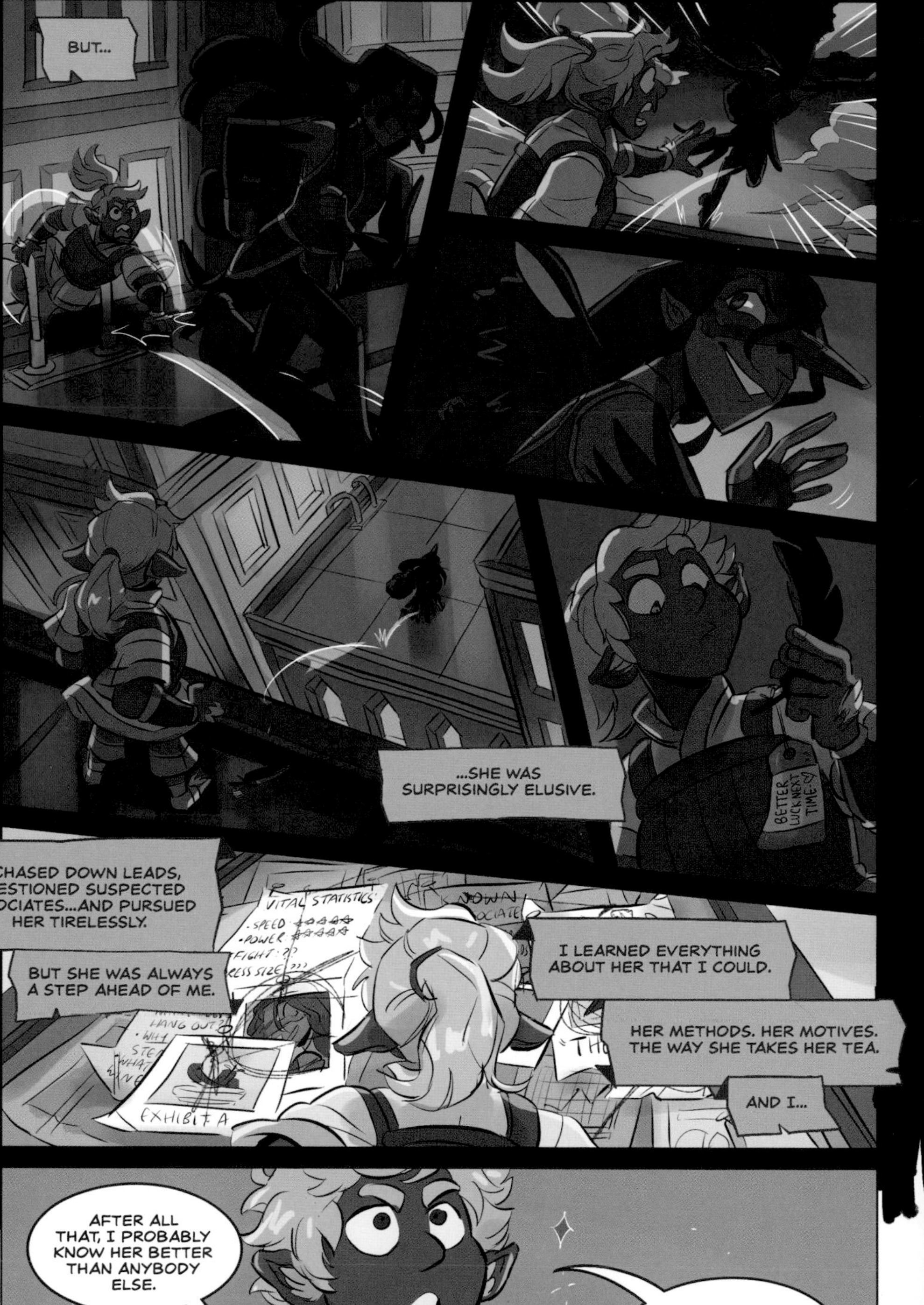
BUT...
...SHE WAS SURPRISINGLY ELUSIVE.
BETTER LUCK NEXT TIME
I CHASED DOWN LEADS, QUESTIONED SUSPECTED ASSOCIATES...AND PURSUED HER TIRELESSLY.
VITAL STATISTICS
SPEED
POWER
BUT SHE WAS ALWAYS A STEP AHEAD OF ME.
EXHIBIT A
I LEARNED EVERYTHING ABOUT HER THAT I COULD.
HER METHODS. HER MOTIVES. THE WAY SHE TAKES HER TEA.
AND I...
AFTER ALL THAT, I PROBABLY KNOW HER BETTER THAN ANYBODY ELSE.
AND I *KNOW* THAT I CAN REACH HER AND SNAP HER OUT OF THIS.

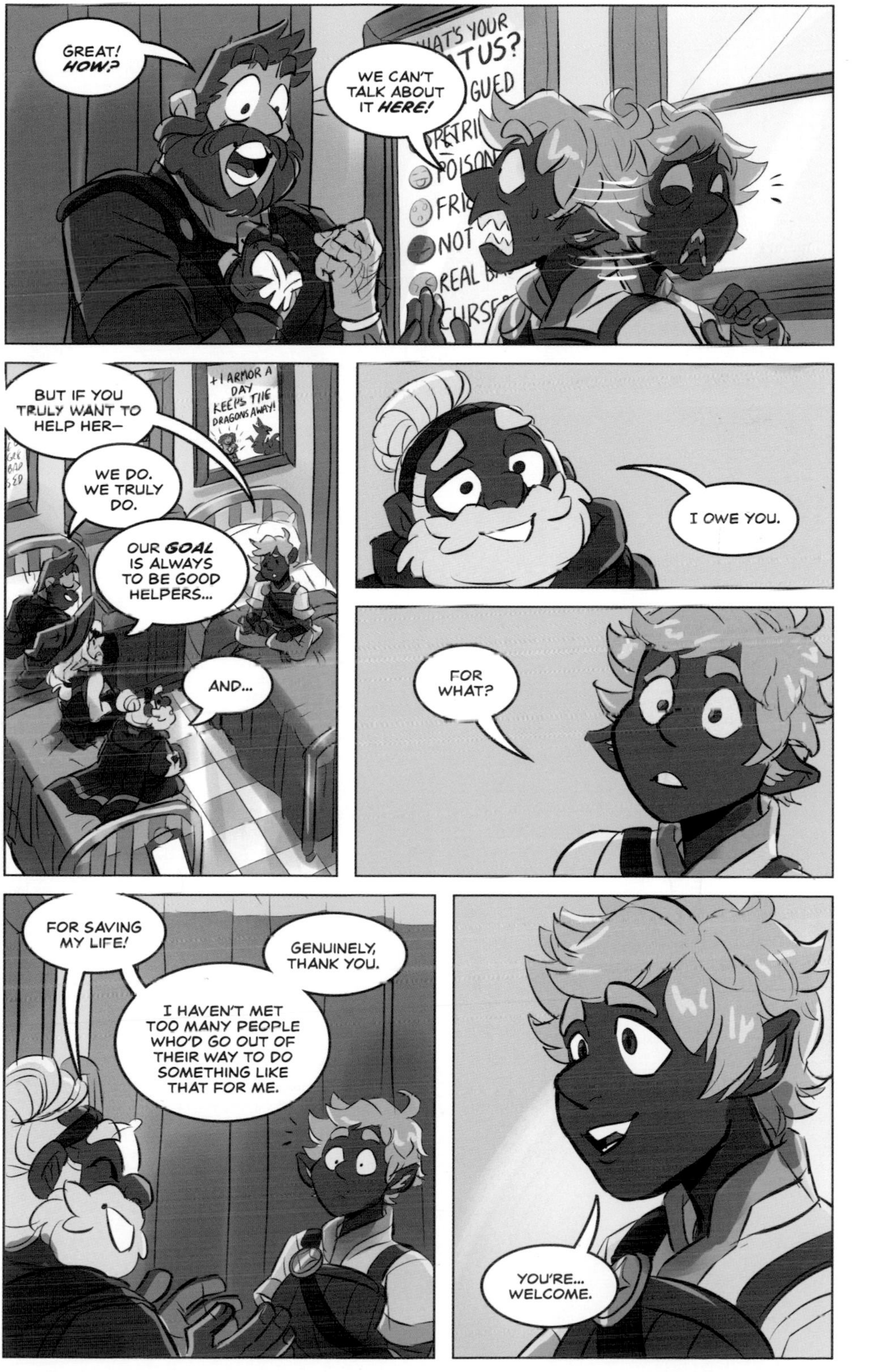
GREAT! HOW?
WHAT'S YOUR ...TUS?
WE CAN'T TALK ABOUT IT HERE!
BUT IF YOU TRULY WANT TO HELP HER—
+1 ARMOR A DAY KEEPS THE DRAGONS AWAY!
WE DO. WE TRULY DO.
OUR GOAL IS ALWAYS TO BE GOOD HELPERS...
AND...
I OWE YOU.
FOR WHAT?
FOR SAVING MY LIFE!
GENUINELY, THANK YOU.
I HAVEN'T MET TOO MANY PEOPLE WHO'D GO OUT OF THEIR WAY TO DO SOMETHING LIKE THAT FOR ME.
YOU'RE... WELCOME.

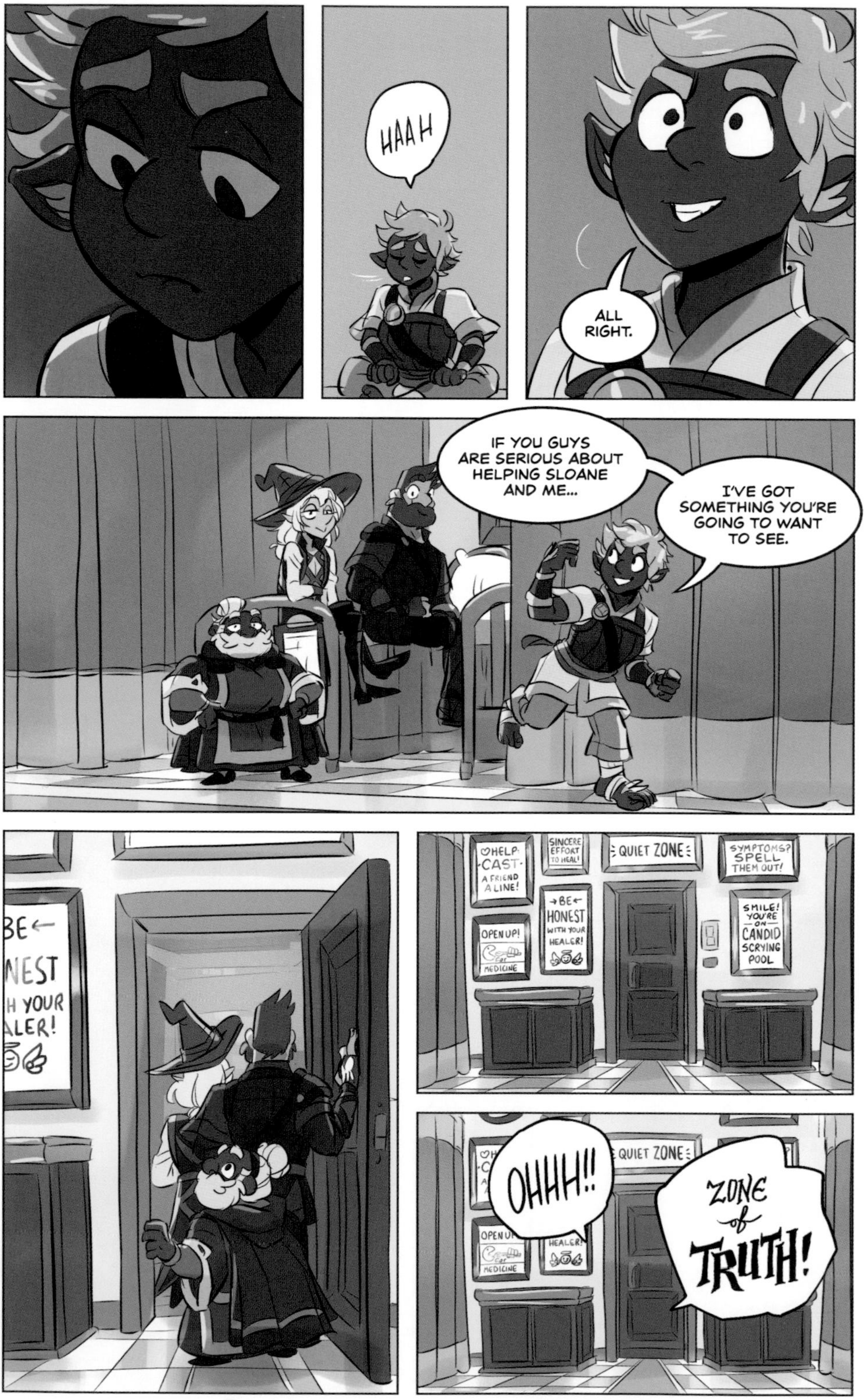
HAAH
ALL RIGHT.
IF YOU GUYS ARE SERIOUS ABOUT HELPING SLOANE AND ME...
I'VE GOT SOMETHING YOU'RE GOING TO WANT TO SEE.
HELP CAST A FRIEND A LINE!
SINCERE EFFORT TO HEAL!
QUIET ZONE
SYMPTOMS? SPELL THEM OUT!
BE HONEST WITH YOUR HEALER!
OPEN UP!
MEDICINE
SMILE! YOU'RE ON CANDID SCRYING POOL
OHHH!!
ZONE of TRUTH!

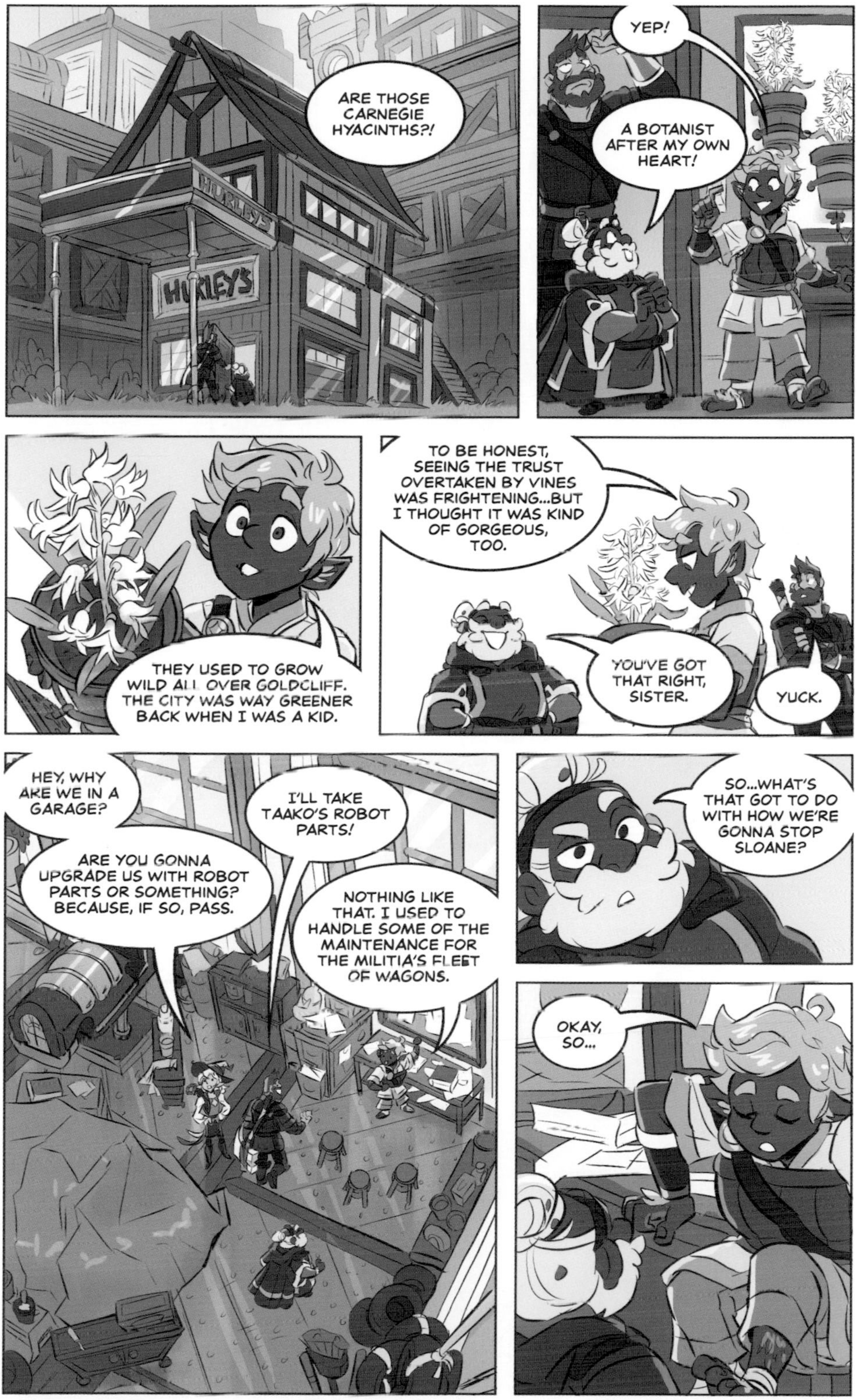
HURLEY'S
HURLEY'S
ARE THOSE CARNEGIE HYACINTHS?!
YEP!
A BOTANIST AFTER MY OWN HEART!
THEY USED TO GROW WILD ALL OVER GOLDCLIFF. THE CITY WAS WAY GREENER BACK WHEN I WAS A KID.
TO BE HONEST, SEEING THE TRUST OVERTAKEN BY VINES WAS FRIGHTENING...BUT I THOUGHT IT WAS KIND OF GORGEOUS, TOO.
YOU'VE GOT THAT RIGHT, SISTER.
YUCK.
HEY, WHY ARE WE IN A GARAGE?
ARE YOU GONNA UPGRADE US WITH ROBOT PARTS OR SOMETHING? BECAUSE, IF SO, PASS.
I'LL TAKE TAAKO'S ROBOT PARTS!
NOTHING LIKE THAT. I USED TO HANDLE SOME OF THE MAINTENANCE FOR THE MILITIA'S FLEET OF WAGONS.
SO...WHAT'S THAT GOT TO DO WITH HOW WE'RE GONNA STOP SLOANE?
OKAY, SO...

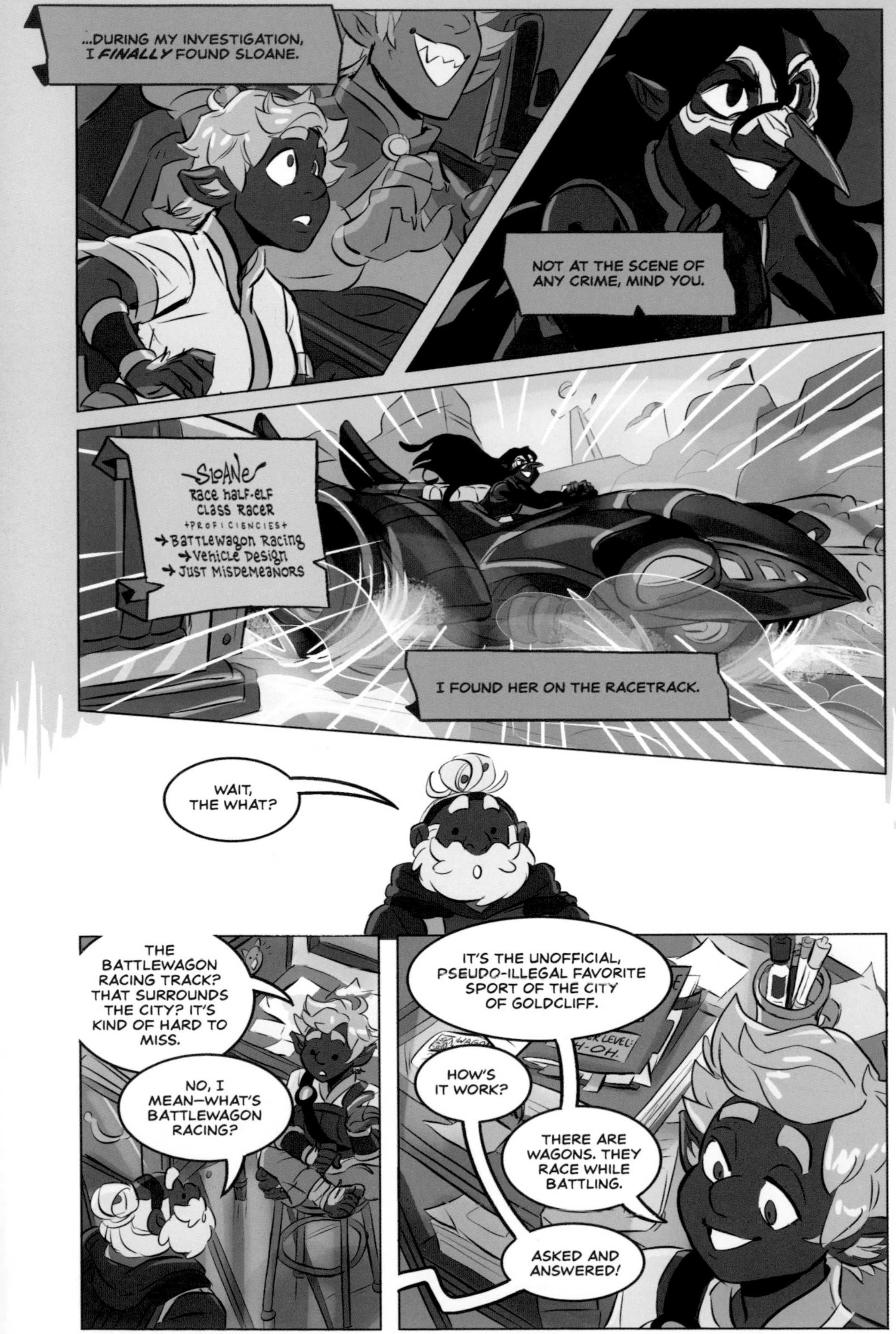
...DURING MY INVESTIGATION, I *FINALLY* FOUND SLOANE.
NOT AT THE SCENE OF ANY CRIME, MIND YOU.
SLOANE
RACE HALF-ELF
CLASS RACER
PROFICIENCIES
→BATTLEWAGON RACING
→VEHICLE DESIGN
→JUST MISDEMEANORS
I FOUND HER ON THE RACETRACK.
WAIT, THE WHAT?
THE BATTLEWAGON RACING TRACK? THAT SURROUNDS THE CITY? IT'S KIND OF HARD TO MISS.
NO, I MEAN—WHAT'S BATTLEWAGON RACING?
IT'S THE UNOFFICIAL, PSEUDO-ILLEGAL FAVORITE SPORT OF THE CITY OF GOLDCLIFF.
HOW'S IT WORK?
THERE ARE WAGONS. THEY RACE WHILE BATTLING.
ASKED AND ANSWERED!

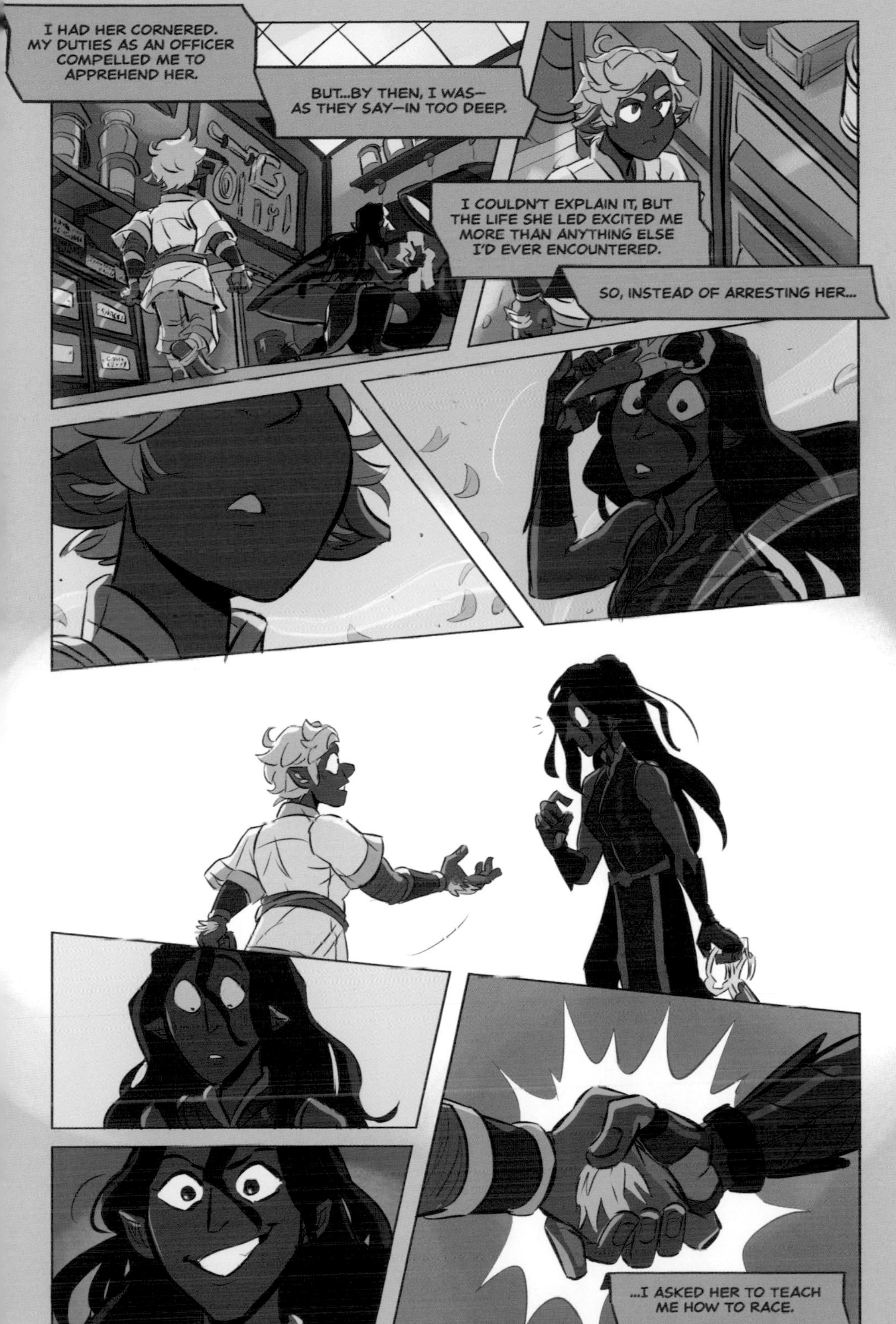
I HAD HER CORNERED. MY DUTIES AS AN OFFICER COMPELLED ME TO APPREHEND HER.
BUT...BY THEN, I WAS—AS THEY SAY—IN TOO DEEP.
I COULDN'T EXPLAIN IT, BUT THE LIFE SHE LED EXCITED ME MORE THAN ANYTHING ELSE I'D EVER ENCOUNTERED.
SO, INSTEAD OF ARRESTING HER...
...I ASKED HER TO TEACH ME HOW TO RACE.

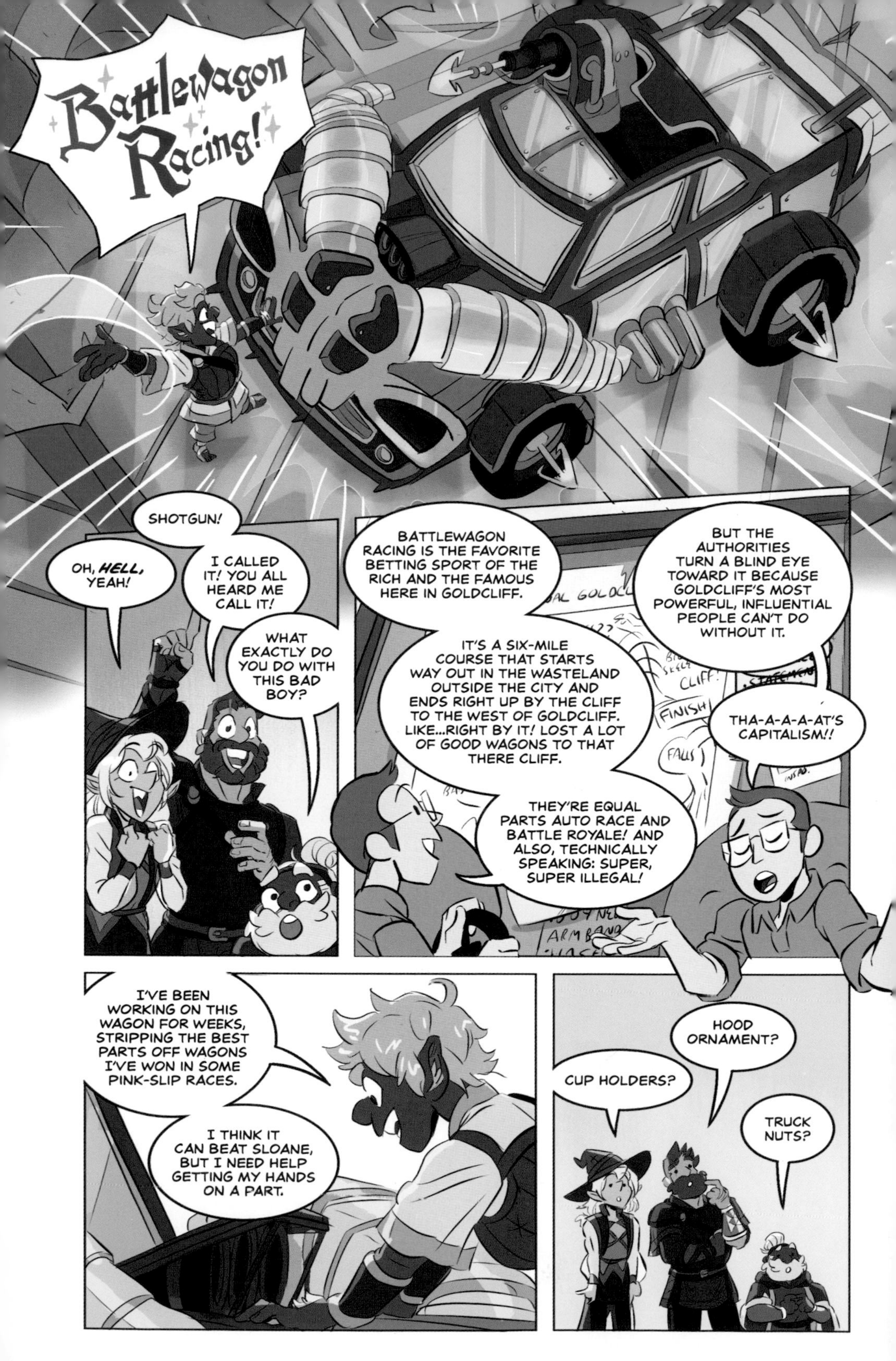
Battlewagon Racing!
SHOTGUN!
OH, HELL, YEAH!
I CALLED IT! YOU ALL HEARD ME CALL IT!
WHAT EXACTLY DO YOU DO WITH THIS BAD BOY?
BATTLEWAGON RACING IS THE FAVORITE BETTING SPORT OF THE RICH AND THE FAMOUS HERE IN GOLDCLIFF.
BUT THE AUTHORITIES TURN A BLIND EYE TOWARD IT BECAUSE GOLDCLIFF'S MOST POWERFUL, INFLUENTIAL PEOPLE CAN'T DO WITHOUT IT.
IT'S A SIX-MILE COURSE THAT STARTS WAY OUT IN THE WASTELAND OUTSIDE THE CITY AND ENDS RIGHT UP BY THE CLIFF TO THE WEST OF GOLDCLIFF. LIKE...RIGHT BY IT! LOST A LOT OF GOOD WAGONS TO THAT THERE CLIFF.
THA-A-A-A-AT'S CAPITALISM!!
THEY'RE EQUAL PARTS AUTO RACE AND BATTLE ROYALE! AND ALSO, TECHNICALLY SPEAKING: SUPER, SUPER ILLEGAL!
I'VE BEEN WORKING ON THIS WAGON FOR WEEKS, STRIPPING THE BEST PARTS OFF WAGONS I'VE WON IN SOME PINK-SLIP RACES.
I THINK IT CAN BEAT SLOANE, BUT I NEED HELP GETTING MY HANDS ON A PART.
CUP HOLDERS?
HOOD ORNAMENT?
TRUCK NUTS?

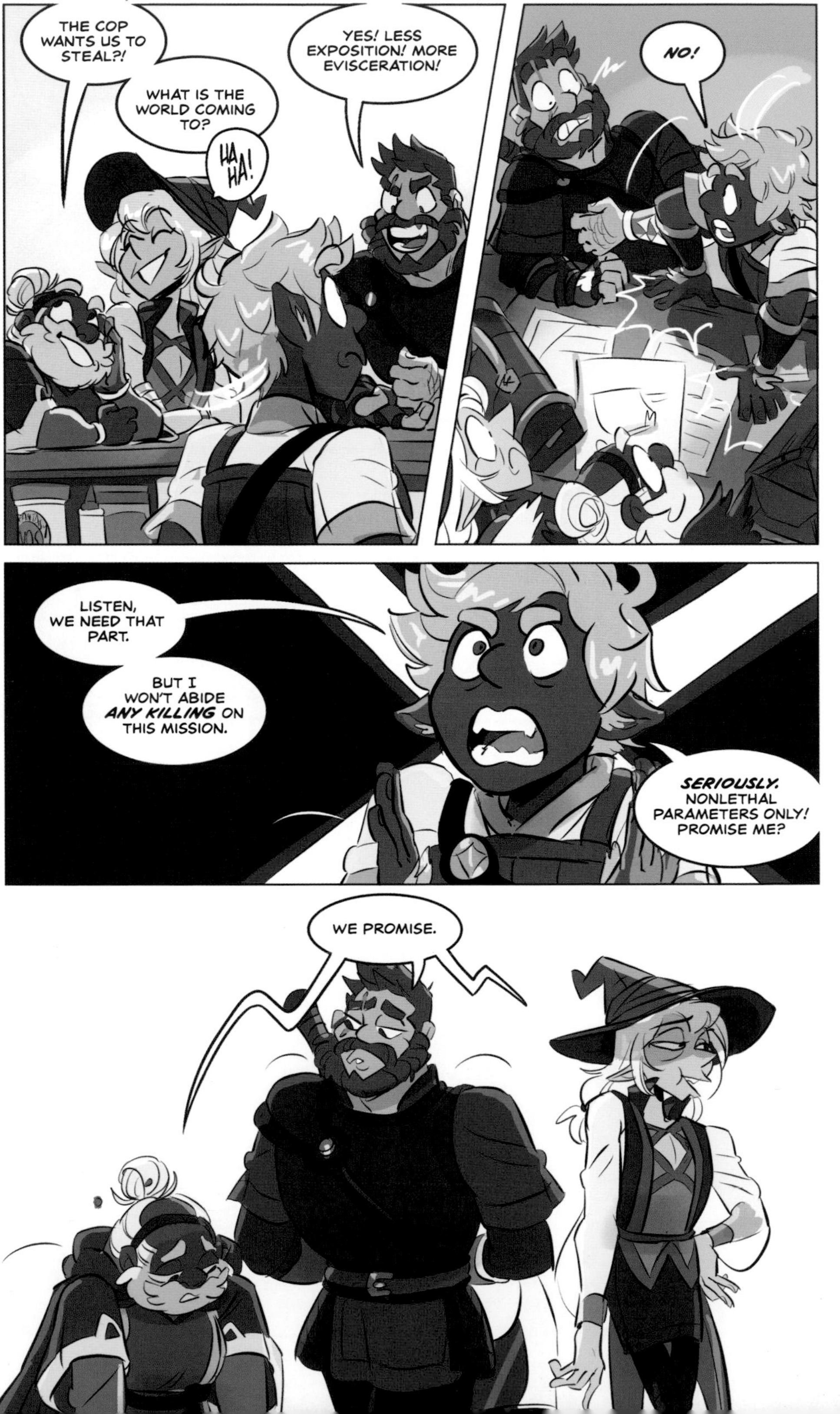
THE COP WANTS US TO STEAL?!
WHAT IS THE WORLD COMING TO?
HA HA!
YES! LESS EXPOSITION! MORE EVISCERATION!
NO!
LISTEN, WE NEED THAT PART.
BUT I WON'T ABIDE ANY KILLING ON THIS MISSION.
SERIOUSLY. NONLETHAL PARAMETERS ONLY! PROMISE ME?
WE PROMISE.

Chapter 4

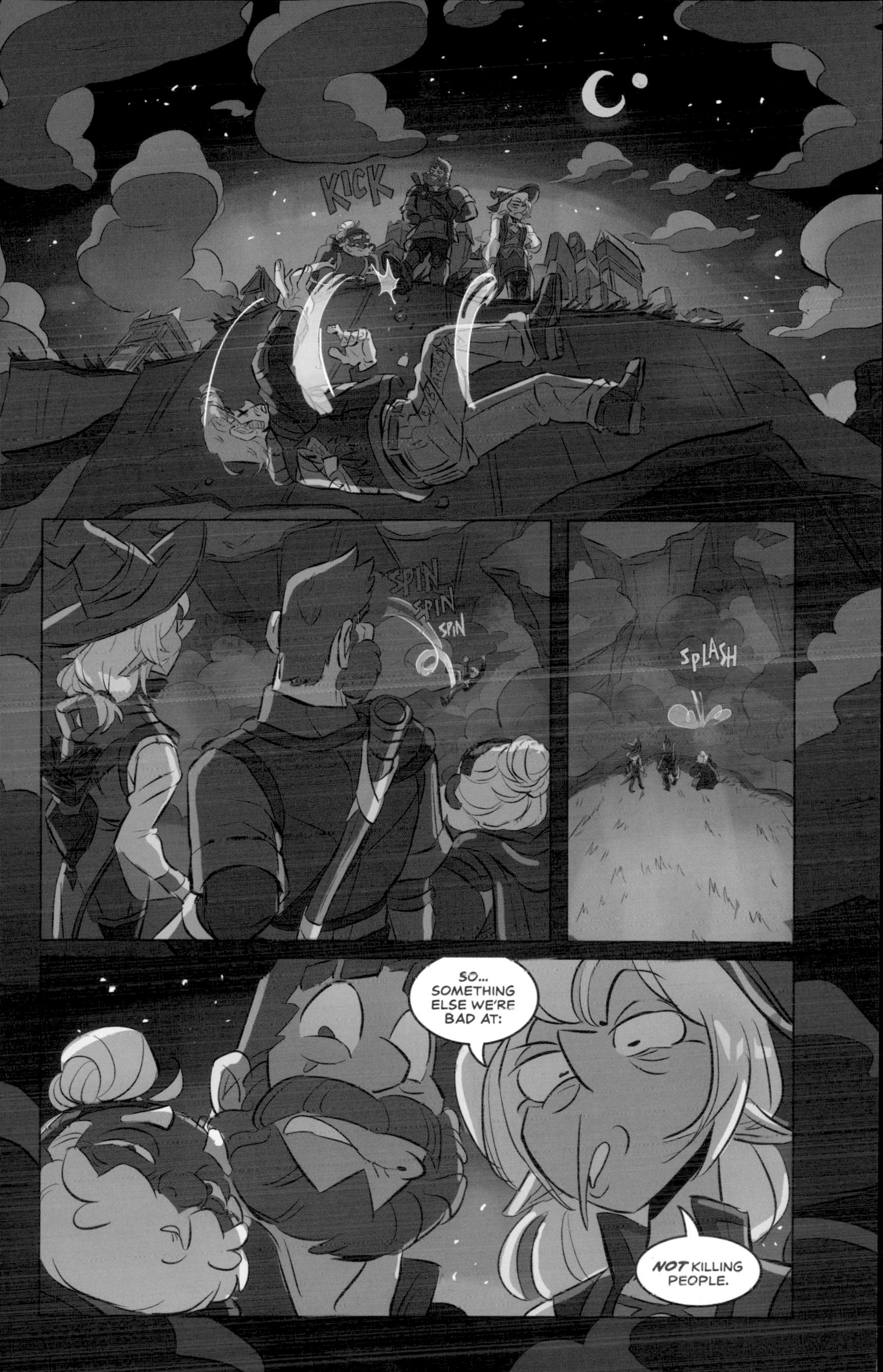
KICK
SPIN
SPIN
SPIN
SPLASH
SO... SOMETHING ELSE WE'RE BAD AT:
NOT KILLING PEOPLE.

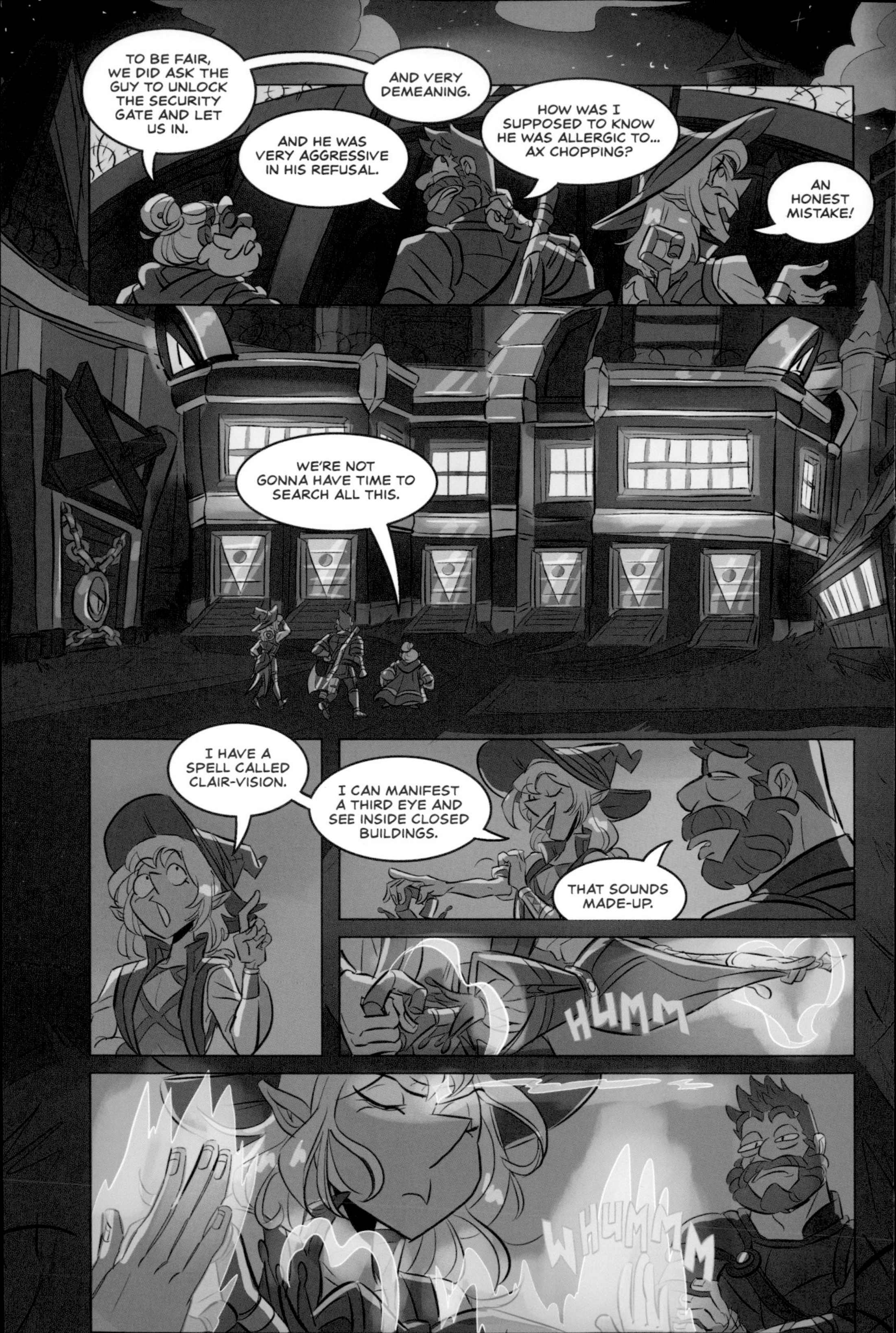
TO BE FAIR, WE DID ASK THE GUY TO UNLOCK THE SECURITY GATE AND LET US IN.
AND HE WAS VERY AGGRESSIVE IN HIS REFUSAL.
AND VERY DEMEANING.
HOW WAS I SUPPOSED TO KNOW HE WAS ALLERGIC TO... AX CHOPPING?
AN HONEST MISTAKE!
WE'RE NOT GONNA HAVE TIME TO SEARCH ALL THIS.
I HAVE A SPELL CALLED CLAIR-VISION.
I CAN MANIFEST A THIRD EYE AND SEE INSIDE CLOSED BUILDINGS.
THAT SOUNDS MADE-UP.
HUMM
WHUMMM

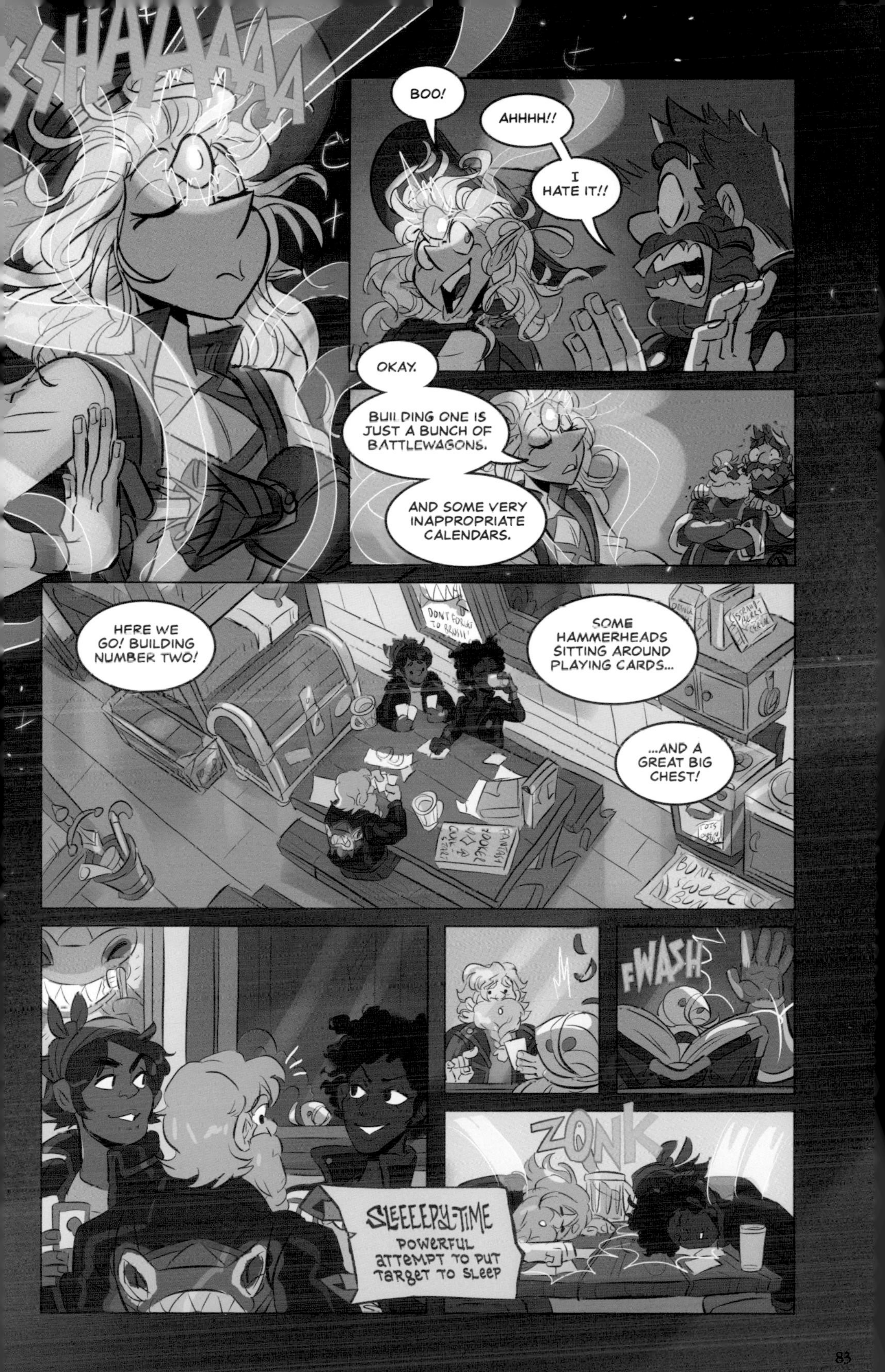
SSHAAAAA
BOO!
AHHHH!!
I HATE IT!!
OKAY.
BUILDING ONE IS JUST A BUNCH OF BATTLEWAGONS.
AND SOME VERY INAPPROPRIATE CALENDARS.
HERE WE GO! BUILDING NUMBER TWO!
SOME HAMMERHEADS SITTING AROUND PLAYING CARDS...
...AND A GREAT BIG CHEST!
DON'T FORGET TO BRUSH!
FWASH
ZONK
SLEEEEPY-TIME
POWERFUL ATTEMPT TO PUT TARGET TO SLEEP

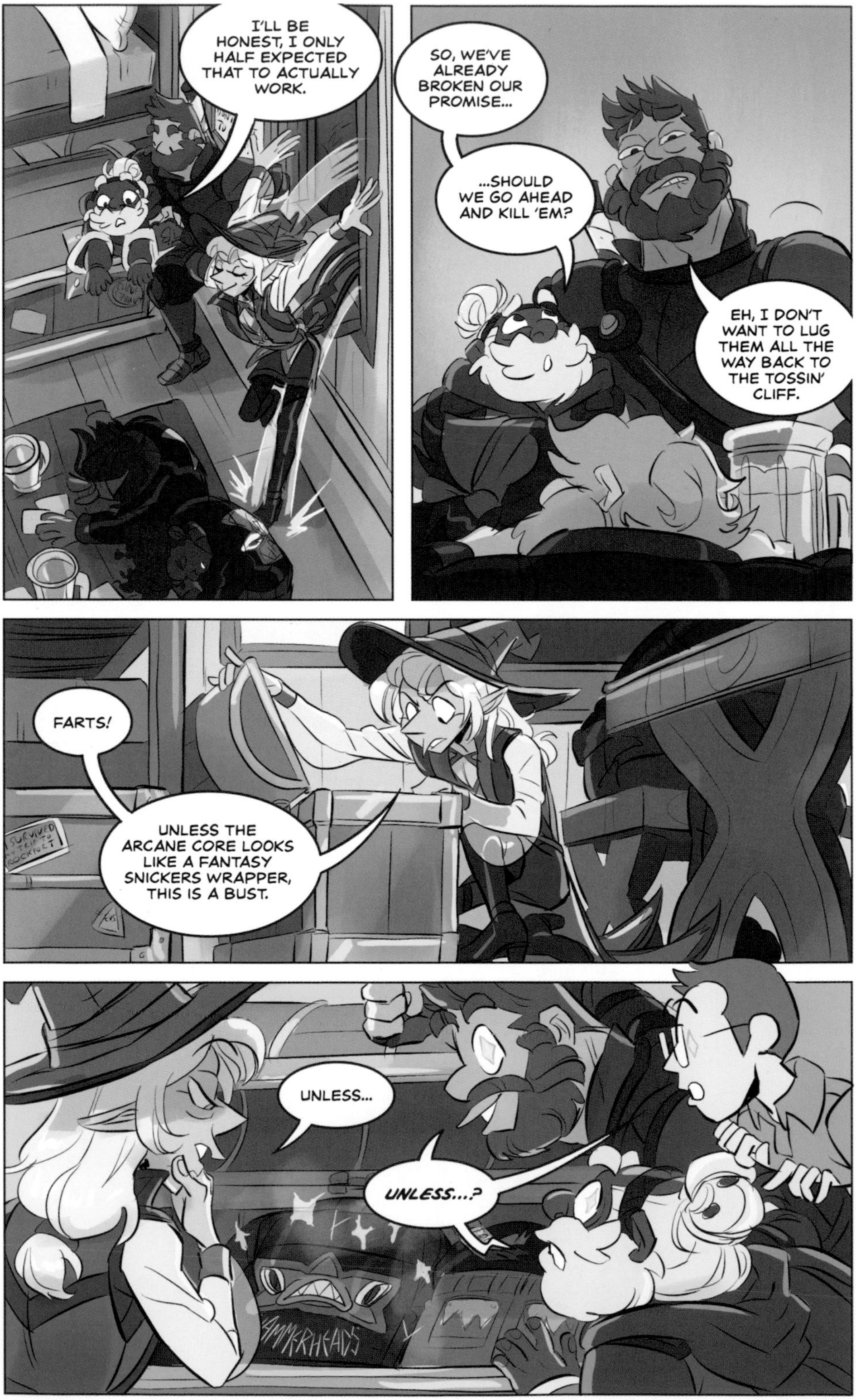
I'LL BE HONEST, I ONLY HALF EXPECTED THAT TO ACTUALLY WORK.
SO, WE'VE ALREADY BROKEN OUR PROMISE...
...SHOULD WE GO AHEAD AND KILL 'EM?
EH, I DON'T WANT TO LUG THEM ALL THE WAY BACK TO THE TOSSIN' CLIFF.
FARTS!
UNLESS THE ARCANE CORE LOOKS LIKE A FANTASY SNICKERS WRAPPER, THIS IS A BUST.
I SURVIVED MY TRIP TO ROCKPORT
UNLESS...
UNLESS...?
HAMMERHEADS

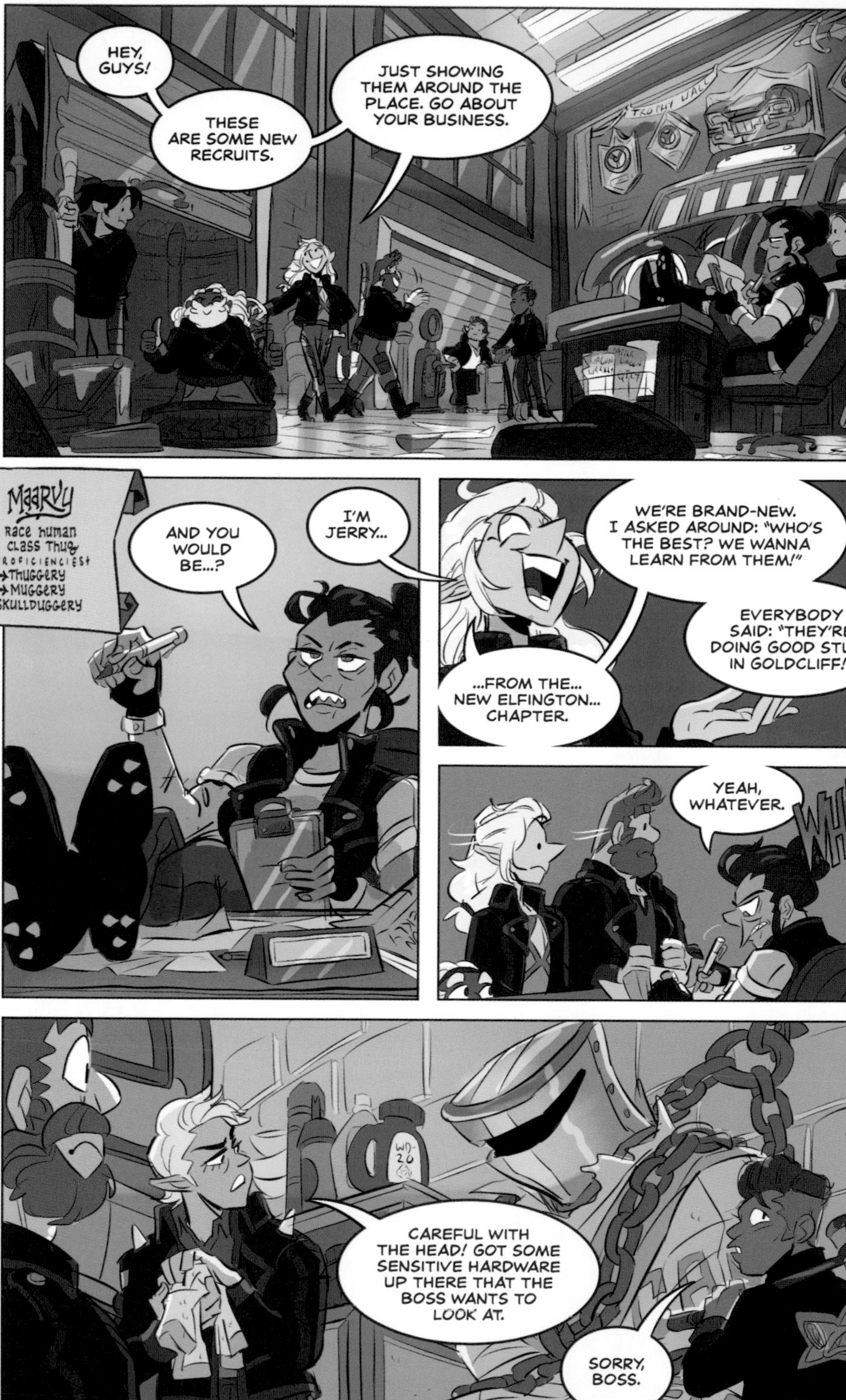
HEY, GUYS!
THESE ARE SOME NEW RECRUITS.
JUST SHOWING THEM AROUND THE PLACE. GO ABOUT YOUR BUSINESS.
TROPHY WALL
MAARVY
RACE HUMAN
CLASS THUG
PROFICIENCIES
→THUGGERY
→MUGGERY
→SKULLDUGGERY
AND YOU WOULD BE...?
I'M JERRY...
...FROM THE... NEW ELFINGTON... CHAPTER.
WE'RE BRAND-NEW. I ASKED AROUND: "WHO'S THE BEST? WE WANNA LEARN FROM THEM!"
EVERYBODY SAID: "THEY'RE DOING GOOD STUFF IN GOLDCLIFF!"
YEAH, WHATEVER.
WHUD!
CAREFUL WITH THE HEAD! GOT SOME SENSITIVE HARDWARE UP THERE THAT THE BOSS WANTS TO LOOK AT.
SORRY, BOSS.

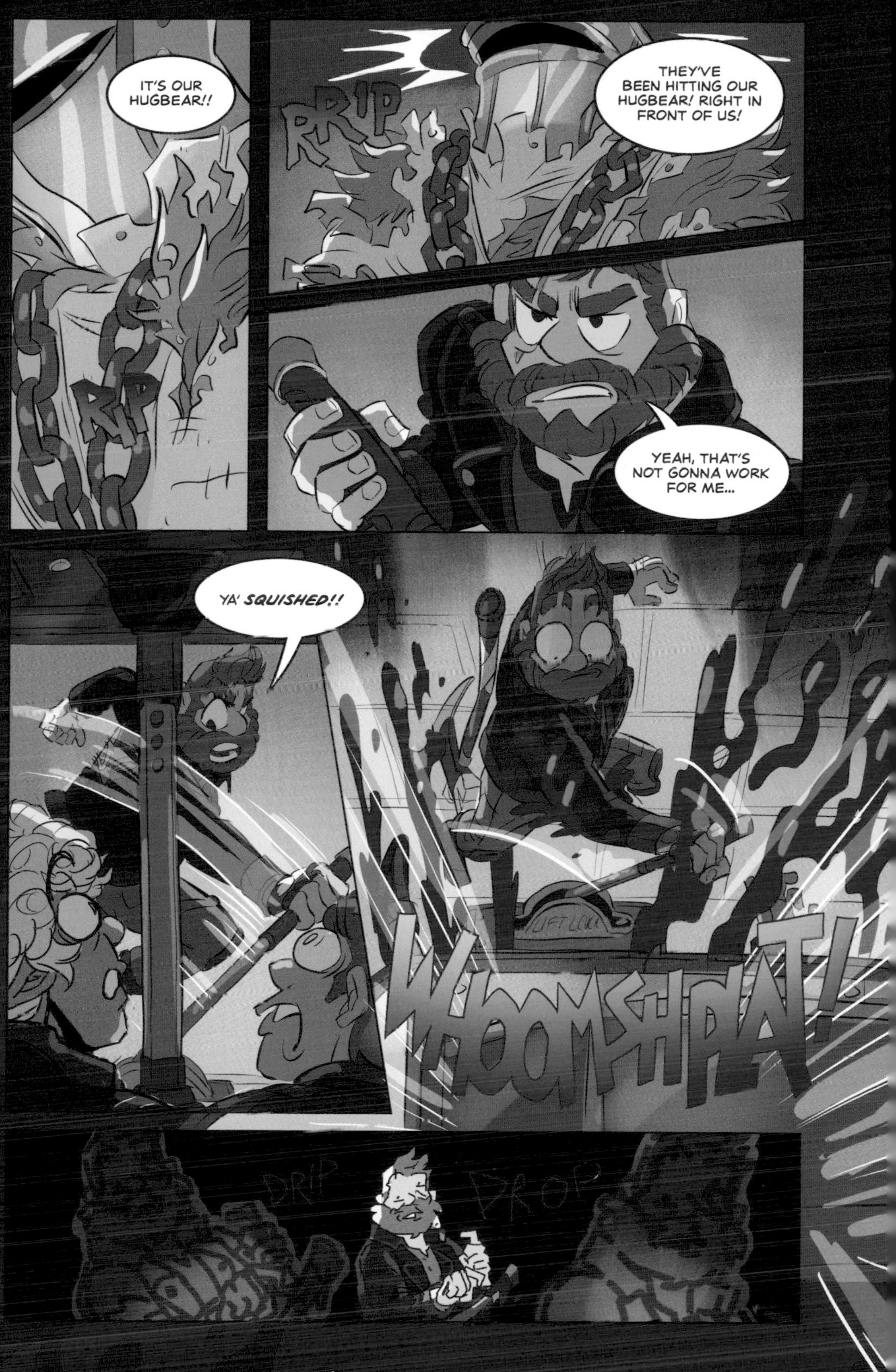
IT'S OUR HUGBEAR!!
RRIP
THEY'VE BEEN HITTING OUR HUGBEAR! RIGHT IN FRONT OF US!
RIP
YEAH, THAT'S NOT GONNA WORK FOR ME...
YA' SQUISHED!!
WHOOMSHPLAT!
DRIP
DROP

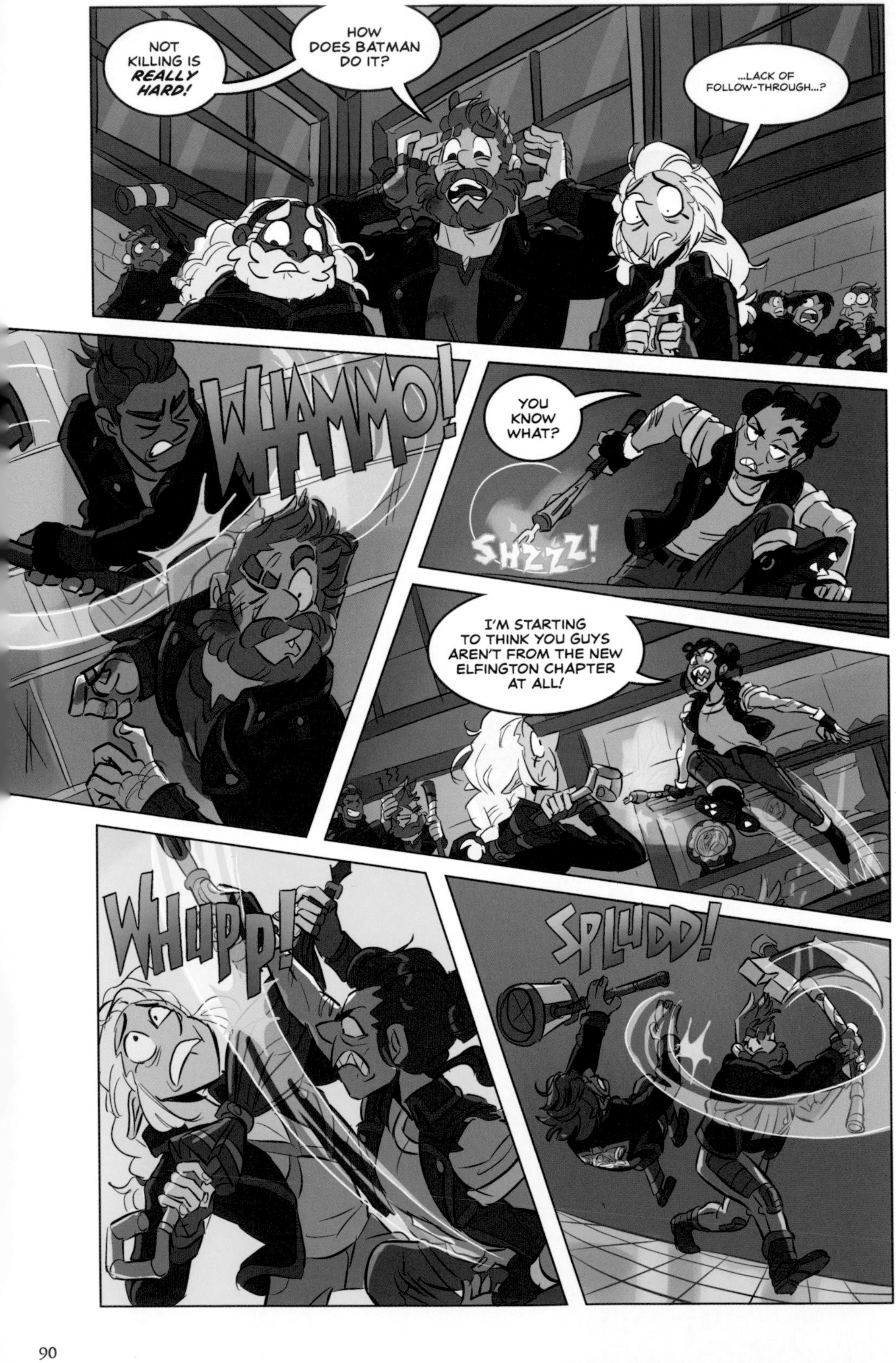
NOT KILLING IS REALLY HARD!
HOW DOES BATMAN DO IT?
...LACK OF FOLLOW-THROUGH...?
WHAMMO!
YOU KNOW WHAT?
SHZZZ!
I'M STARTING TO THINK YOU GUYS AREN'T FROM THE NEW ELFINGTON CHAPTER AT ALL!
WHUPP!
SPLUDD!

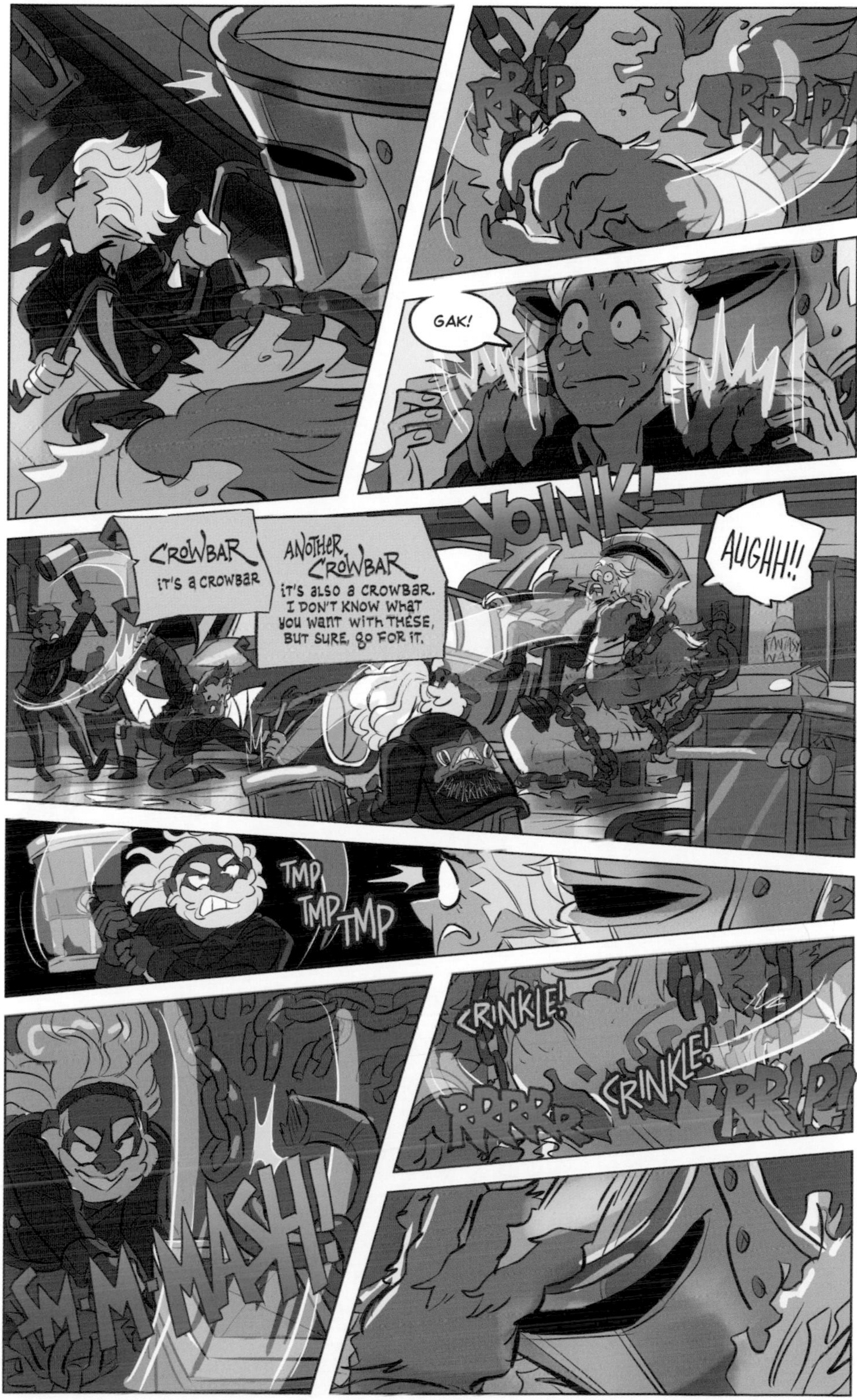
RRIP
RRIP!
GAK!
YOINK!
AUGHH!!
CROWBAR
IT'S A CROWBAR
ANOTHER CROWBAR
IT'S ALSO A CROWBAR. I DON'T KNOW WHAT YOU WANT WITH THESE, BUT SURE, GO FOR IT.
TMP TMP TMP TMP
CRINKLE!
CRINKLE!
RRRRR
RRIP!
SMMMASH!

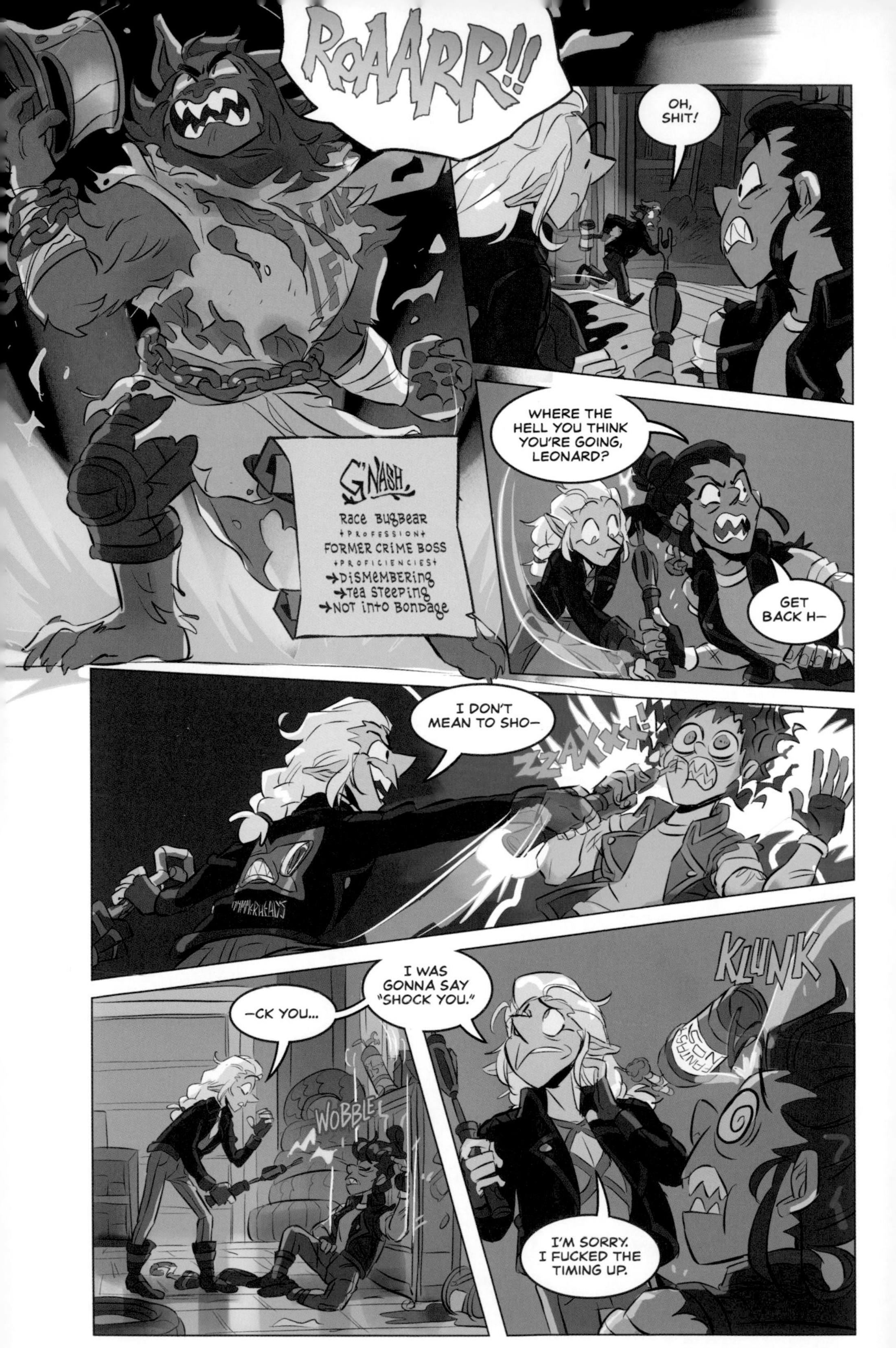
ROAARR!!
OH, SHIT!
G'NASH
Race Bugbear
Profession
FORMER CRIME BOSS
Proficiencies
→DISMEMBERING
→TEA STEEPING
→NOT INTO BONDAGE
WHERE THE HELL YOU THINK YOU'RE GOING, LEONARD?
GET BACK H—
I DON'T MEAN TO SHO—
ZZAXX!!
—CK YOU...
I WAS GONNA SAY "SHOCK YOU."
KLUNK
WOBBLE
I'M SORRY. I FUCKED THE TIMING UP.

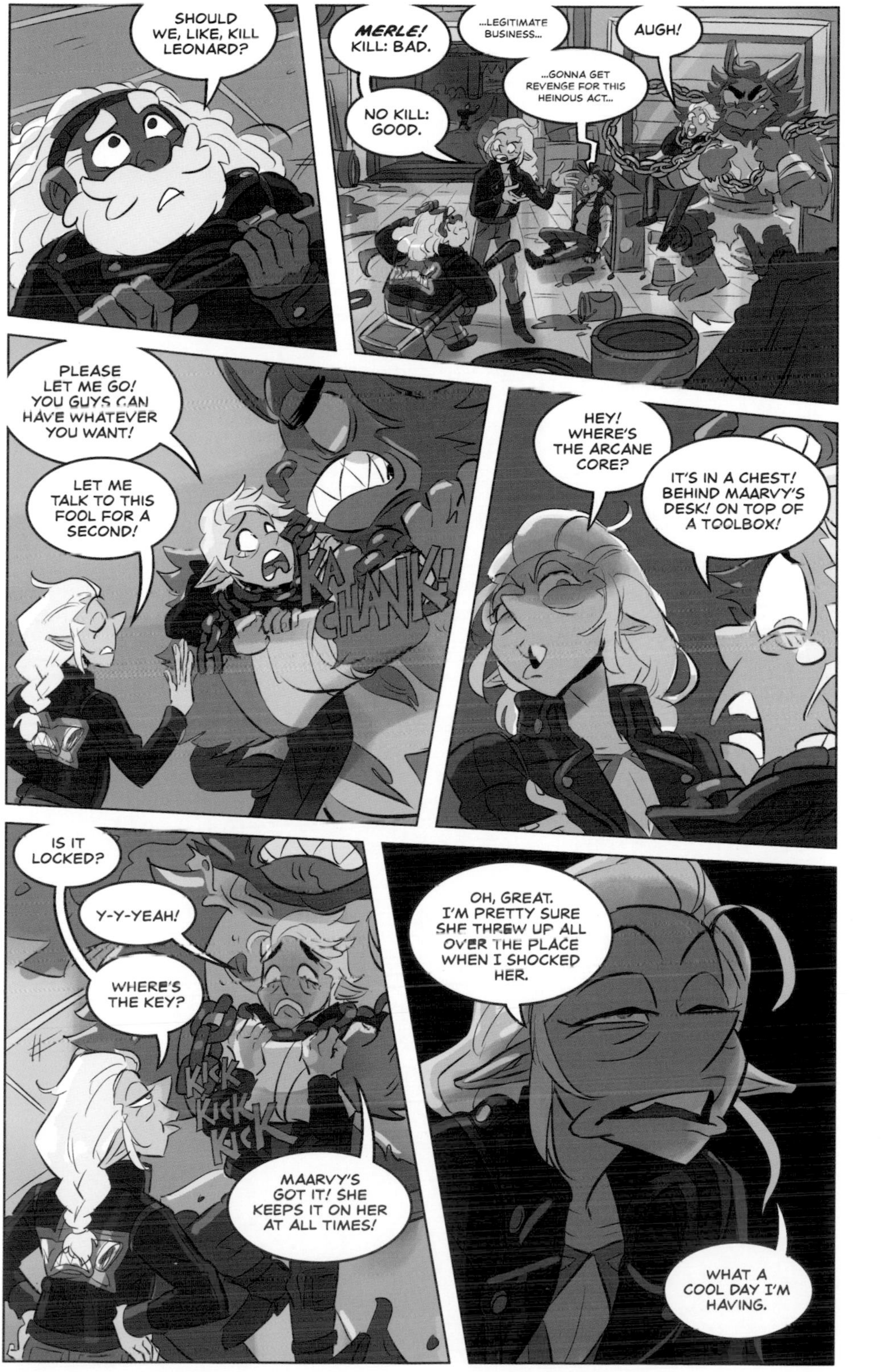
SHOULD WE, LIKE, KILL LEONARD?
MERLE! KILL: BAD.
...LEGITIMATE BUSINESS...
AUGH!
...GONNA GET REVENGE FOR THIS HEINOUS ACT...
NO KILL: GOOD.
PLEASE LET ME GO! YOU GUYS CAN HAVE WHATEVER YOU WANT!
LET ME TALK TO THIS FOOL FOR A SECOND!
KA CHANK!
HEY! WHERE'S THE ARCANE CORE?
IT'S IN A CHEST! BEHIND MAARVY'S DESK! ON TOP OF A TOOLBOX!
IS IT LOCKED?
Y-Y-YEAH!
WHERE'S THE KEY?
KICK KICK KICK
MAARVY'S GOT IT! SHE KEEPS IT ON HER AT ALL TIMES!
OH, GREAT. I'M PRETTY SURE SHE THREW UP ALL OVER THE PLACE WHEN I SHOCKED HER.
WHAT A COOL DAY I'M HAVING.

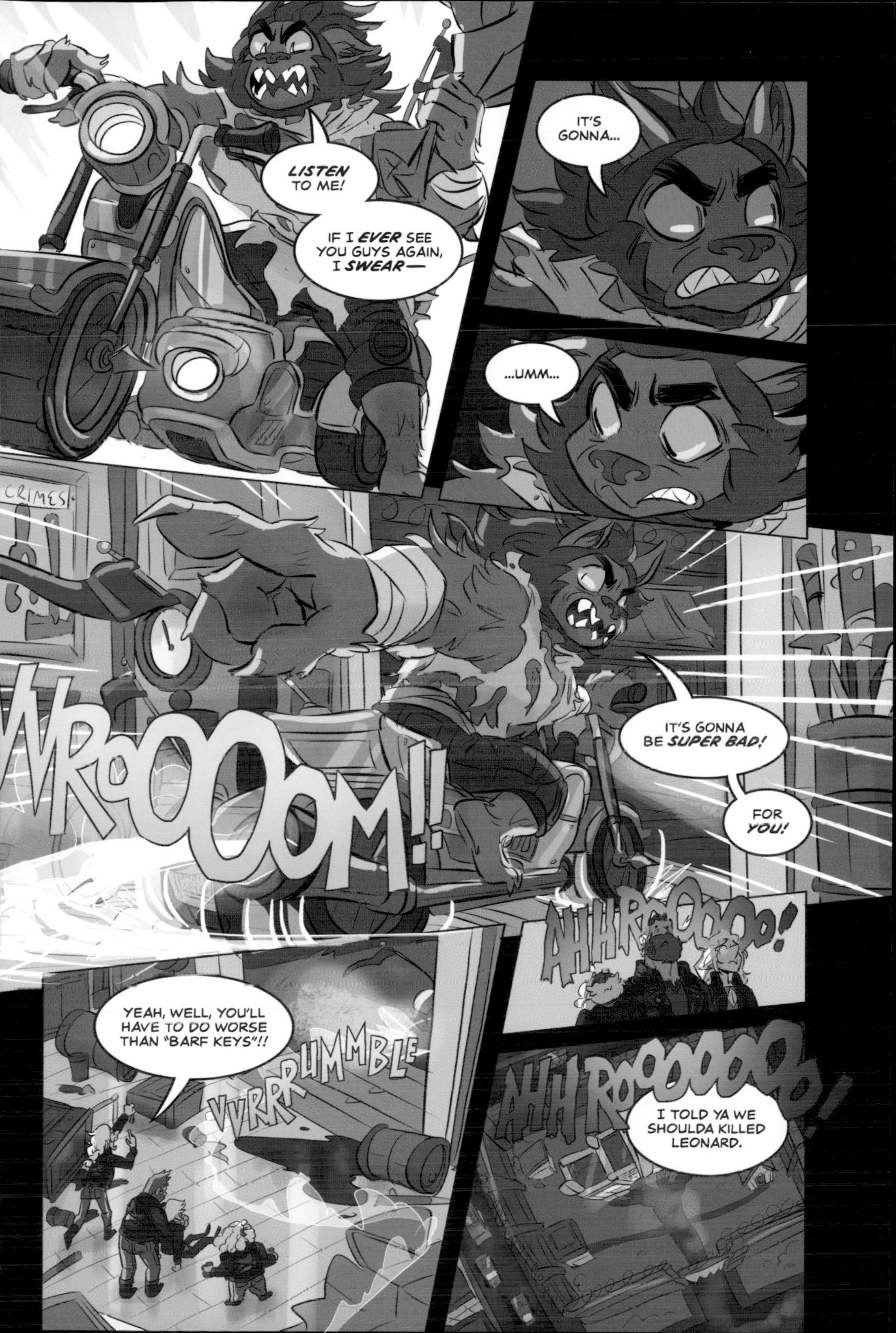
LISTEN TO ME!
IF I EVER SEE YOU GUYS AGAIN, I SWEAR—
IT'S GONNA...
...UMM...
CRIMES
VROOOOM!!
IT'S GONNA BE SUPER BAD!
FOR YOU!
AHHROOOOO!
YEAH, WELL, YOU'LL HAVE TO DO WORSE THAN "BARF KEYS"!!
VVRRRUMMBLE
AHHROOOOOO!
I TOLD YA WE SHOULDA KILLED LEONARD.

Chapter 5

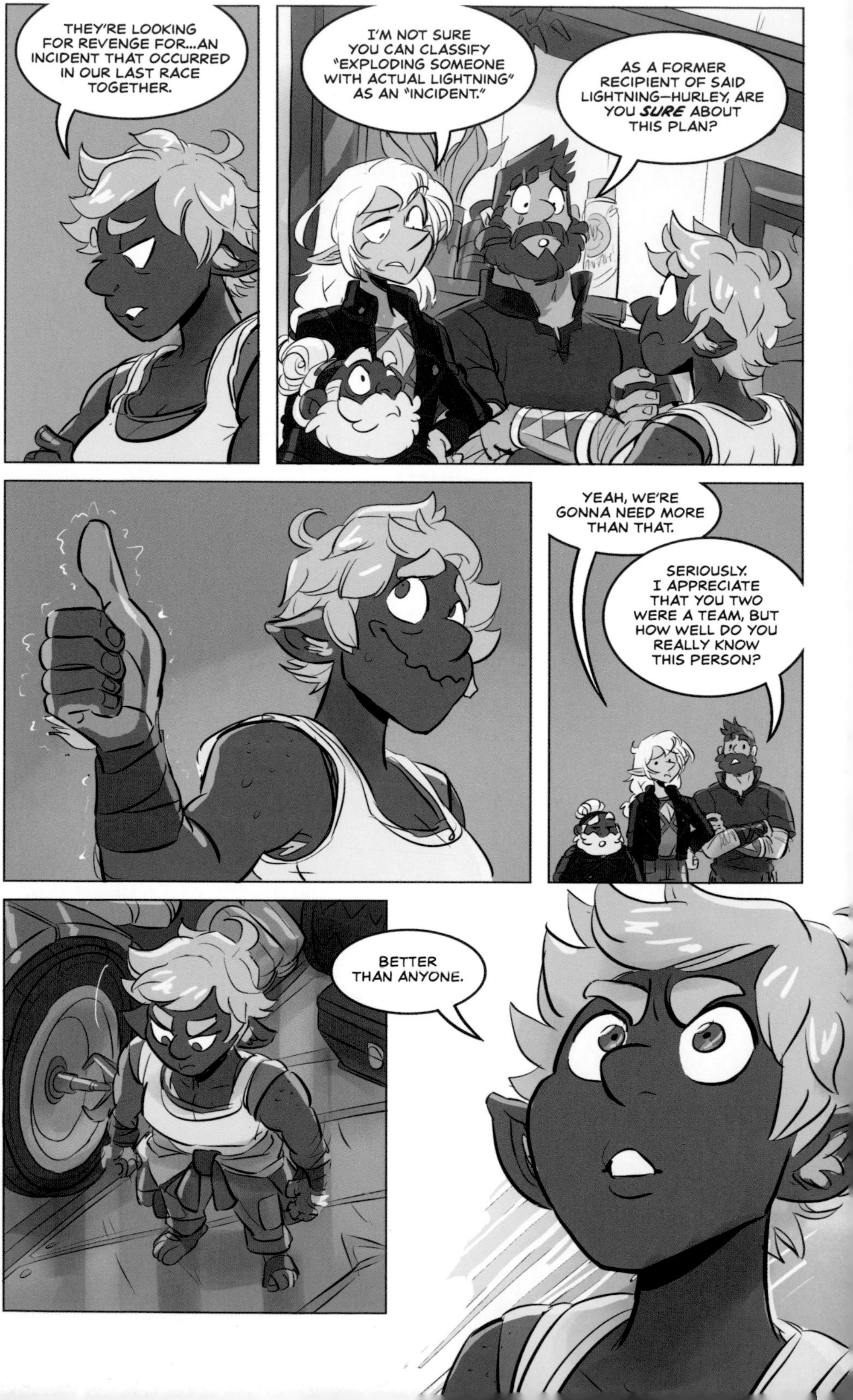
THEY'RE LOOKING FOR REVENGE FOR...AN INCIDENT THAT OCCURRED IN OUR LAST RACE TOGETHER.
I'M NOT SURE YOU CAN CLASSIFY "EXPLODING SOMEONE WITH ACTUAL LIGHTNING" AS AN "INCIDENT."
AS A FORMER RECIPIENT OF SAID LIGHTNING—HURLEY, ARE YOU ***SURE*** ABOUT THIS PLAN?
YEAH, WE'RE GONNA NEED MORE THAN THAT.
SERIOUSLY. I APPRECIATE THAT YOU TWO WERE A TEAM, BUT HOW WELL DO YOU REALLY KNOW THIS PERSON?
BETTER THAN ANYONE.

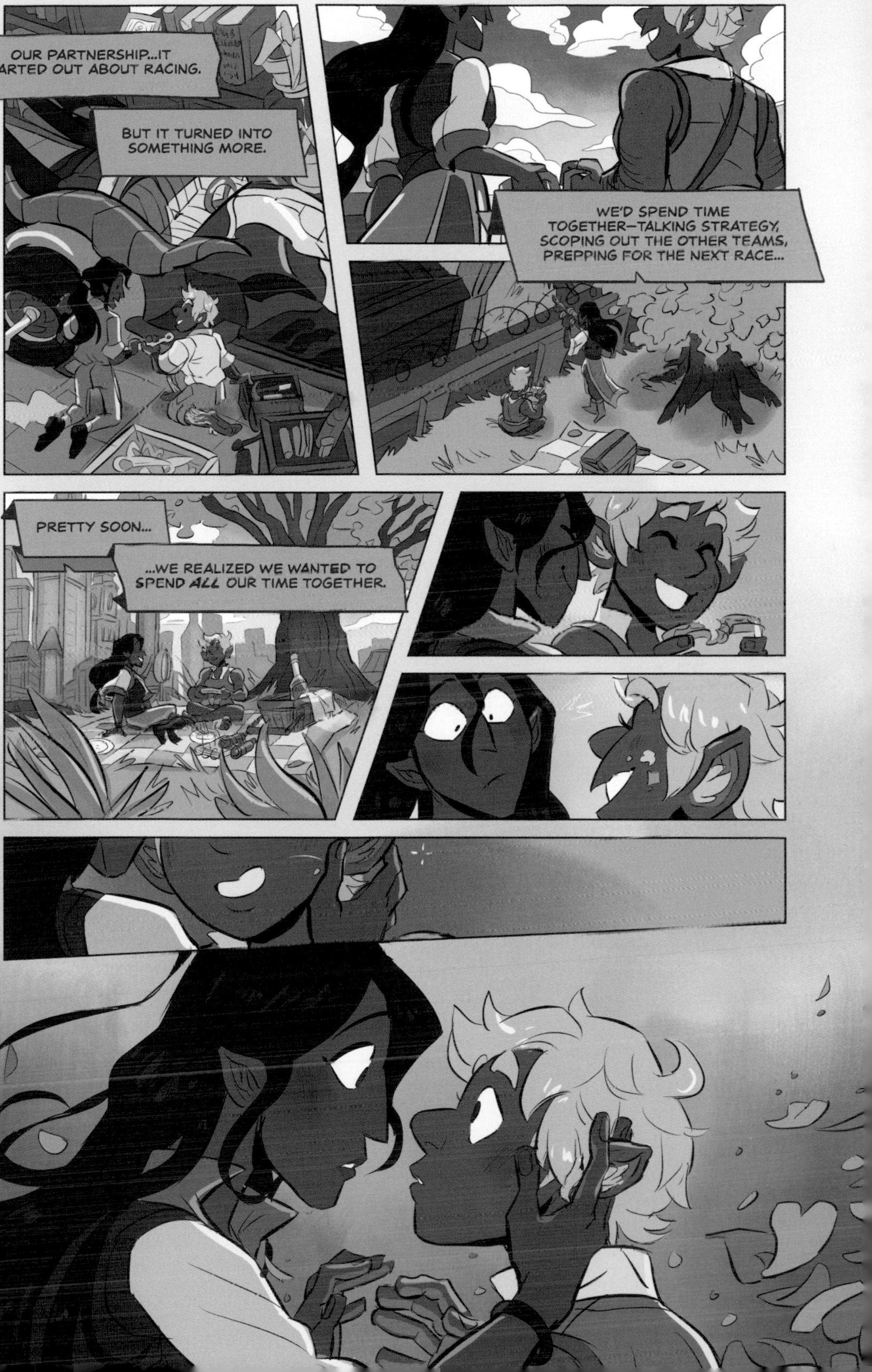
OUR PARTNERSHIP...IT STARTED OUT ABOUT RACING.
BUT IT TURNED INTO SOMETHING MORE.
WE'D SPEND TIME TOGETHER—TALKING STRATEGY, SCOPING OUT THE OTHER TEAMS, PREPPING FOR THE NEXT RACE...
PRETTY SOON...
...WE REALIZED WE WANTED TO SPEND ALL OUR TIME TOGETHER.

WE STARTED DATING A COUPLE MONTHS IN.

THINGS WERE COMPLICATED, OF COURSE. IT TOOK WORK TO BRING OUR WORLDS TOGETHER.

WE WERE COMING FROM DIFFERENT, UH... *PROFESSIONS*...

BUT WE BOTH WANTED TO MAKE THIS CITY BETTER.

AND SHE'S JUST...

I LOVE HOW FIERCE AND DETERMINED SHE IS.

SHE MAKES ME WANT TO BE BRAVER.

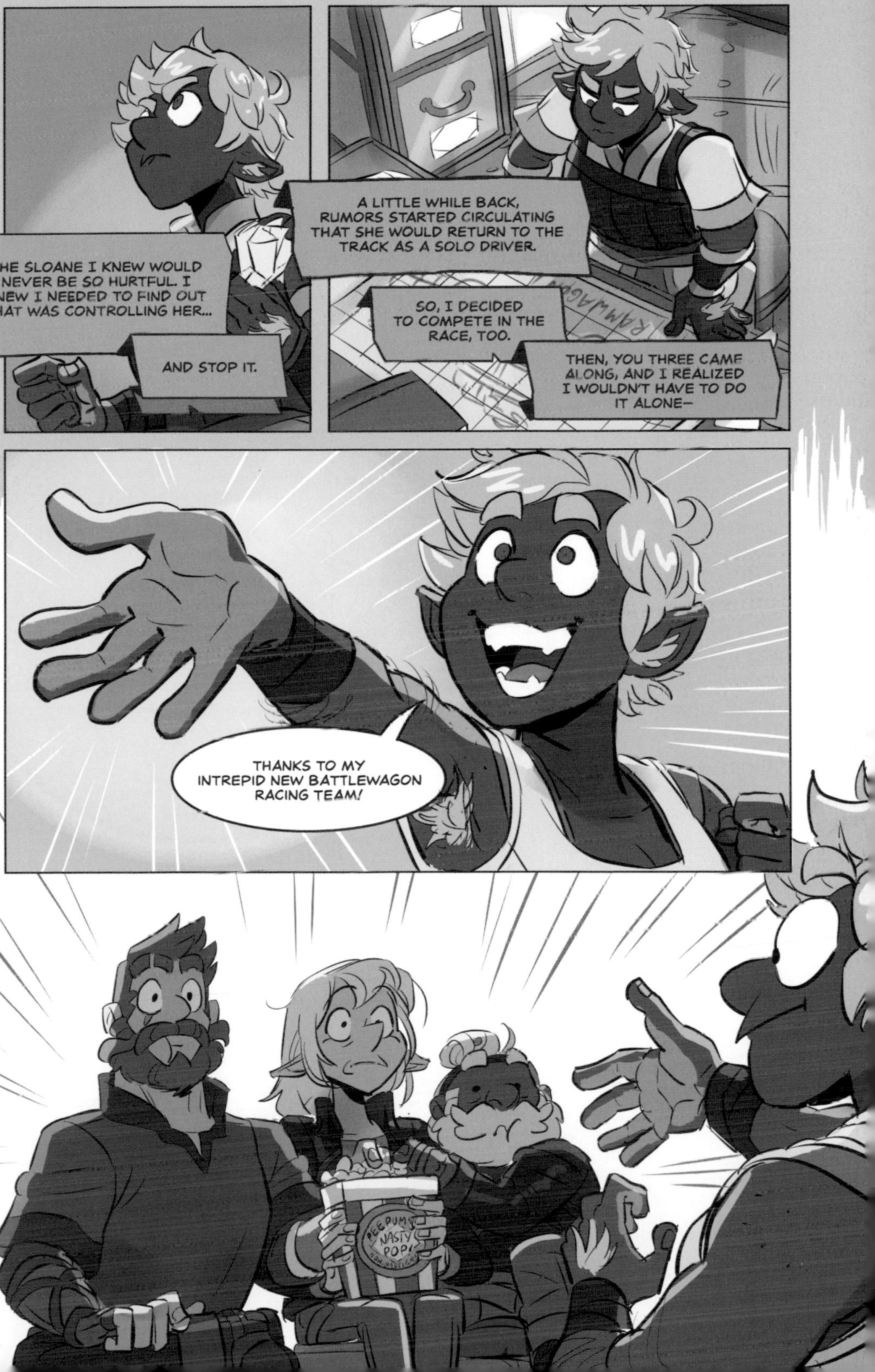
THE SLOANE I KNEW WOULD NEVER BE SO HURTFUL. I KNEW I NEEDED TO FIND OUT WHAT WAS CONTROLLING HER...
AND STOP IT.
A LITTLE WHILE BACK, RUMORS STARTED CIRCULATING THAT SHE WOULD RETURN TO THE TRACK AS A SOLO DRIVER.
SO, I DECIDED TO COMPETE IN THE RACE, TOO.
THEN, YOU THREE CAME ALONG, AND I REALIZED I WOULDN'T HAVE TO DO IT ALONE—
THANKS TO MY INTREPID NEW BATTLEWAGON RACING TEAM!

107

Chapter 6

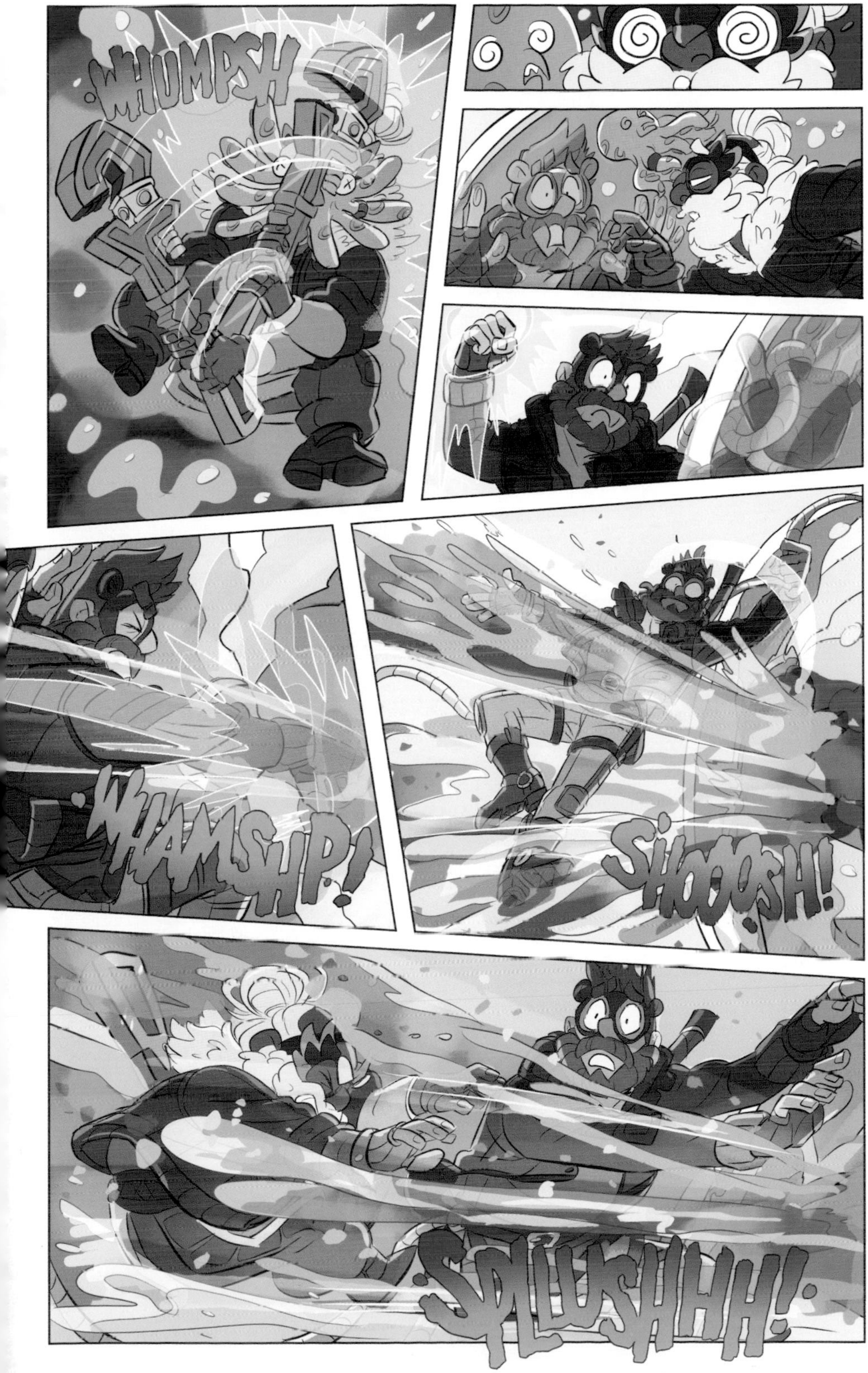
WHUMPSH
WHAMSHP!
SHOOOSH!
SPLUSHHH!

135

141

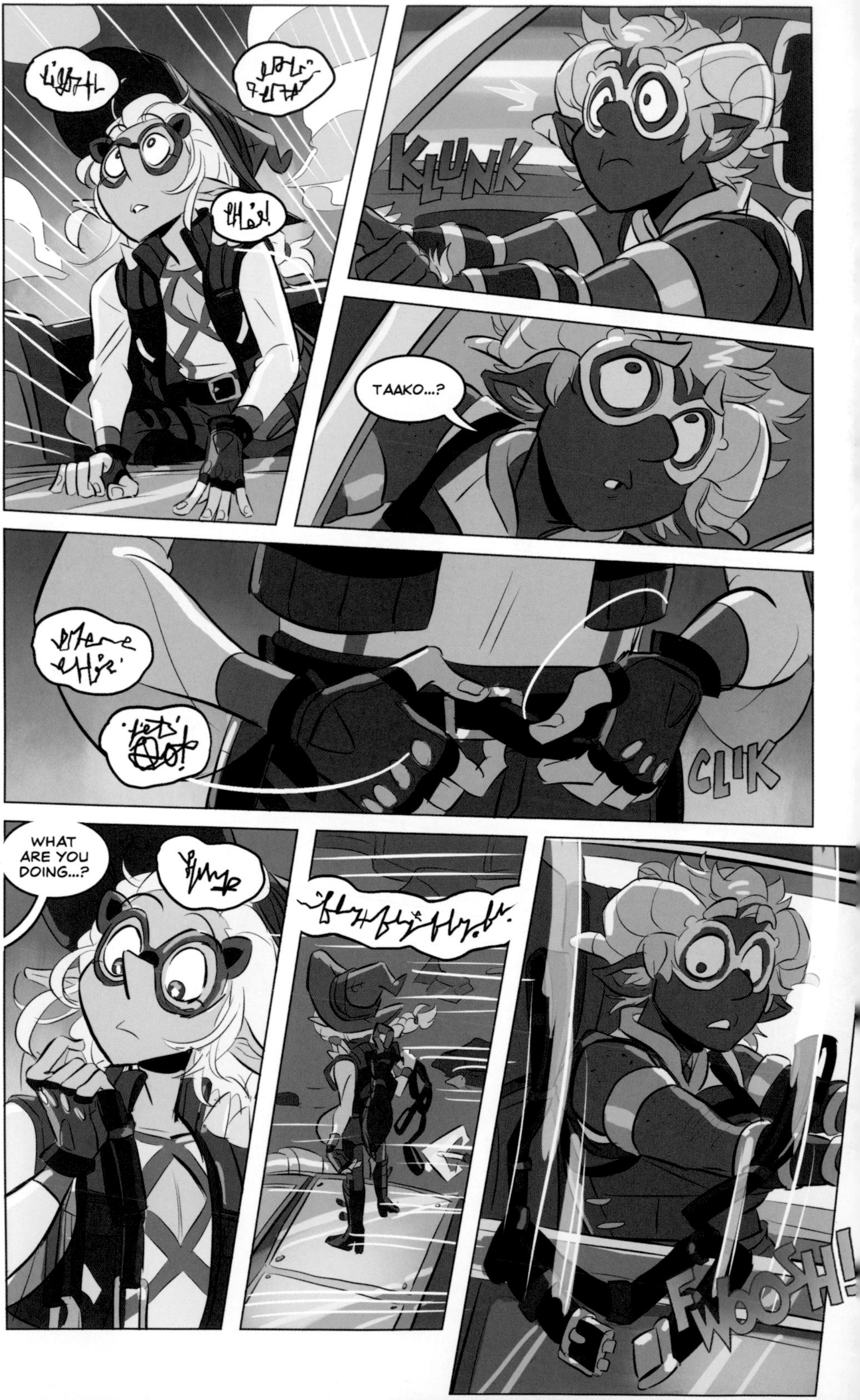
KLUNK
TAAKO...?
CLIK
WHAT ARE YOU DOING...?
FWOOSH!

147

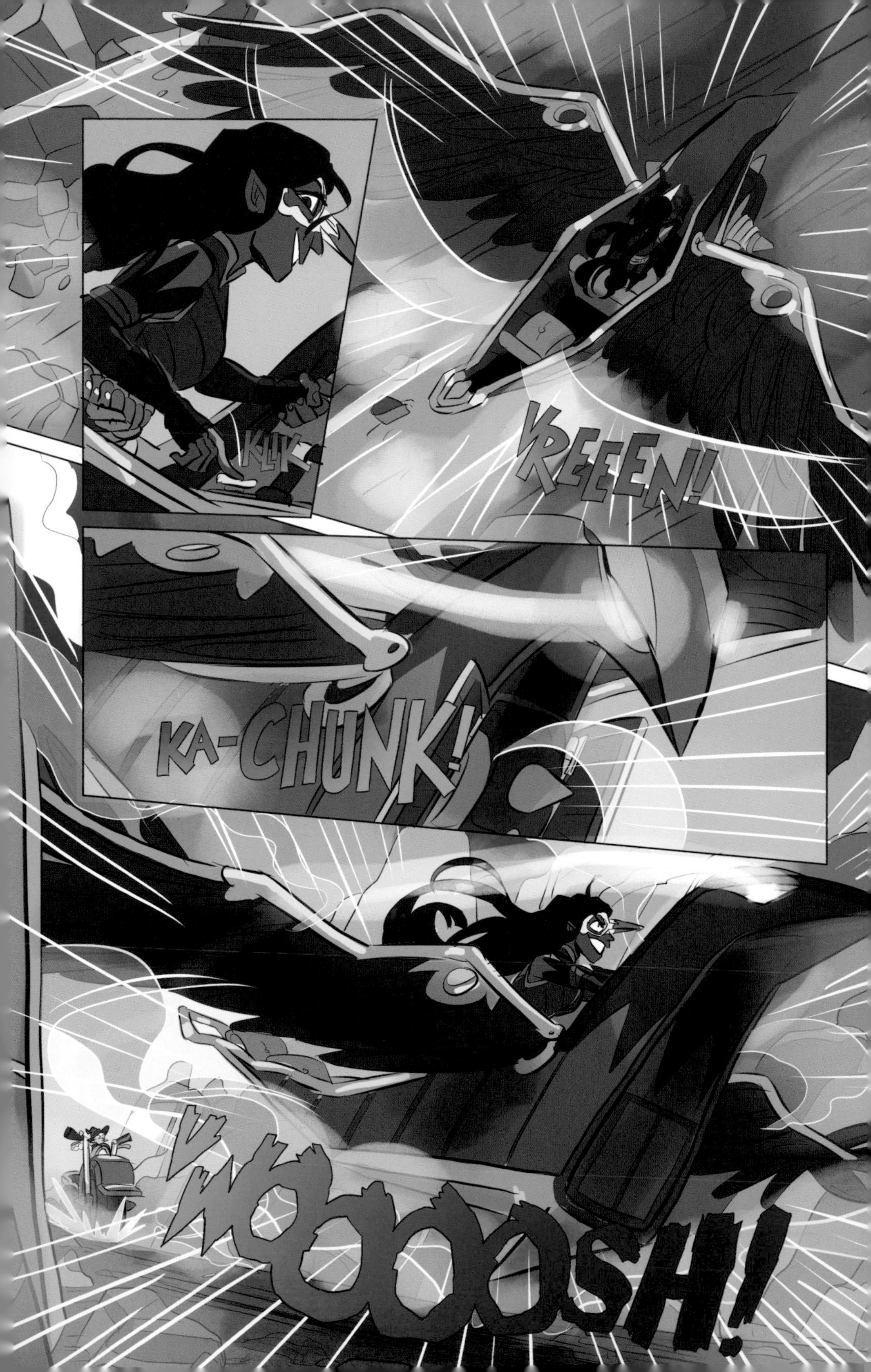
KLIK
VREEEN!
KA-CHUNK!
VWOOOOSH!

161

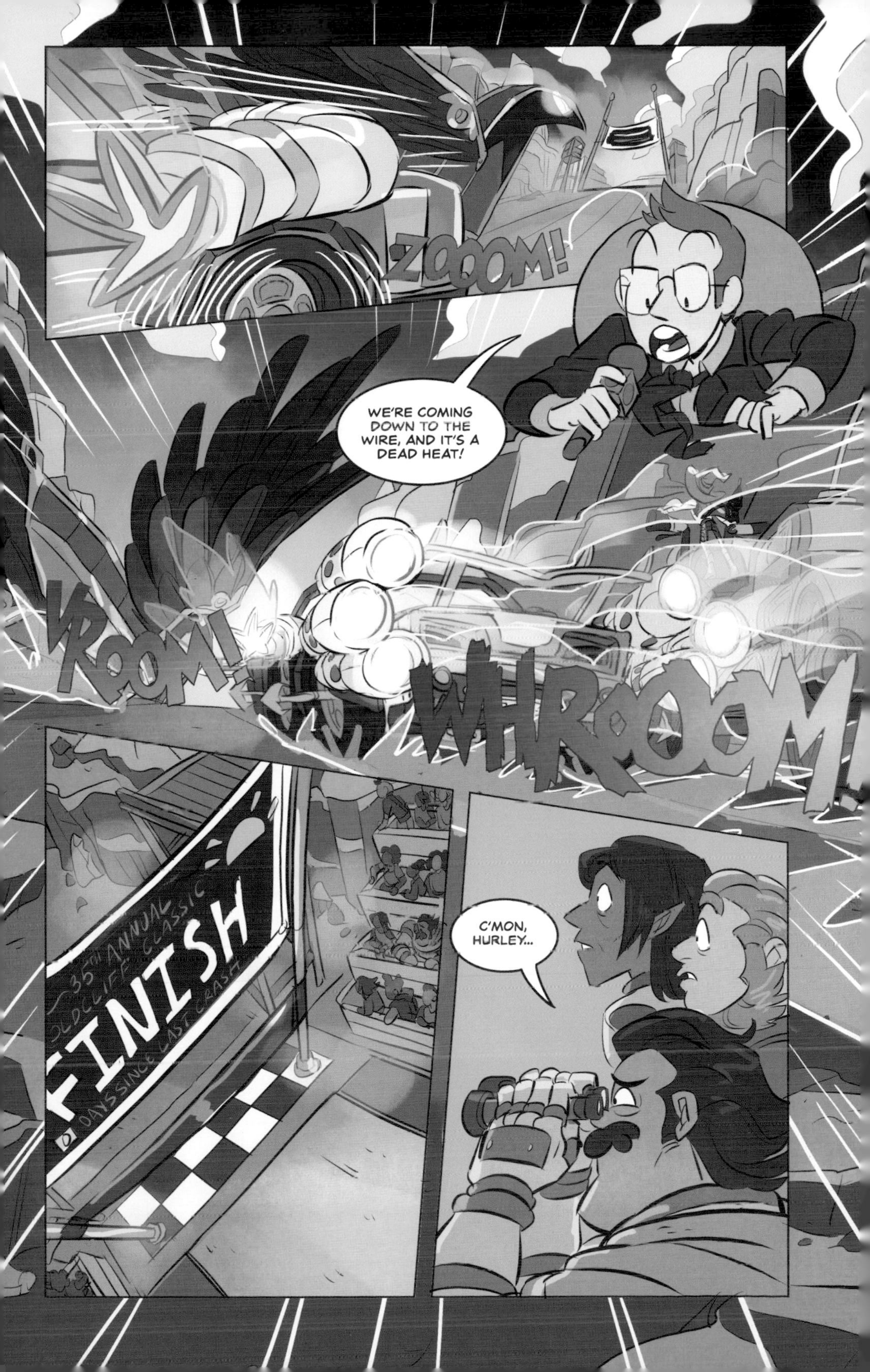
ZOOOM!
WE'RE COMING DOWN TO THE WIRE, AND IT'S A DEAD HEAT!
VROOM!
WHROOM!
35TH ANNUAL
OLDCLIFF CLASSIC
FINISH
0 DAYS SINCE LAST CRASH
C'MON, HURLEY...

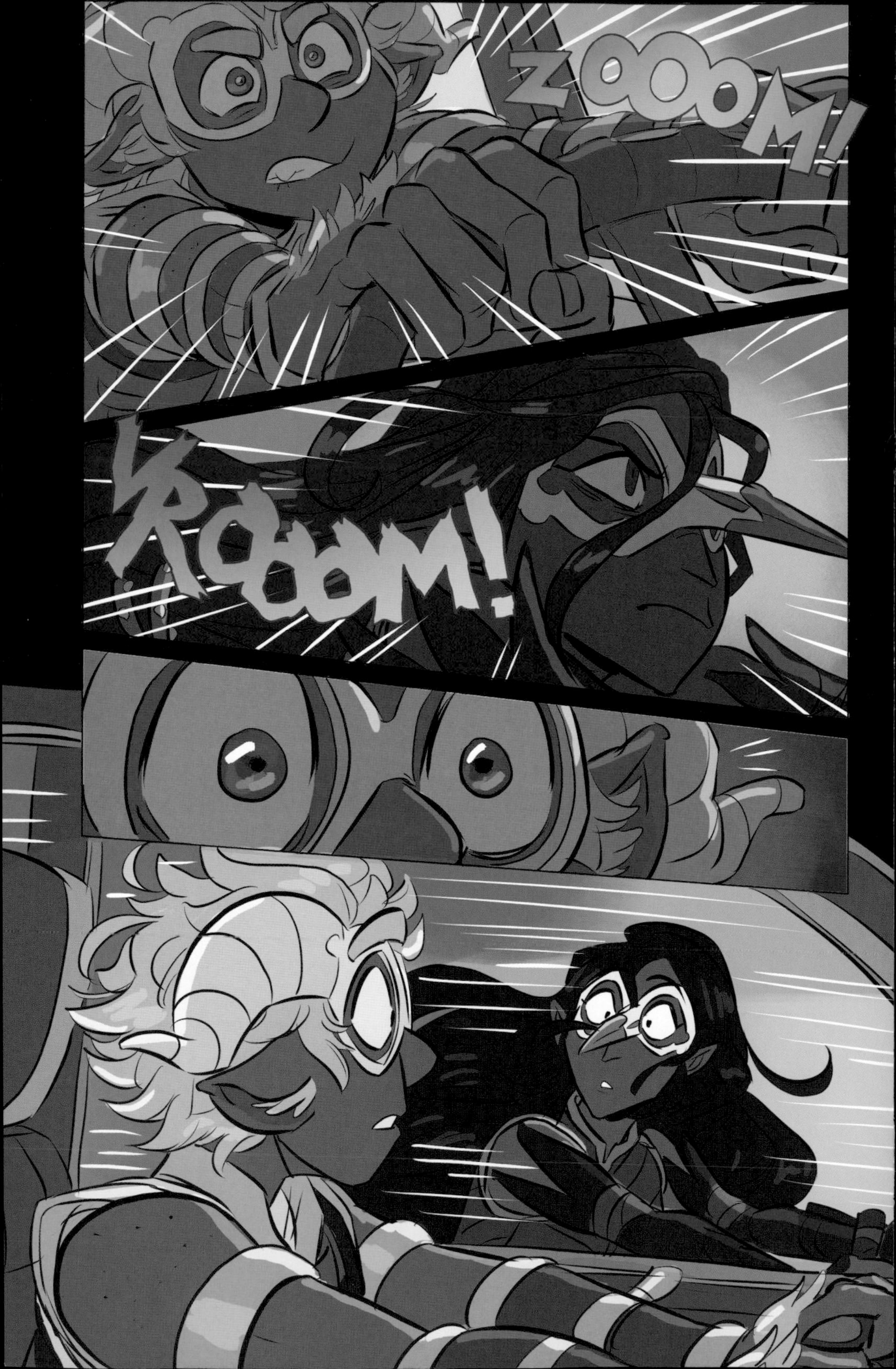
ZOOOOM!
VROOOM!

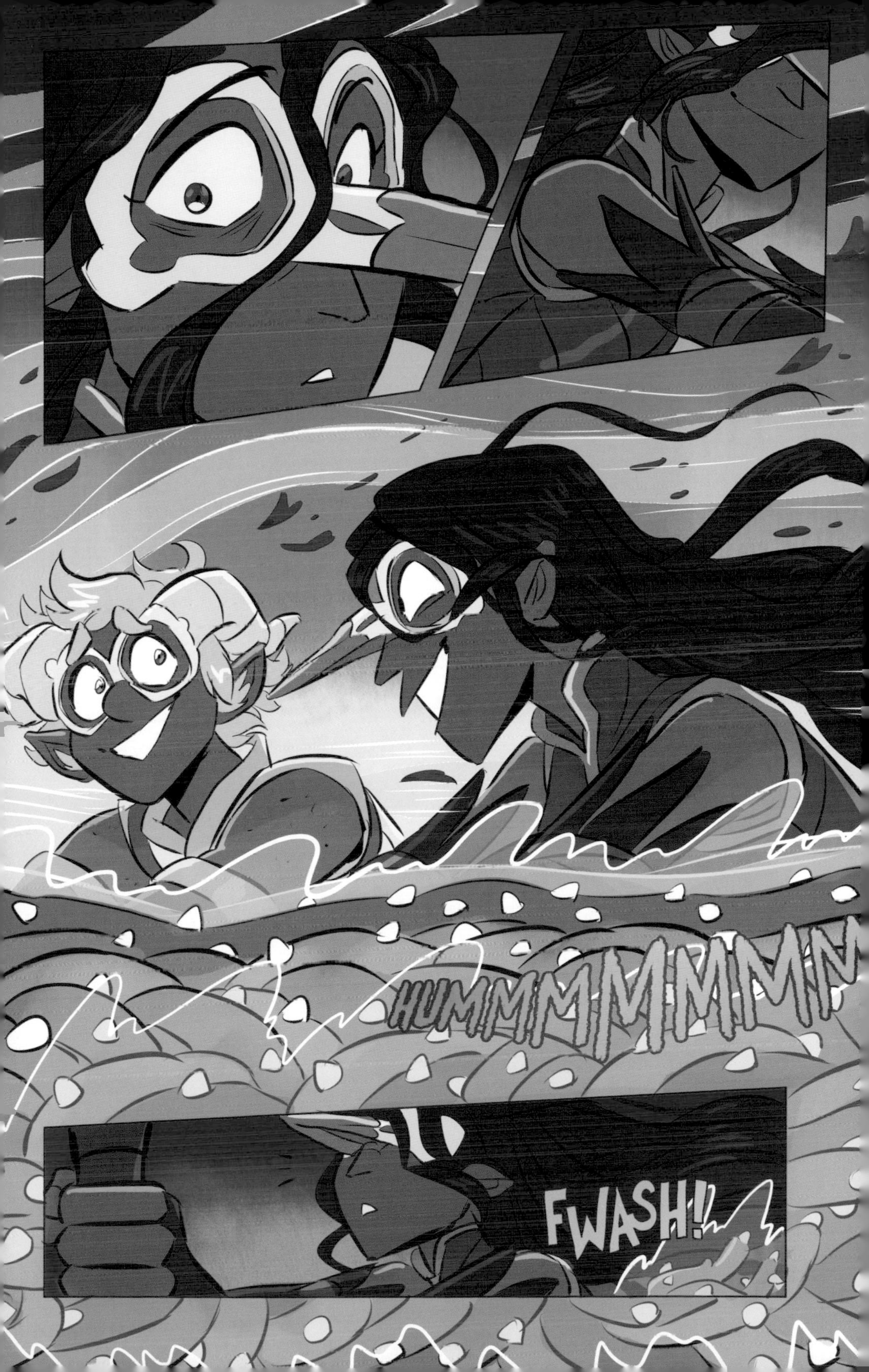
HUMMMMMMMMN
FWASH!!

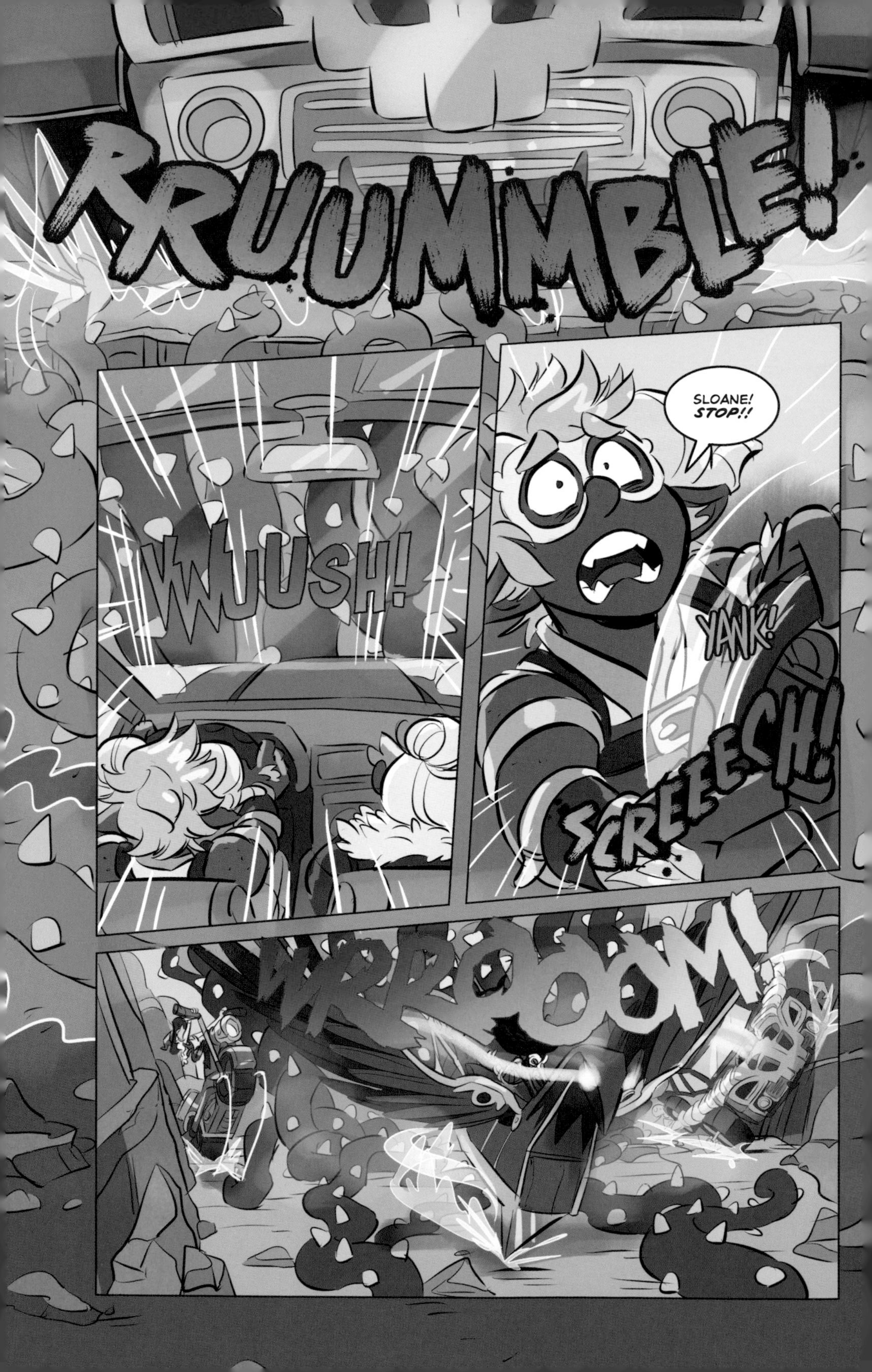
RRUUMMBLE!
WUUUSH!
SLOANE! STOP!!
YANK!
SCREEECH!
WRROOOM!

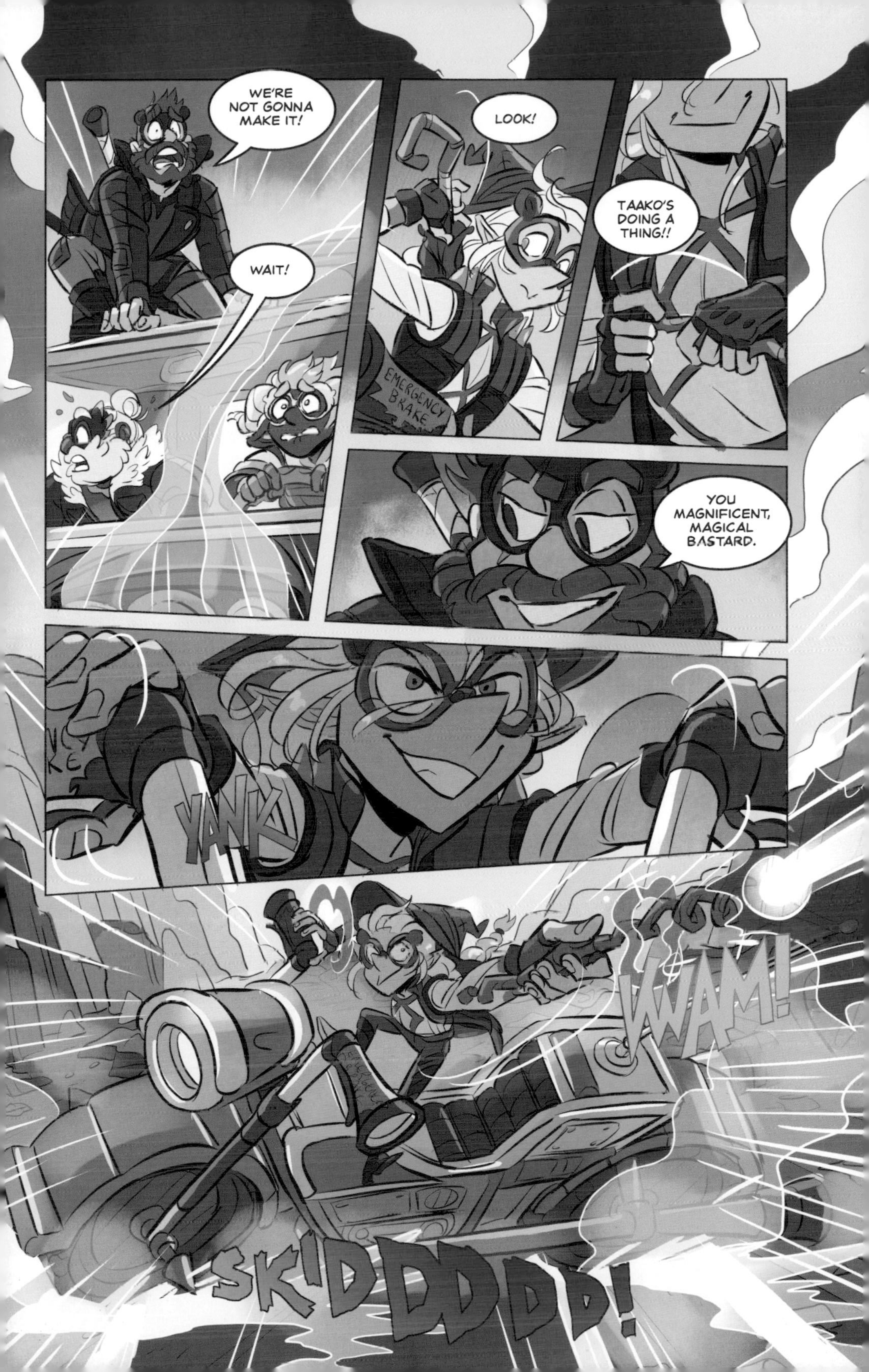
WE'RE NOT GONNA MAKE IT!
WAIT!
LOOK!
EMERGENCY BRAKE
TAAKO'S DOING A THING!!
YOU MAGNIFICENT, MAGICAL BASTARD.
YANK
WAM!
SKIDDDDD!

Chapter 7

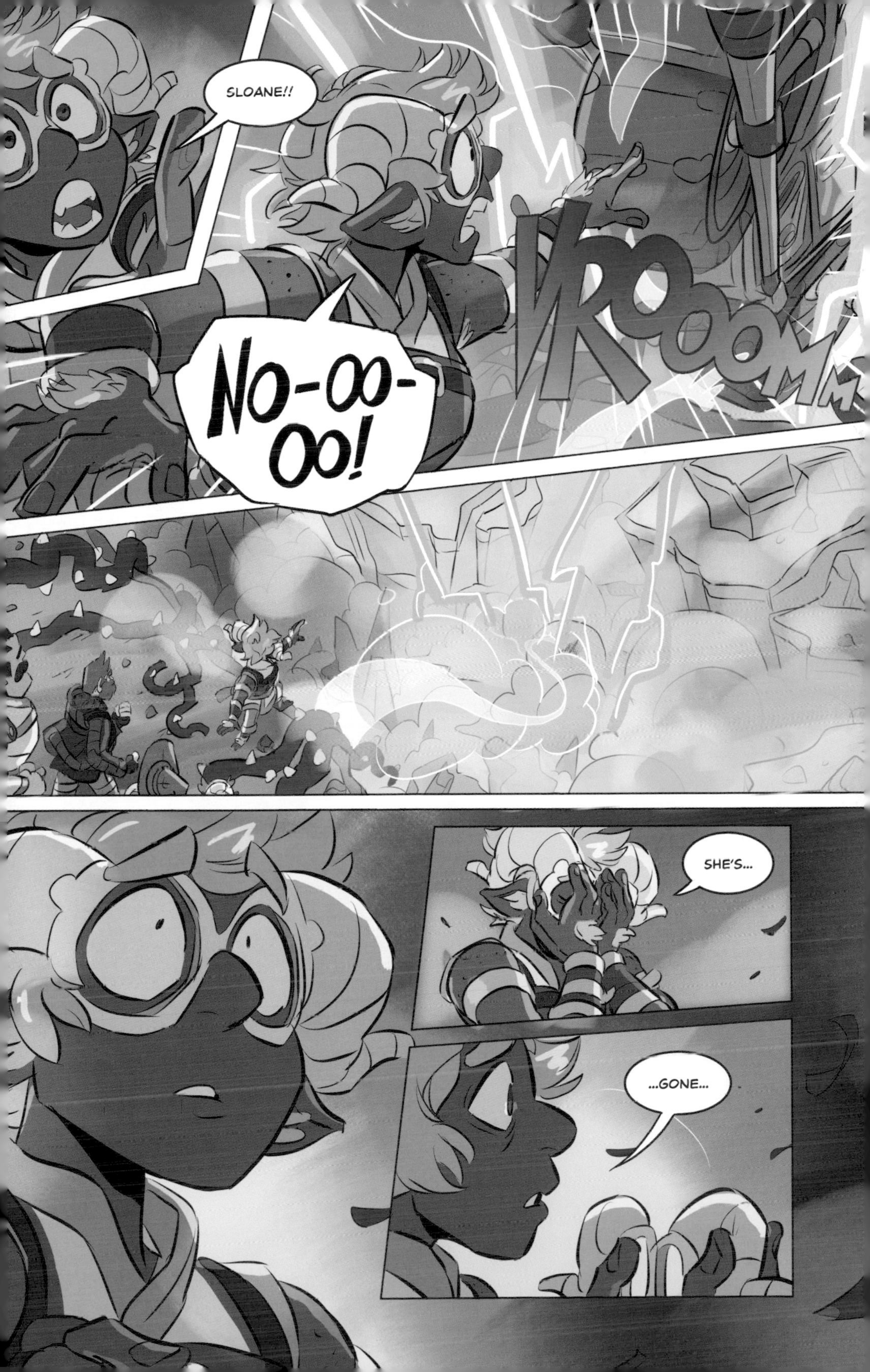
SLOANE!!
NO-OO-OO!
VROOOOMM
SHE'S...
...GONE...

177

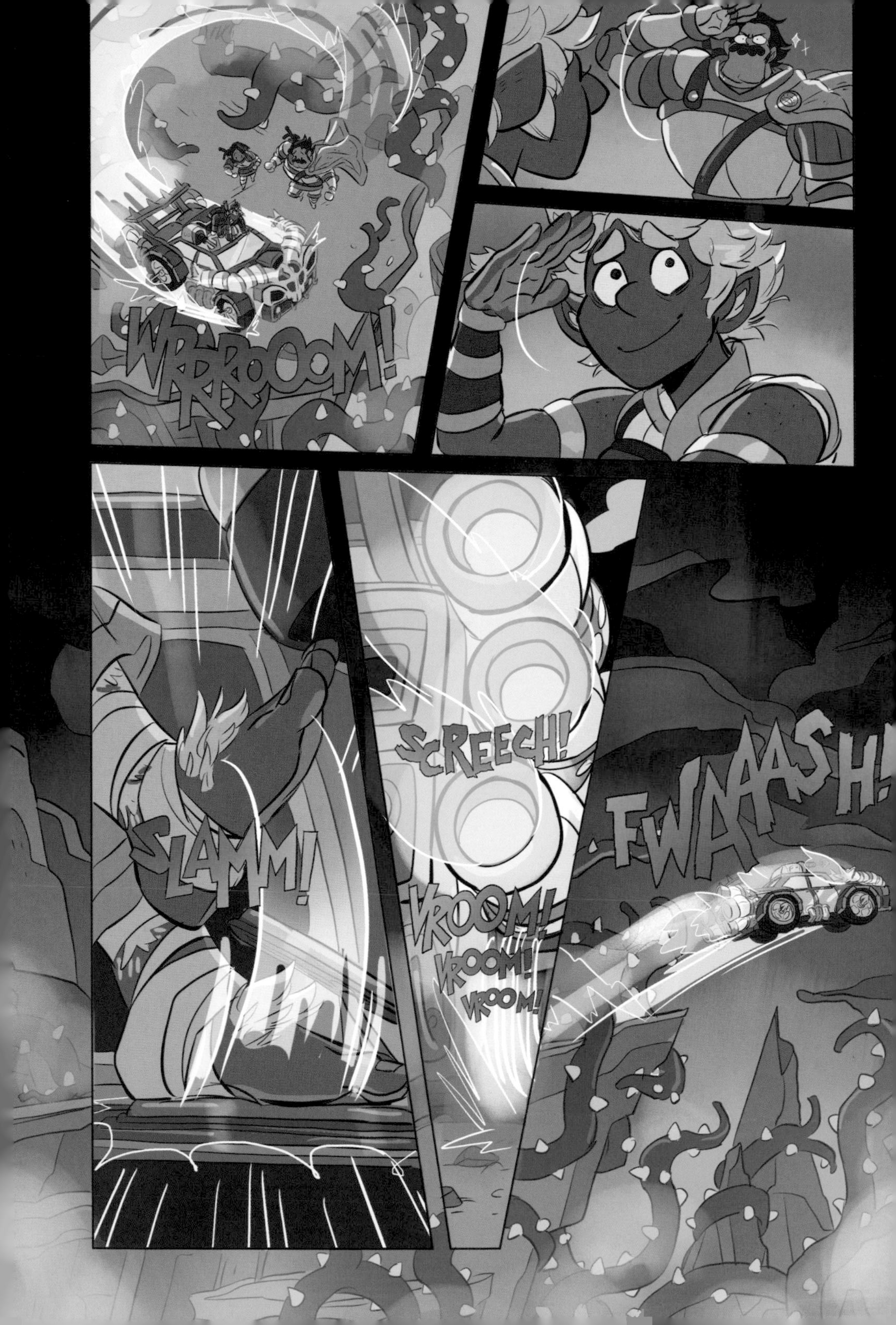
WRRROOOM!
SLAMM!
SCREECH!
VROOM!
VROOM!
VROOM!
FWAAASH!

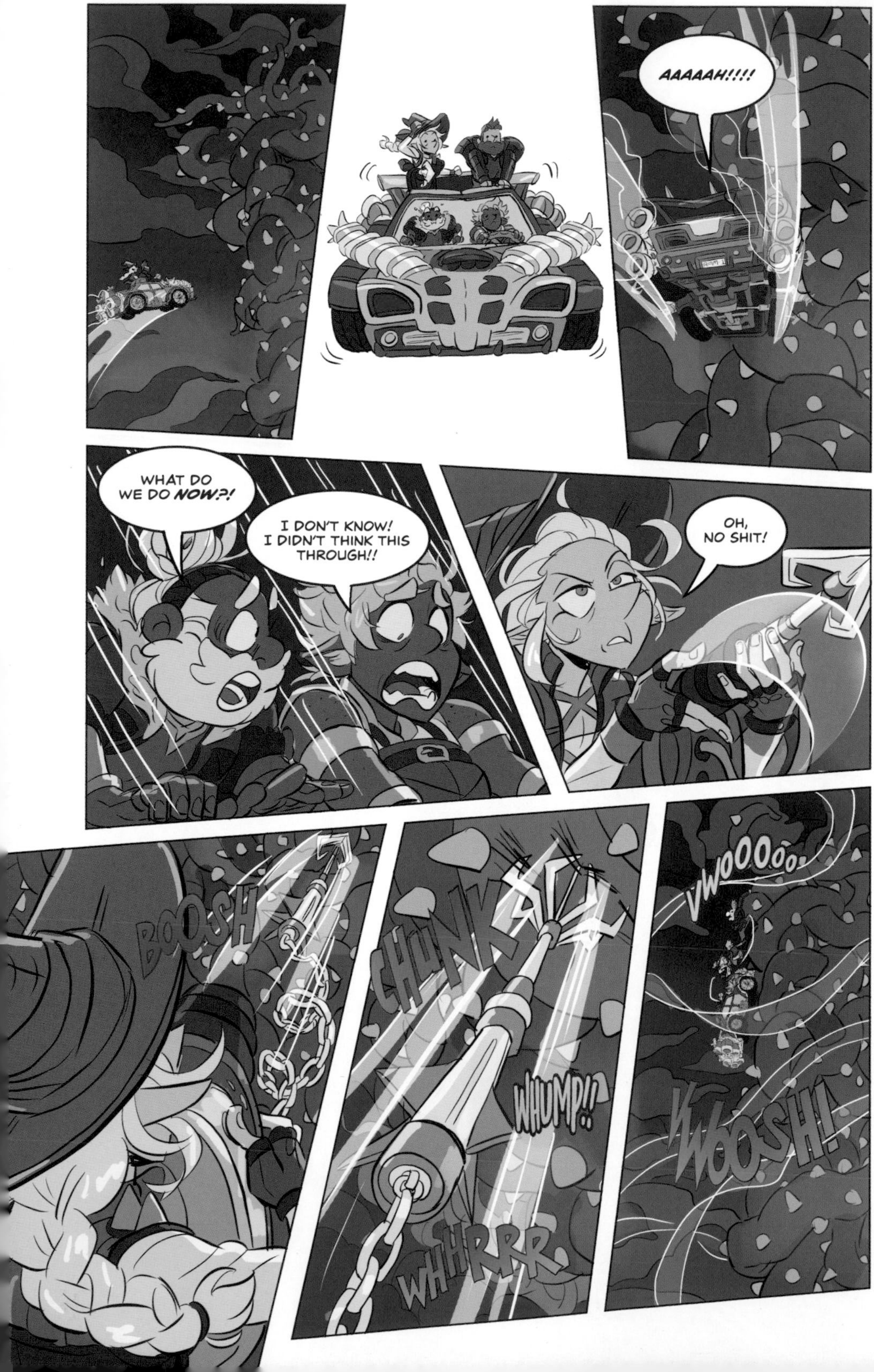
AAAAAH!!!!
WHAT DO WE DO NOW?!
I DON'T KNOW! I DIDN'T THINK THIS THROUGH!!
OH, NO SHIT!
BOOSH
CHUNK
WHUMP!!
WHRRR
VWOOOOoo
WOOSH!

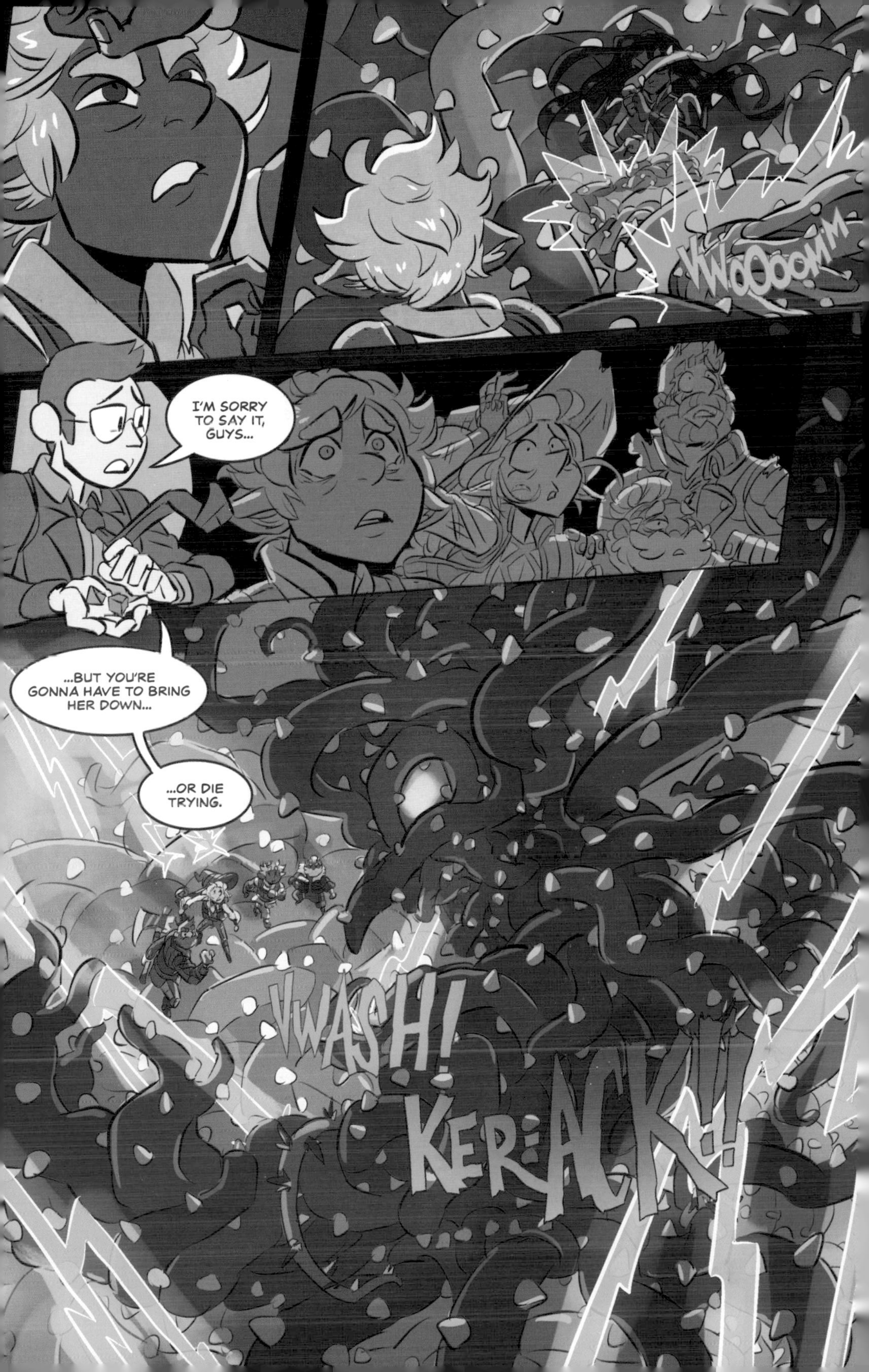
VWOOOOMM
I'M SORRY TO SAY IT, GUYS...
...BUT YOU'RE GONNA HAVE TO BRING HER DOWN...
...OR DIE TRYING.
VWASH!
KER-ACK!!

184

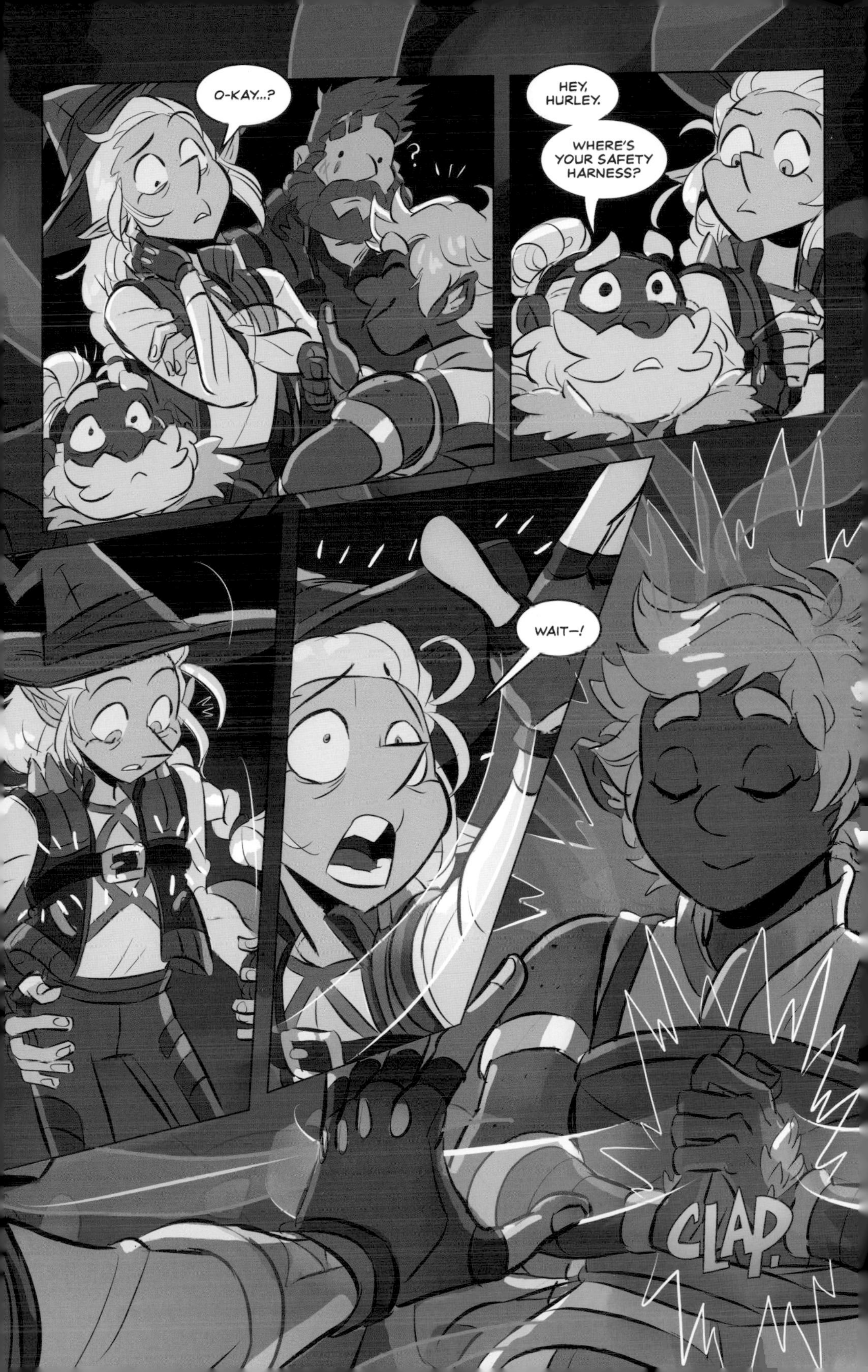
O-KAY...?
?
HEY, HURLEY.
WHERE'S YOUR SAFETY HARNESS?
WAIT-!
CLAP.

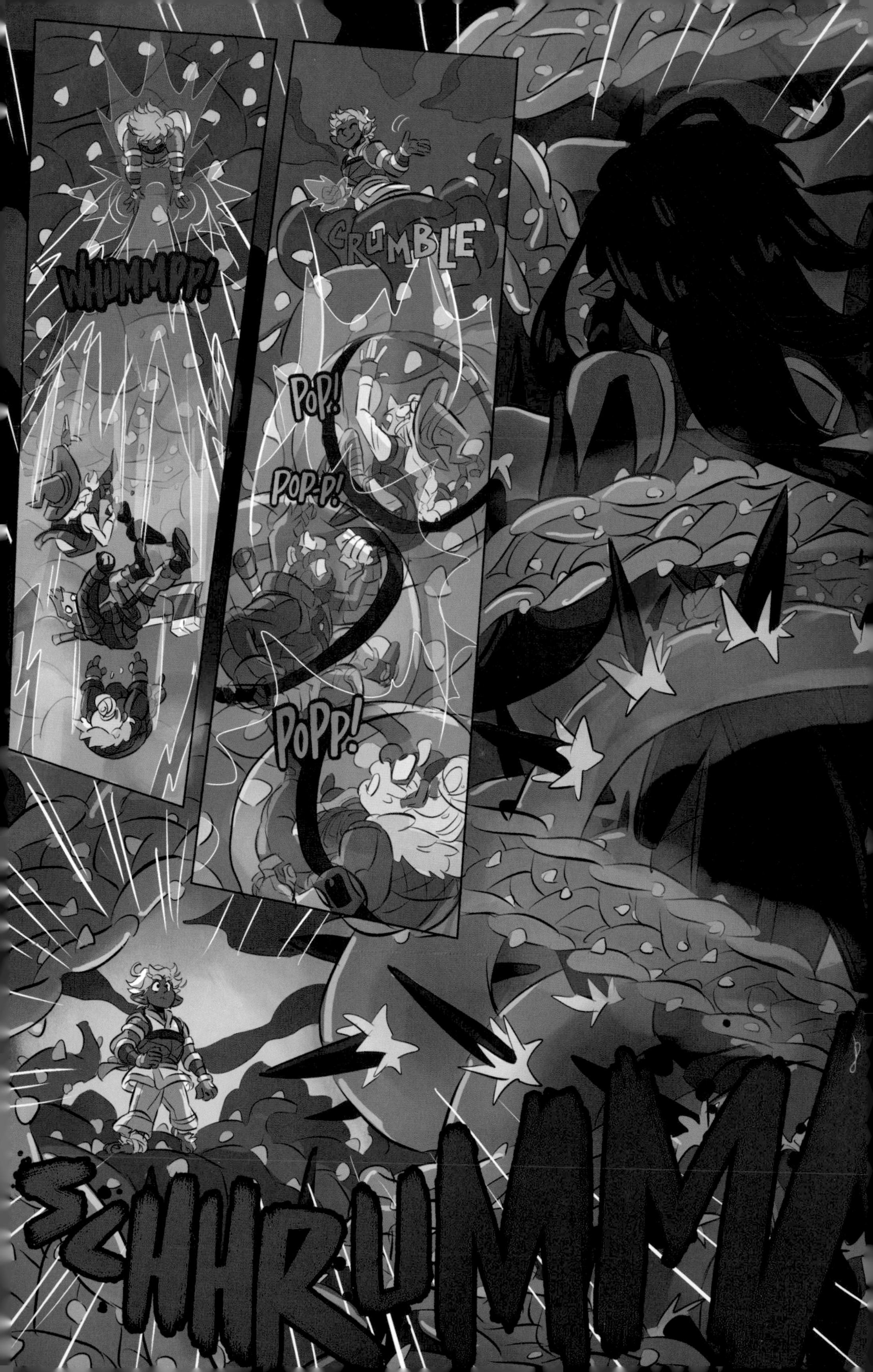
WHUMMPP!
CRUMBLE
POP!
POP-P!
POPP!
SCHHRUMMM

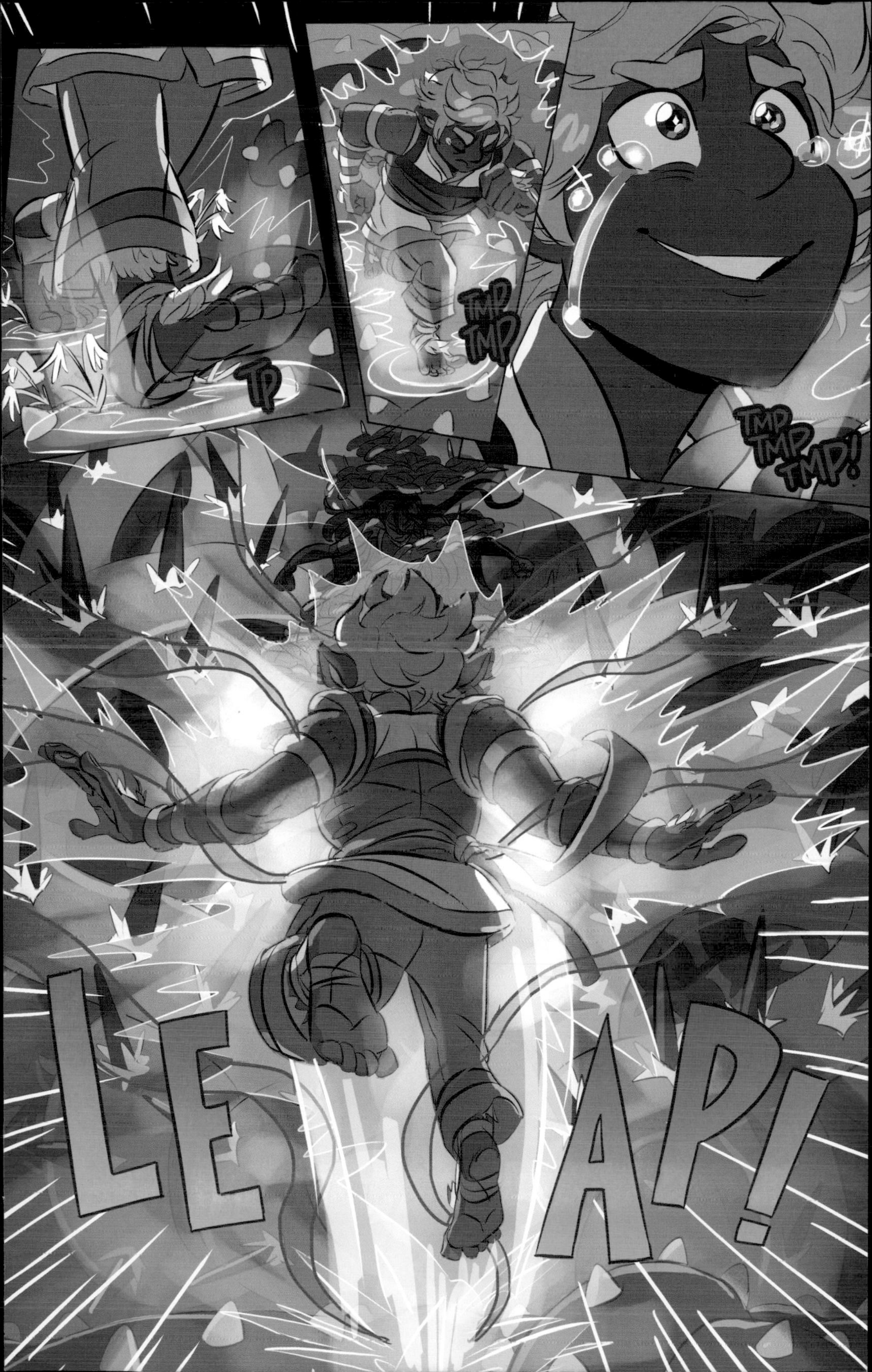
TP
TMP
TMP
TMP
TMP
TMP!
LEAP!

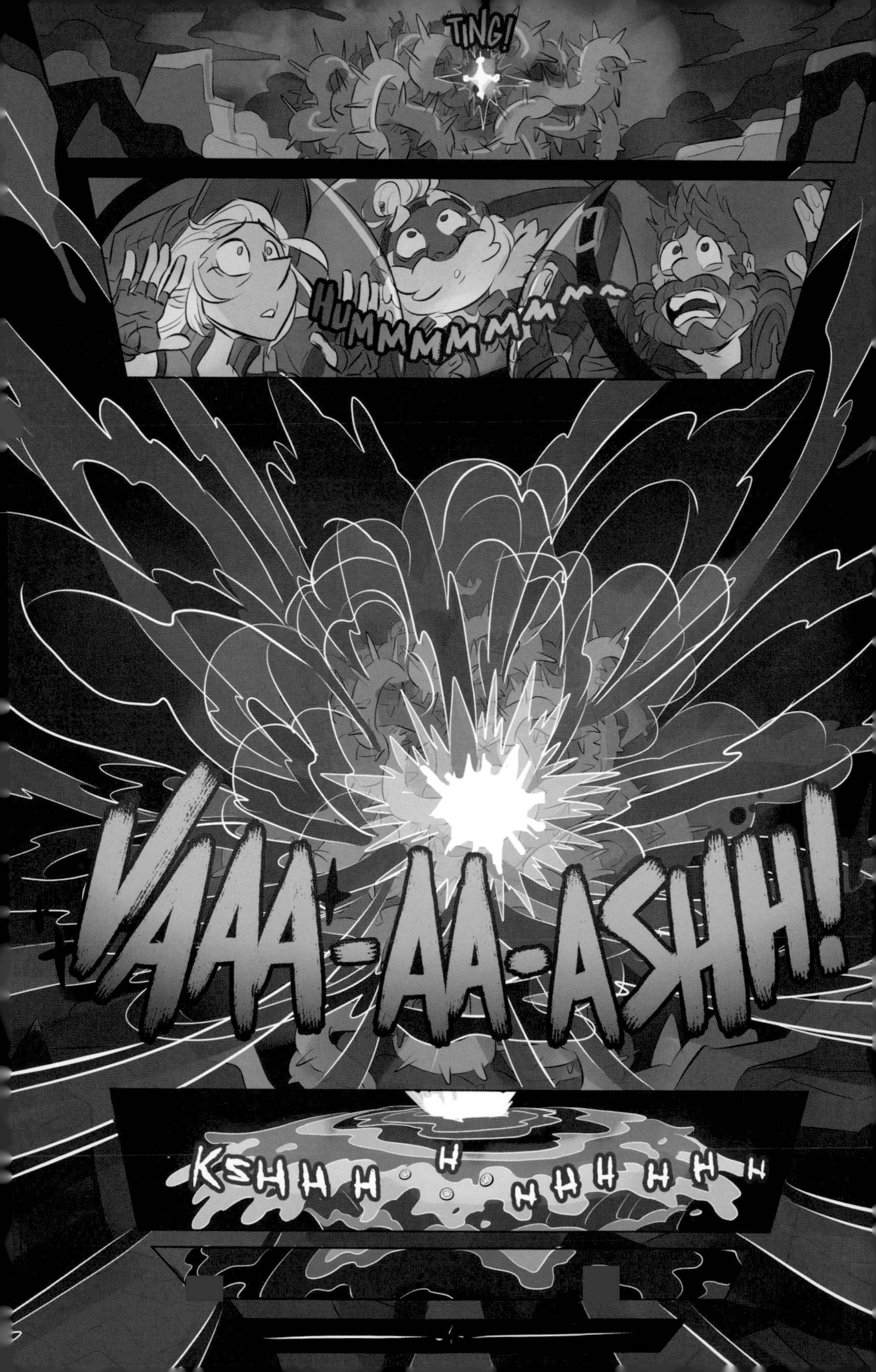
TING!
HUMMMMMMMMMM
VAAA-AA-ASHH!
KSHHHH H HHHHHHH

Chapter 8

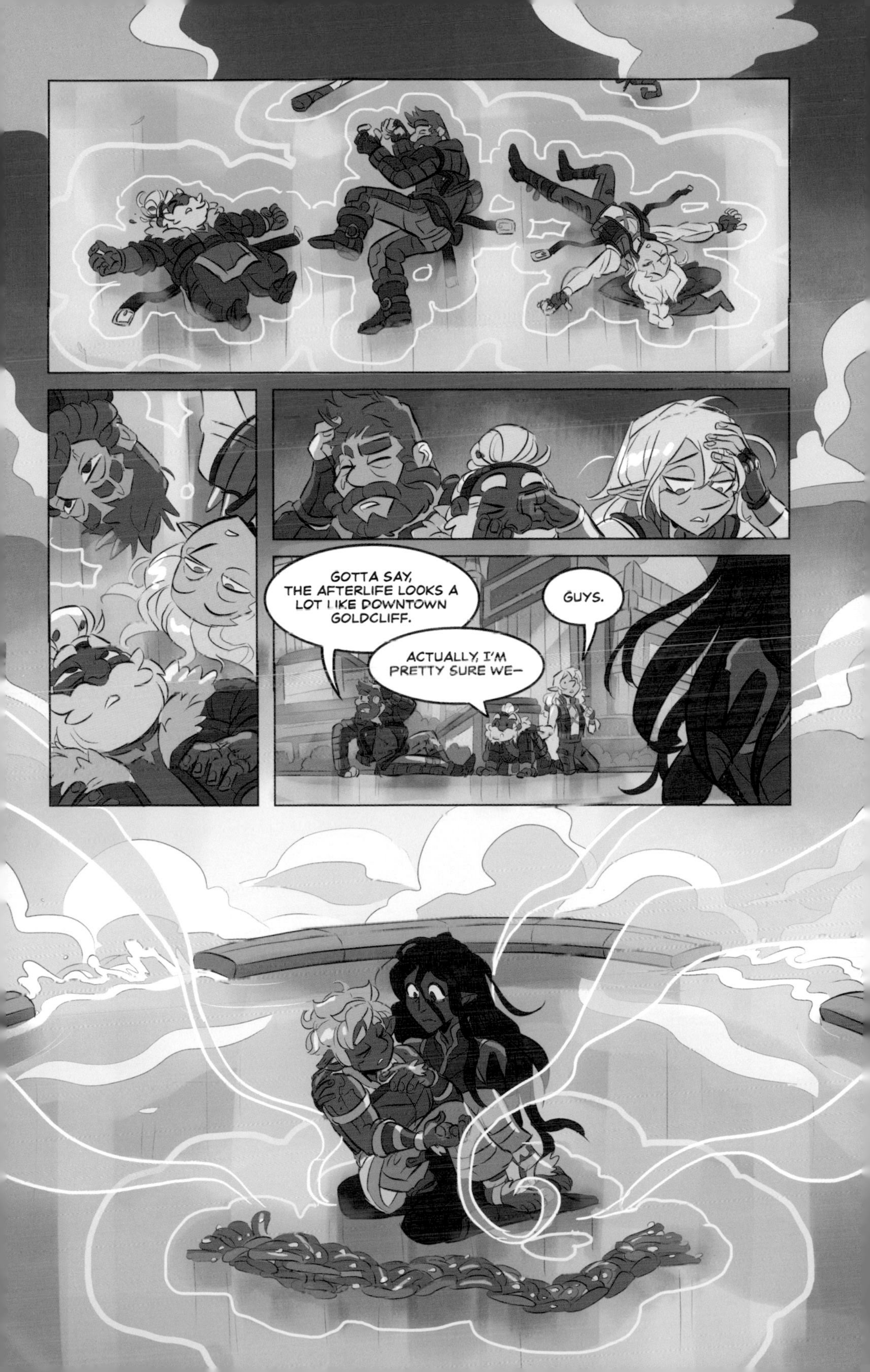
GOTTA SAY, THE AFTERLIFE LOOKS A LOT LIKE DOWNTOWN GOLDCLIFF.
ACTUALLY, I'M PRETTY SURE WE—
GUYS.

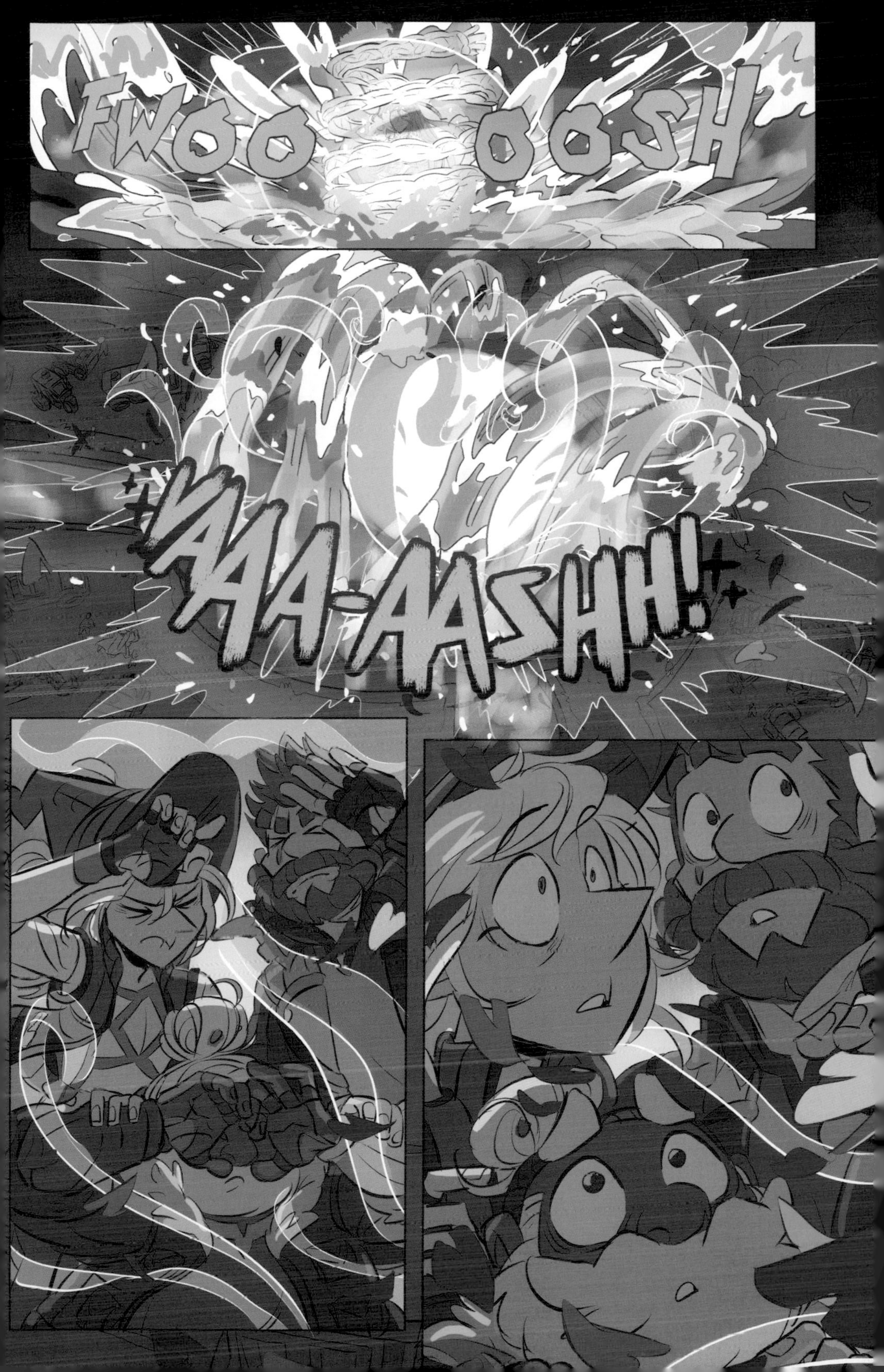
FWOOOOOSH
VAAA-AASHH!

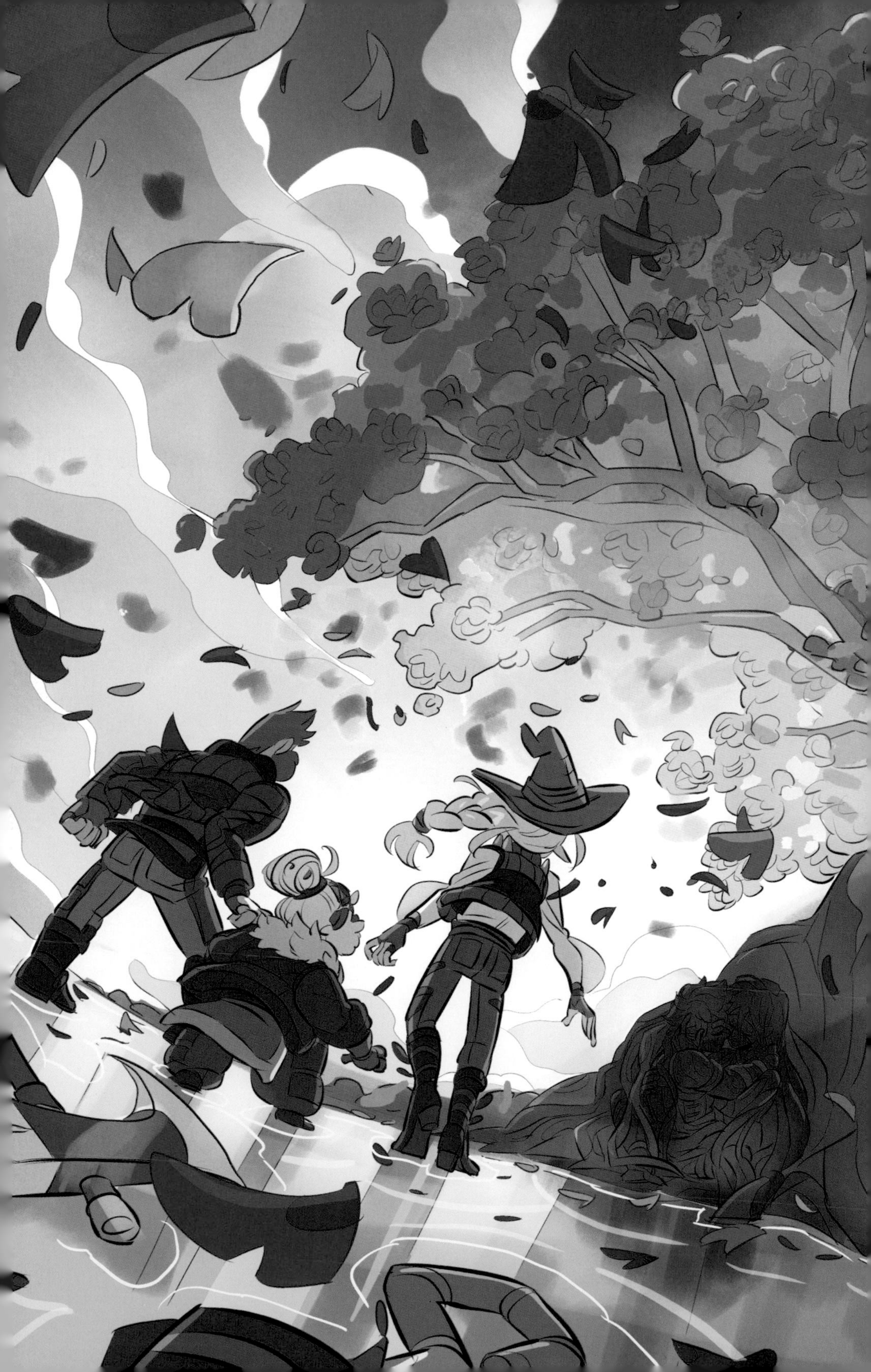

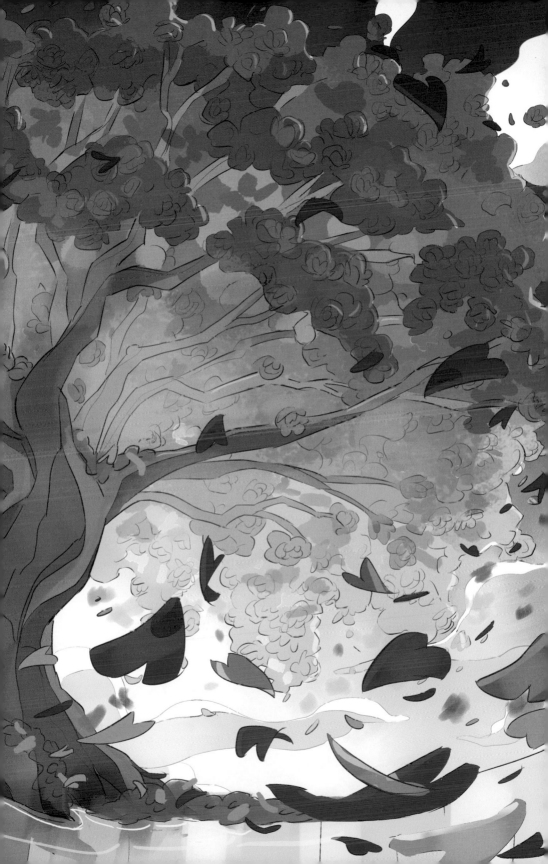

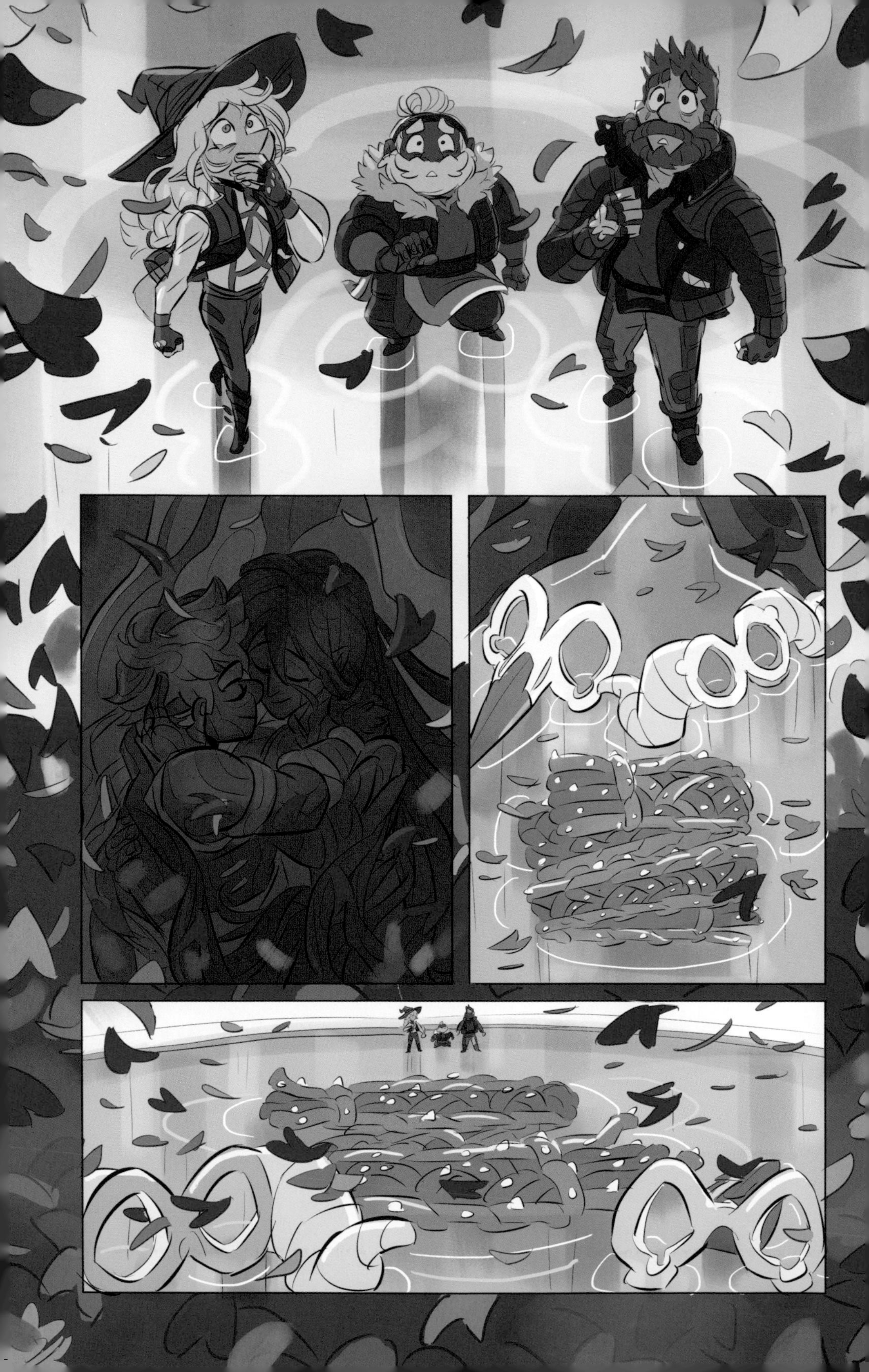

NUDGE

NUDGE NUDGE

TP TP

EASY THERE, LITTLE BELT.

NO SUDDEN MOVEMENTS, OKAY?

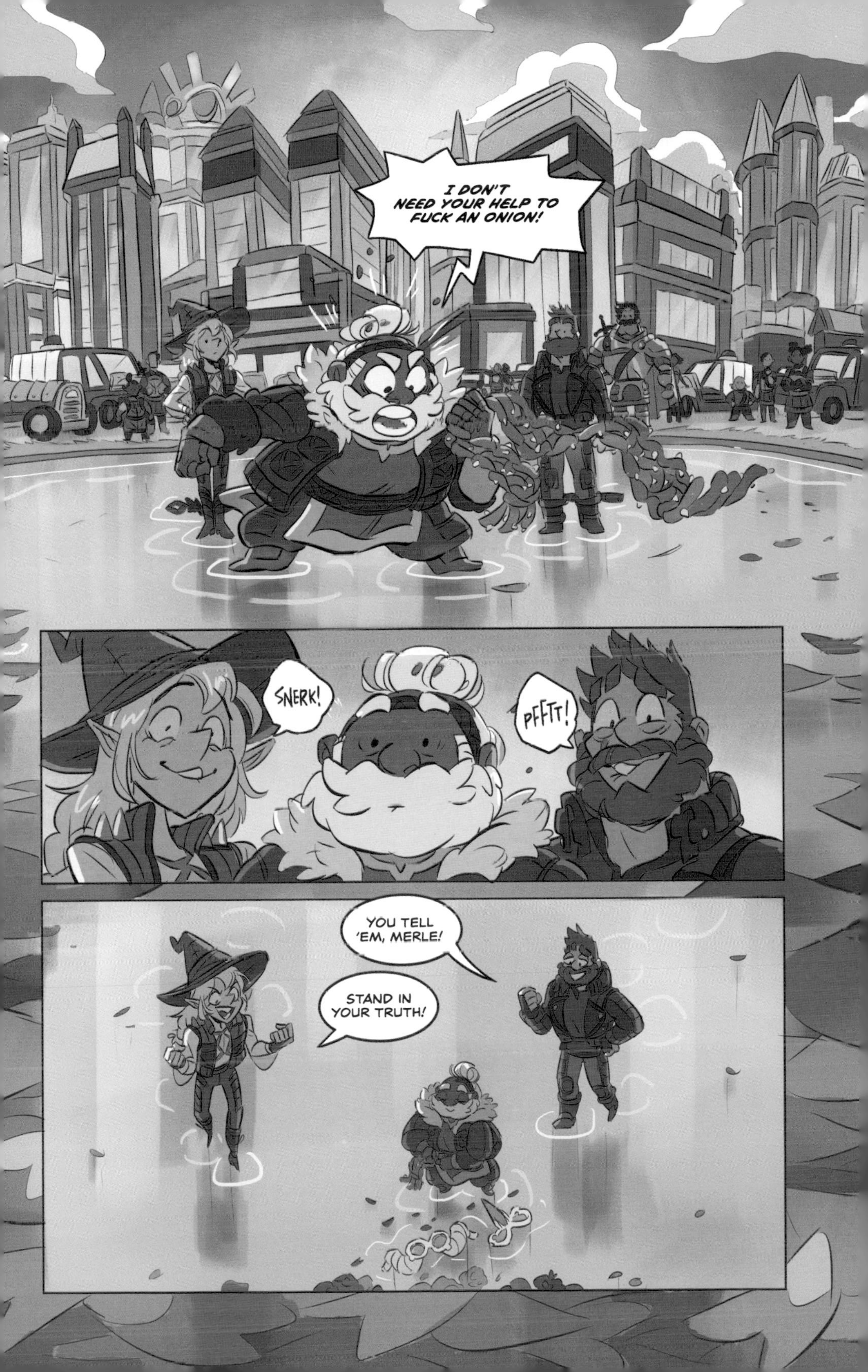
I DON'T NEED YOUR HELP TO FUCK AN ONION!
SNERK!
PFFTT!
YOU TELL 'EM, MERLE!
STAND IN YOUR TRUTH!

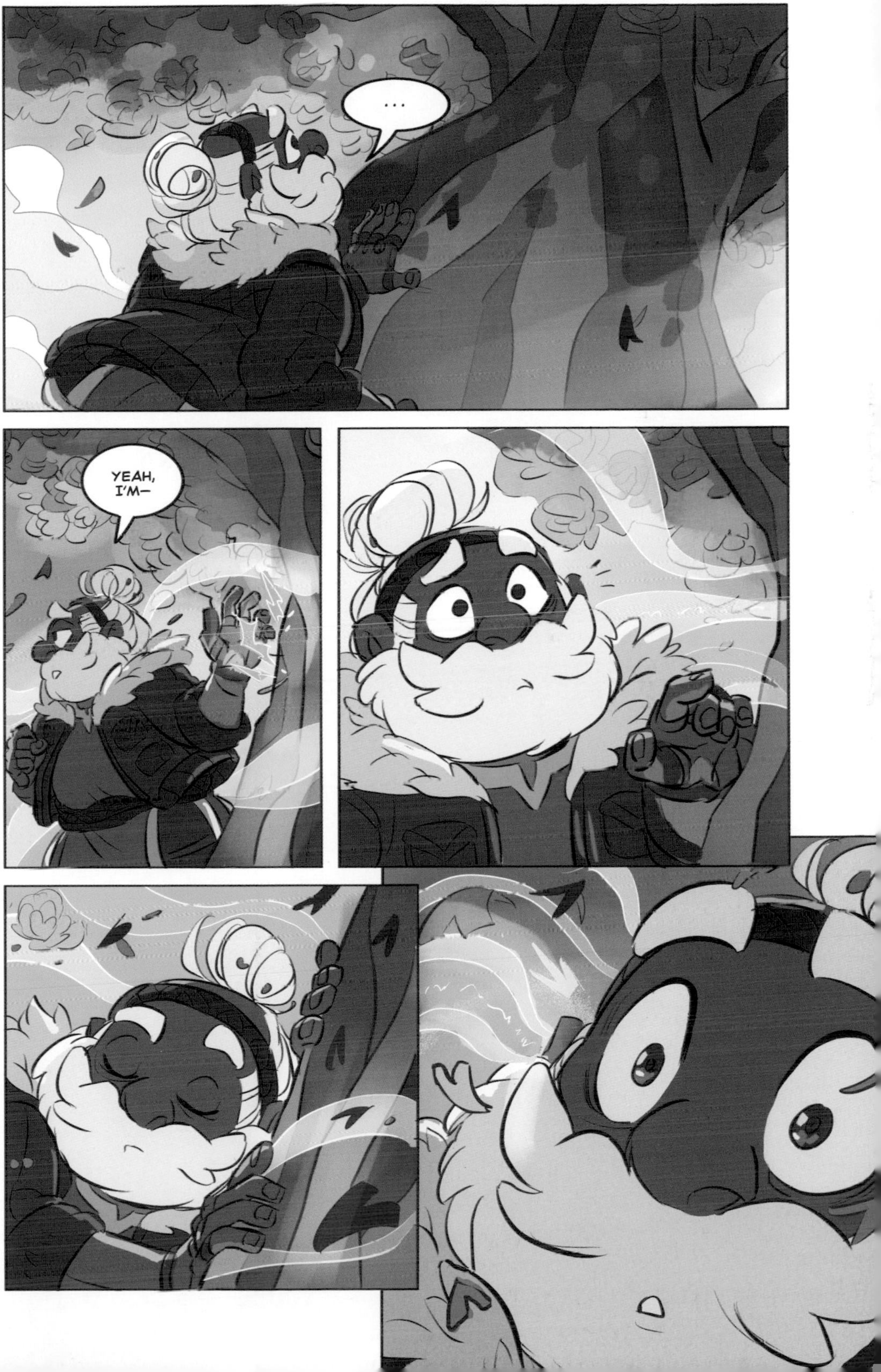
...
YEAH, I'M—

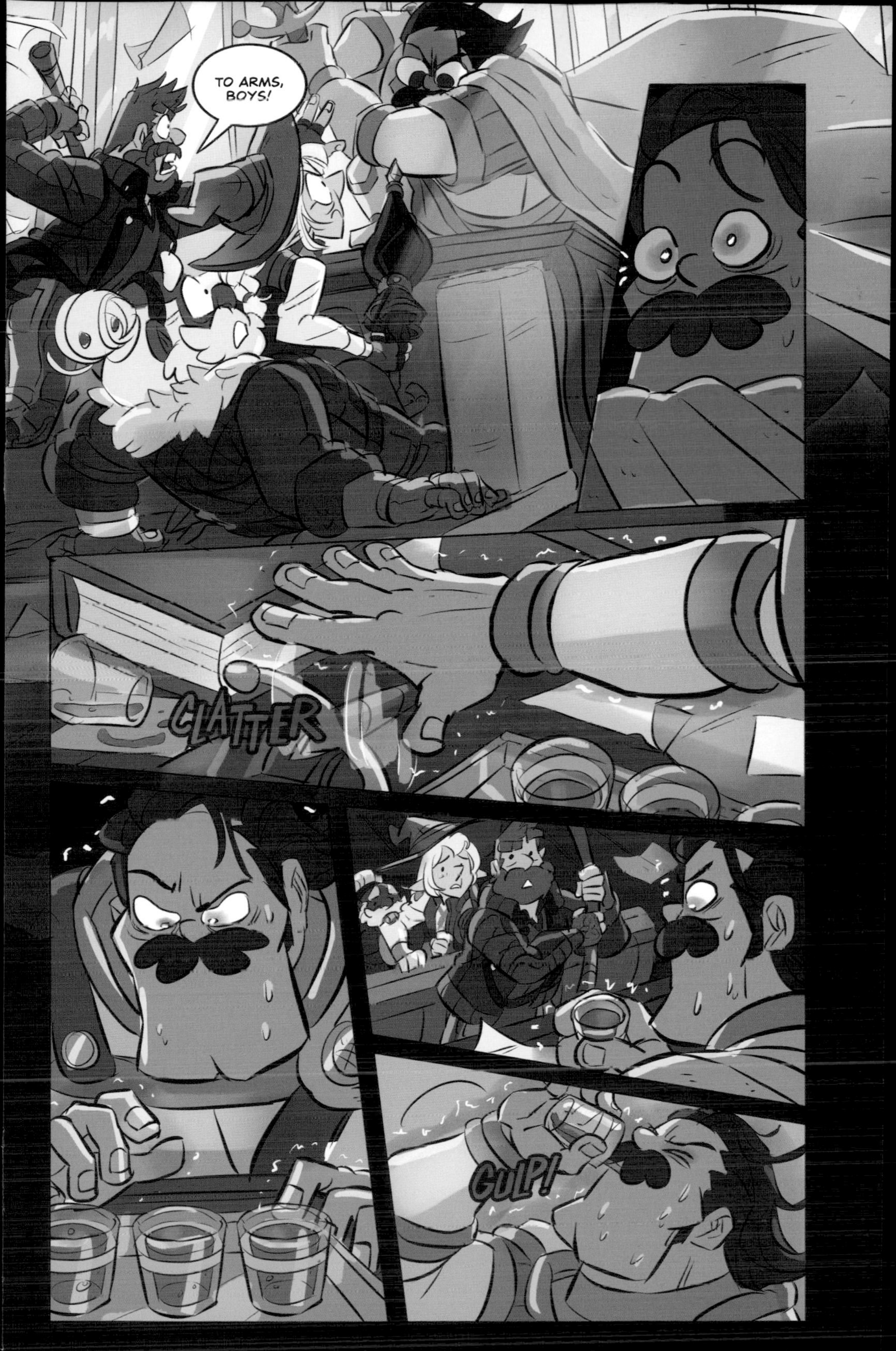
TO ARMS, BOYS!
CLATTER
GULP!

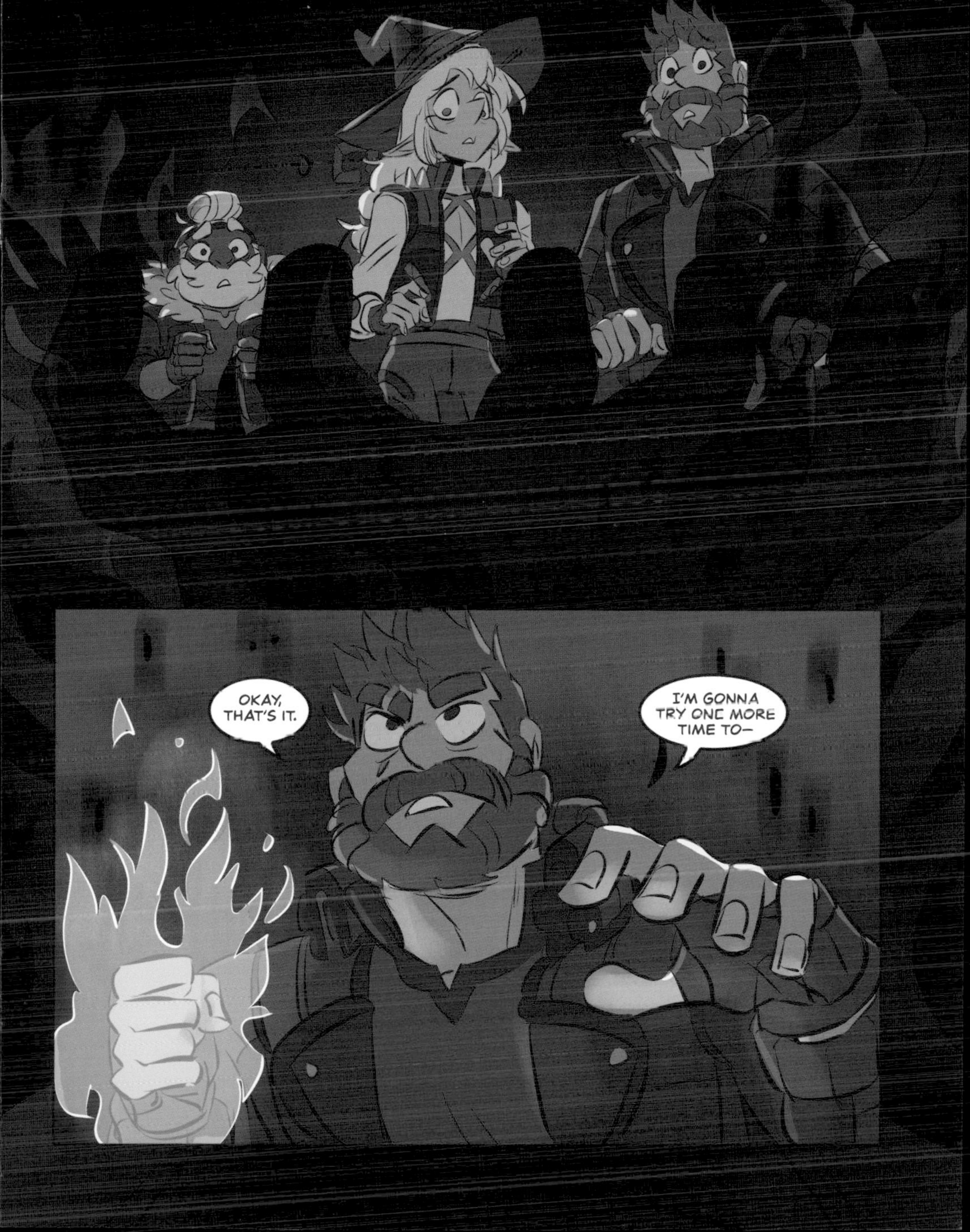
OKAY, THAT'S IT.
I'M GONNA TRY ONE MORE TIME TO—

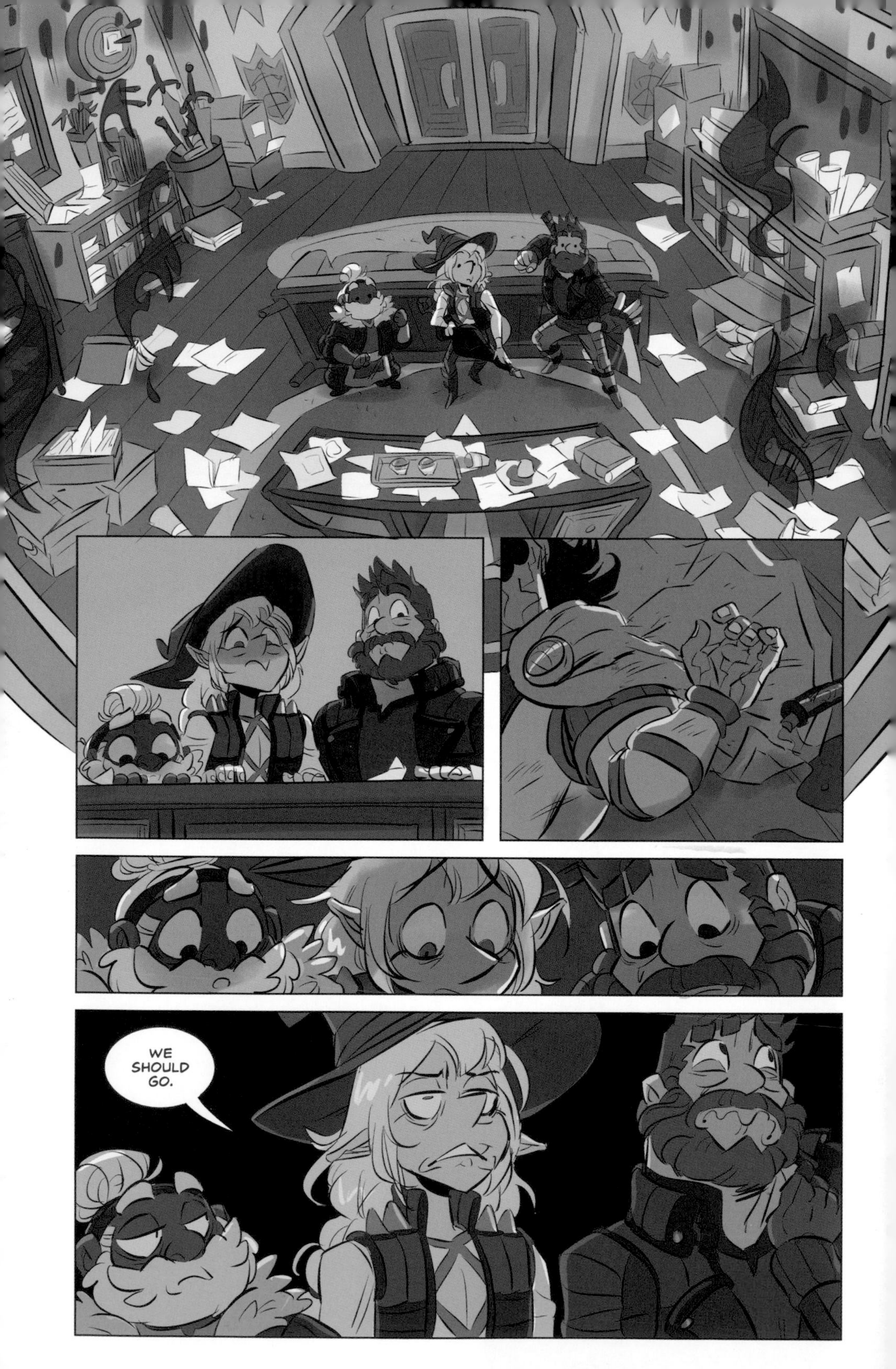
WE SHOULD GO.

Chapter 9

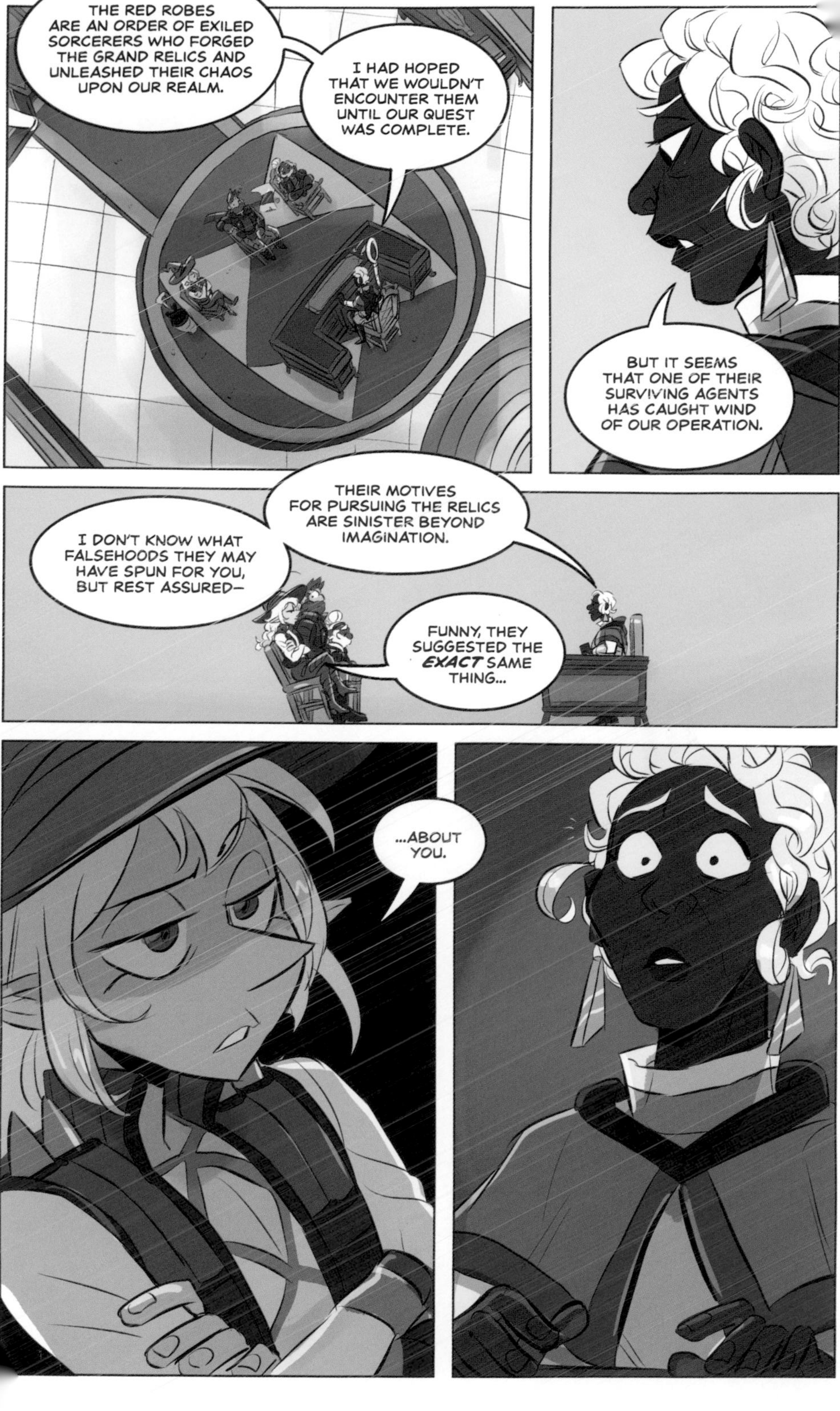
THE RED ROBES ARE AN ORDER OF EXILED SORCERERS WHO FORGED THE GRAND RELICS AND UNLEASHED THEIR CHAOS UPON OUR REALM.
I HAD HOPED THAT WE WOULDN'T ENCOUNTER THEM UNTIL OUR QUEST WAS COMPLETE.
BUT IT SEEMS THAT ONE OF THEIR SURVIVING AGENTS HAS CAUGHT WIND OF OUR OPERATION.
THEIR MOTIVES FOR PURSUING THE RELICS ARE SINISTER BEYOND IMAGINATION.
I DON'T KNOW WHAT FALSEHOODS THEY MAY HAVE SPUN FOR YOU, BUT REST ASSURED—
FUNNY, THEY SUGGESTED THE *EXACT* SAME THING...
...ABOUT YOU.

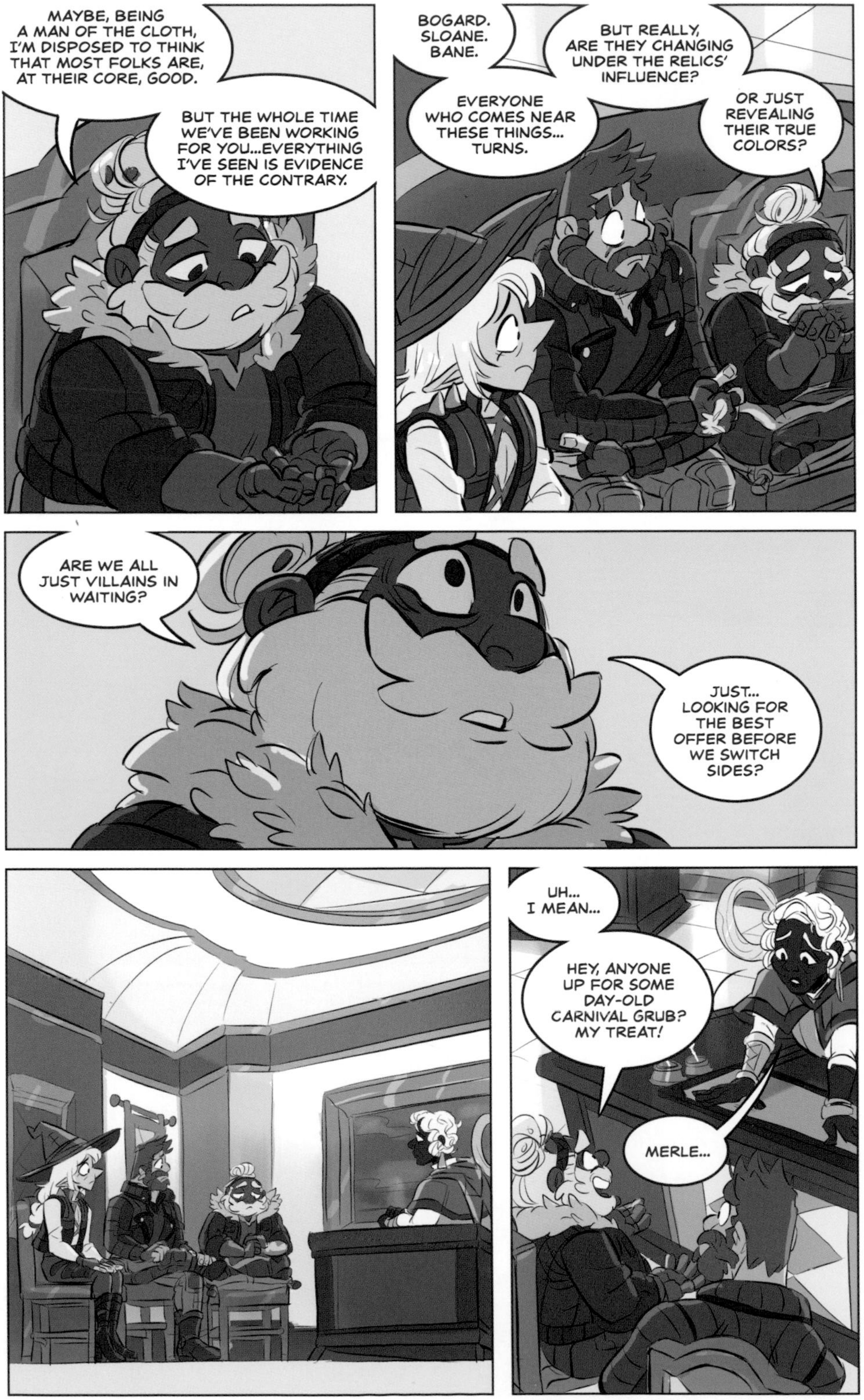
MAYBE, BEING A MAN OF THE CLOTH, I'M DISPOSED TO THINK THAT MOST FOLKS ARE, AT THEIR CORE, GOOD.
BUT THE WHOLE TIME WE'VE BEEN WORKING FOR YOU...EVERYTHING I'VE SEEN IS EVIDENCE OF THE CONTRARY.
BOGARD. SLOANE. BANE.
EVERYONE WHO COMES NEAR THESE THINGS... TURNS.
BUT REALLY, ARE THEY CHANGING UNDER THE RELICS' INFLUENCE?
OR JUST REVEALING THEIR TRUE COLORS?
ARE WE ALL JUST VILLAINS IN WAITING?
JUST... LOOKING FOR THE BEST OFFER BEFORE WE SWITCH SIDES?
UH... I MEAN...
HEY, ANYONE UP FOR SOME DAY-OLD CARNIVAL GRUB? MY TREAT!
MERLE...

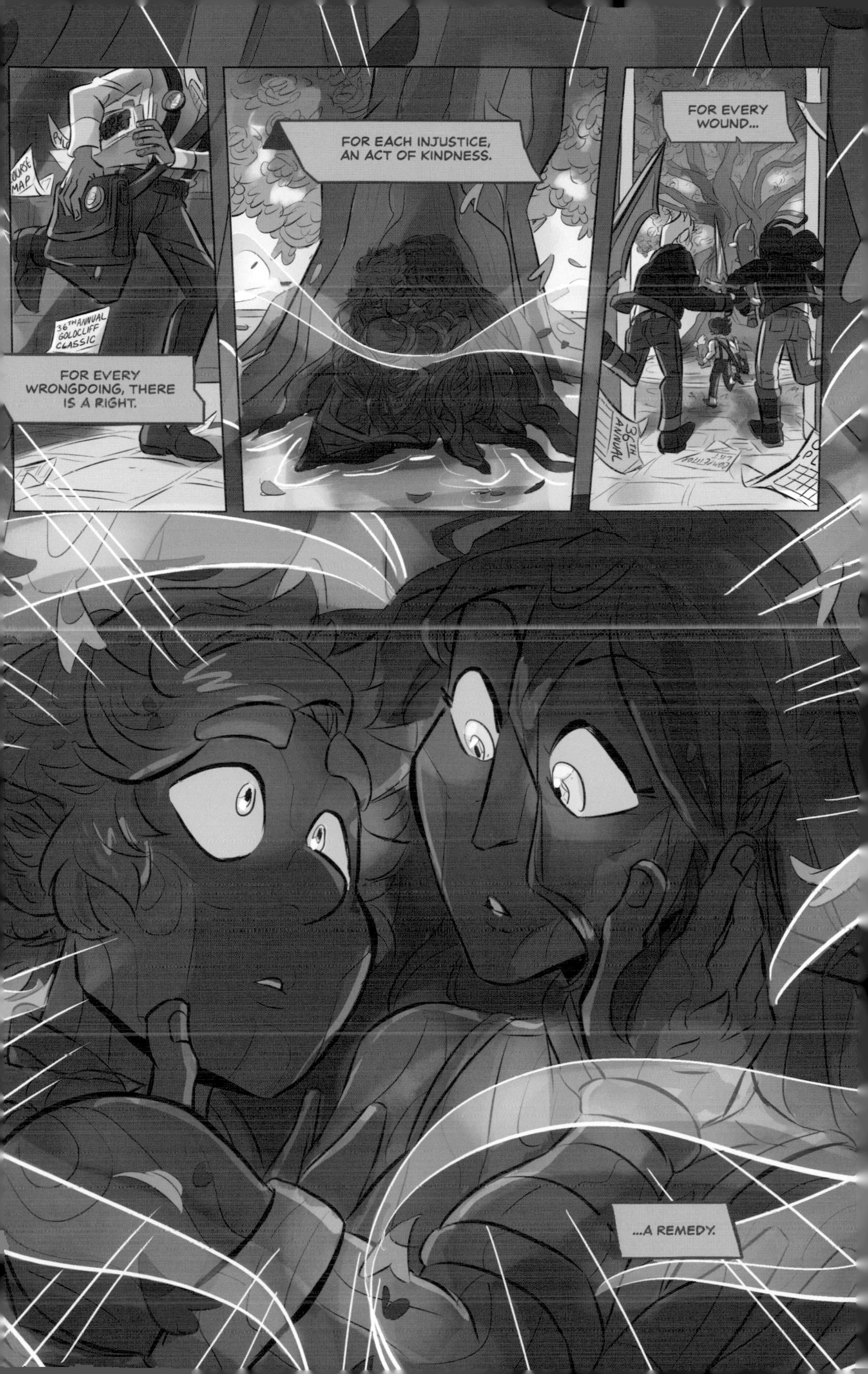

TOP SECRET
COURSE MAP
36TH ANNUAL GOLDCLIFF CLASSIC
FOR EVERY WRONGDOING, THERE IS A RIGHT.
FOR EACH INJUSTICE, AN ACT OF KINDNESS.
FOR EVERY WOUND...
36TH ANNUAL
COMPETITOR LIST
...A REMEDY.

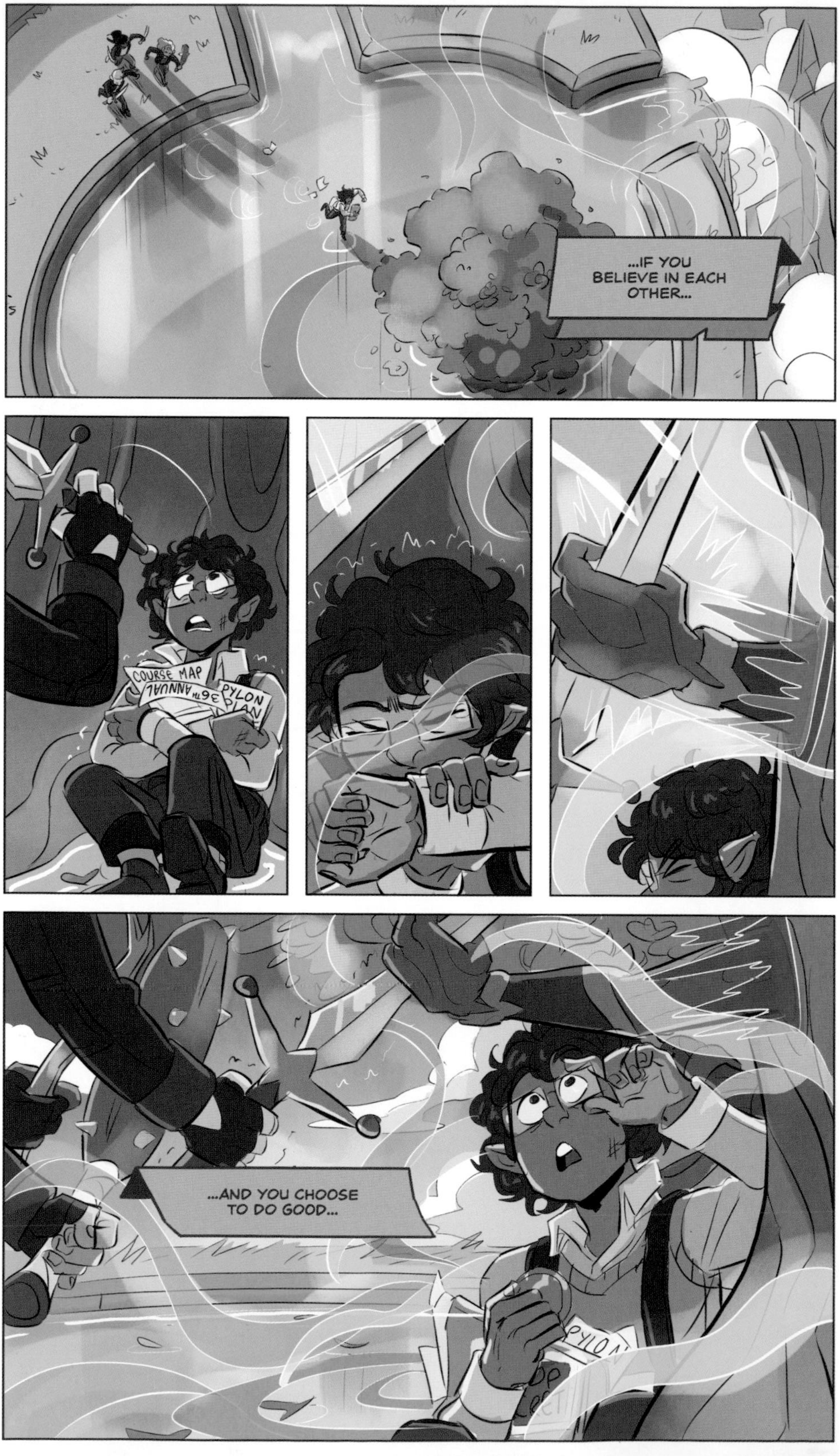
...IF YOU BELIEVE IN EACH OTHER...
COURSE MAP
36TH ANNUAL
PYLON PLAN
...AND YOU CHOOSE TO DO GOOD...
PYLON

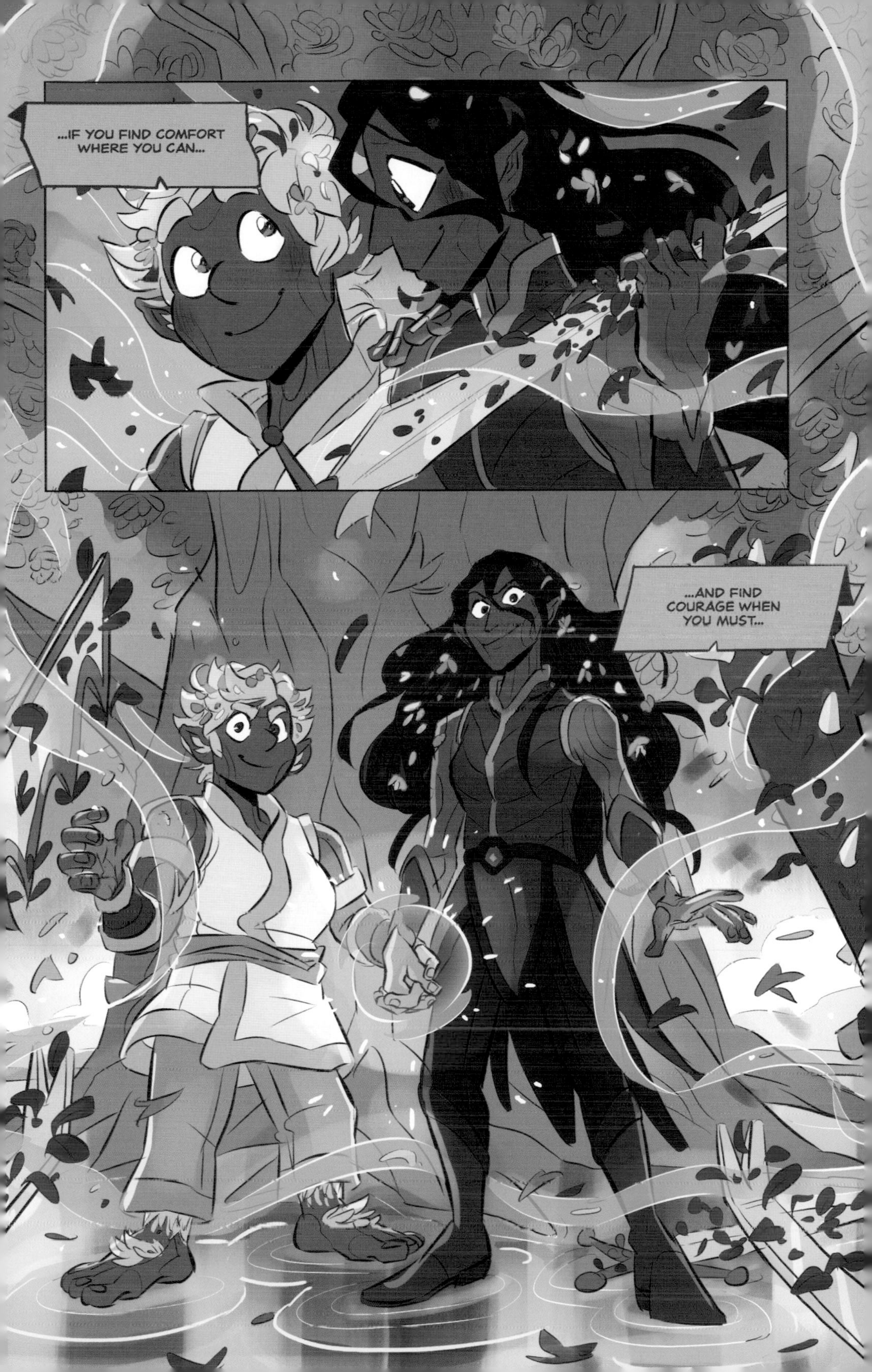
...IF YOU FIND COMFORT WHERE YOU CAN...
...AND FIND COURAGE WHEN YOU MUST...

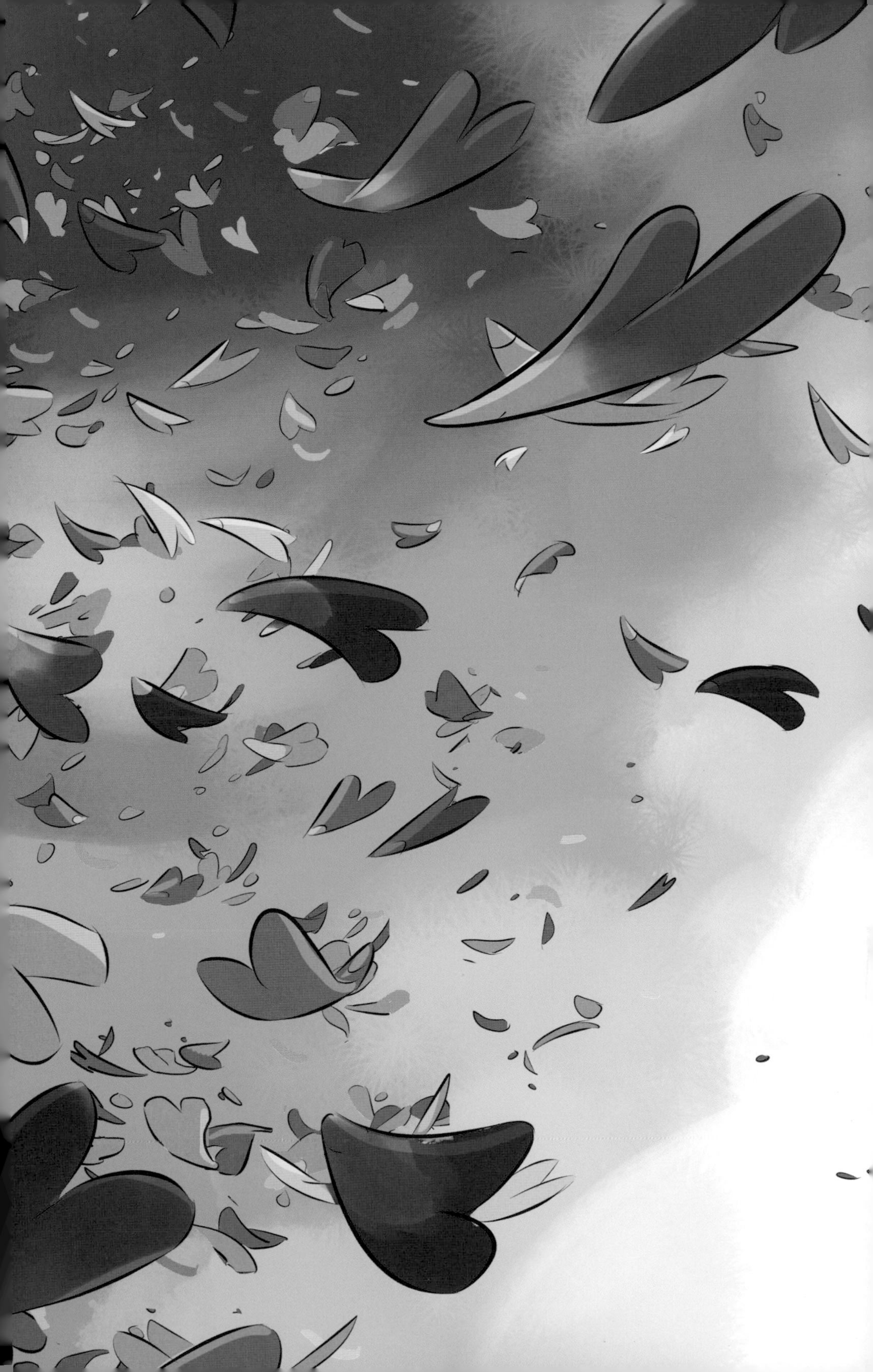

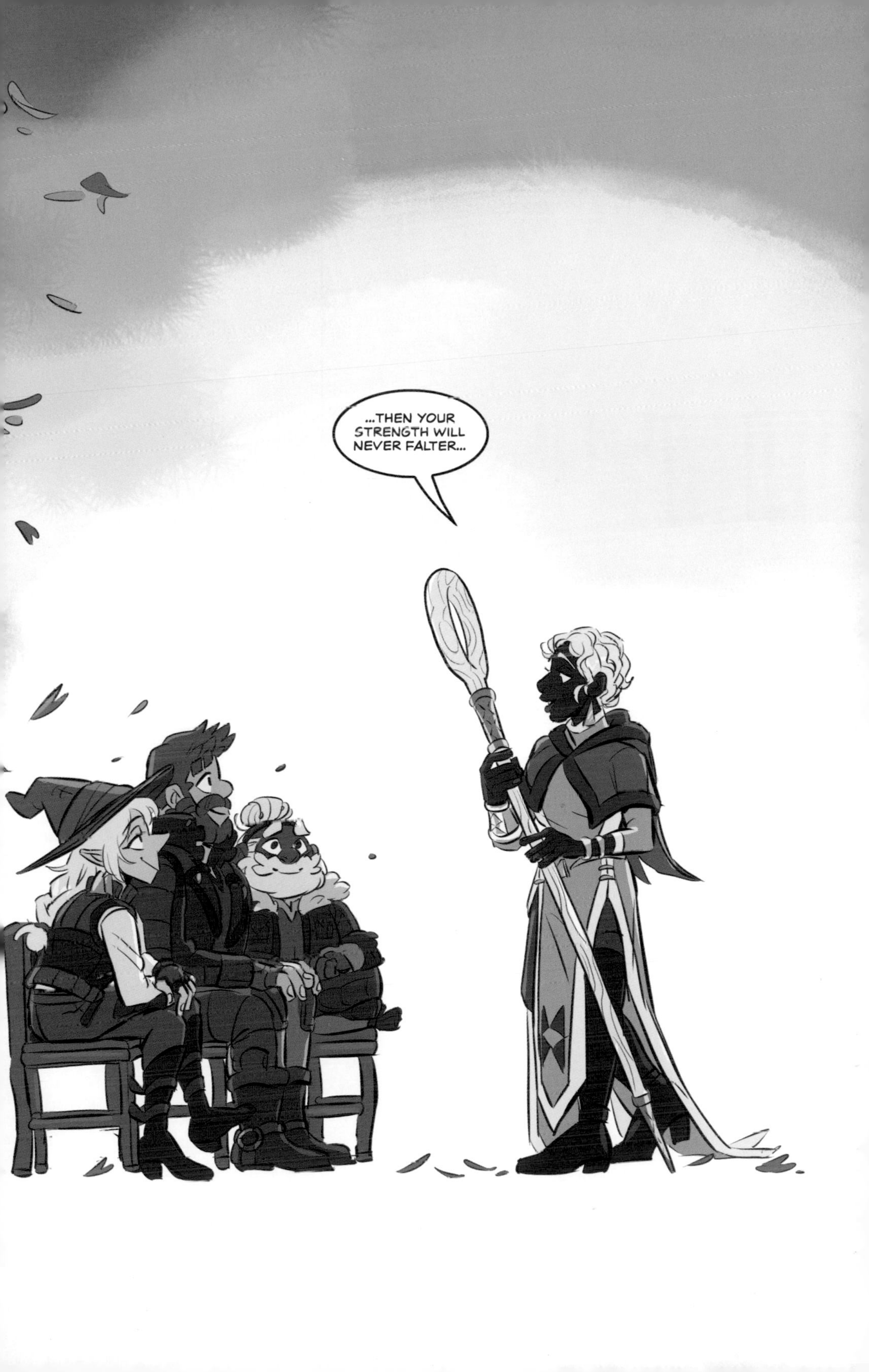
...THEN YOUR STRENGTH WILL NEVER FALTER...

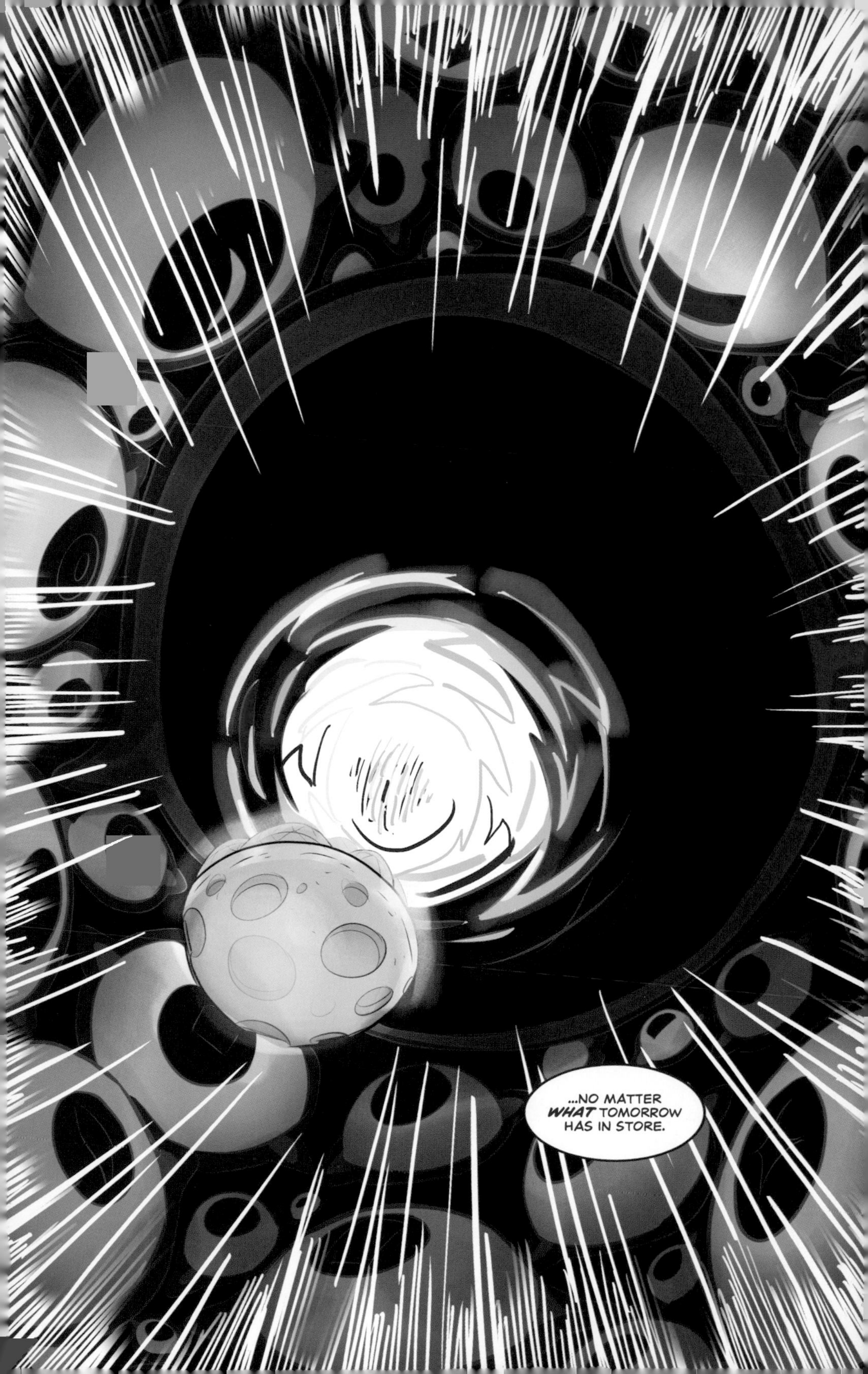
...NO MATTER WHAT TOMORROW HAS IN STORE.

The ADVENTURE CONTINUES in

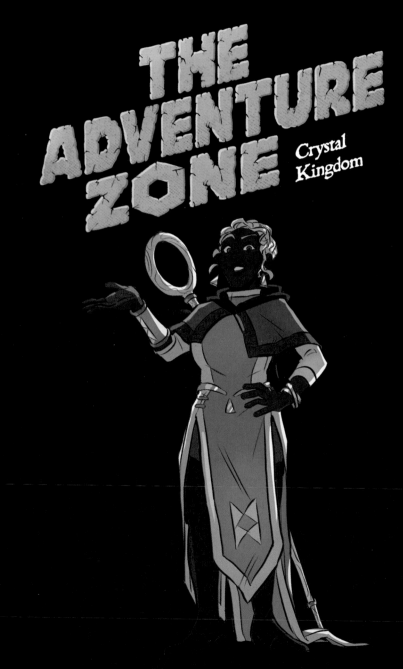

THE ADVENTURE ZONE
Crystal Kingdom

Coming Soon!

Fan Art Gallery

The Adventure Zone has been lucky enough to garner a passionate and deeply creative fandom. Many thanks to the fan artists who contributed pieces to this gallery—and to all the writers, artists, creators, and fans of all stripes who have made *The Adventure Zone* what it is.

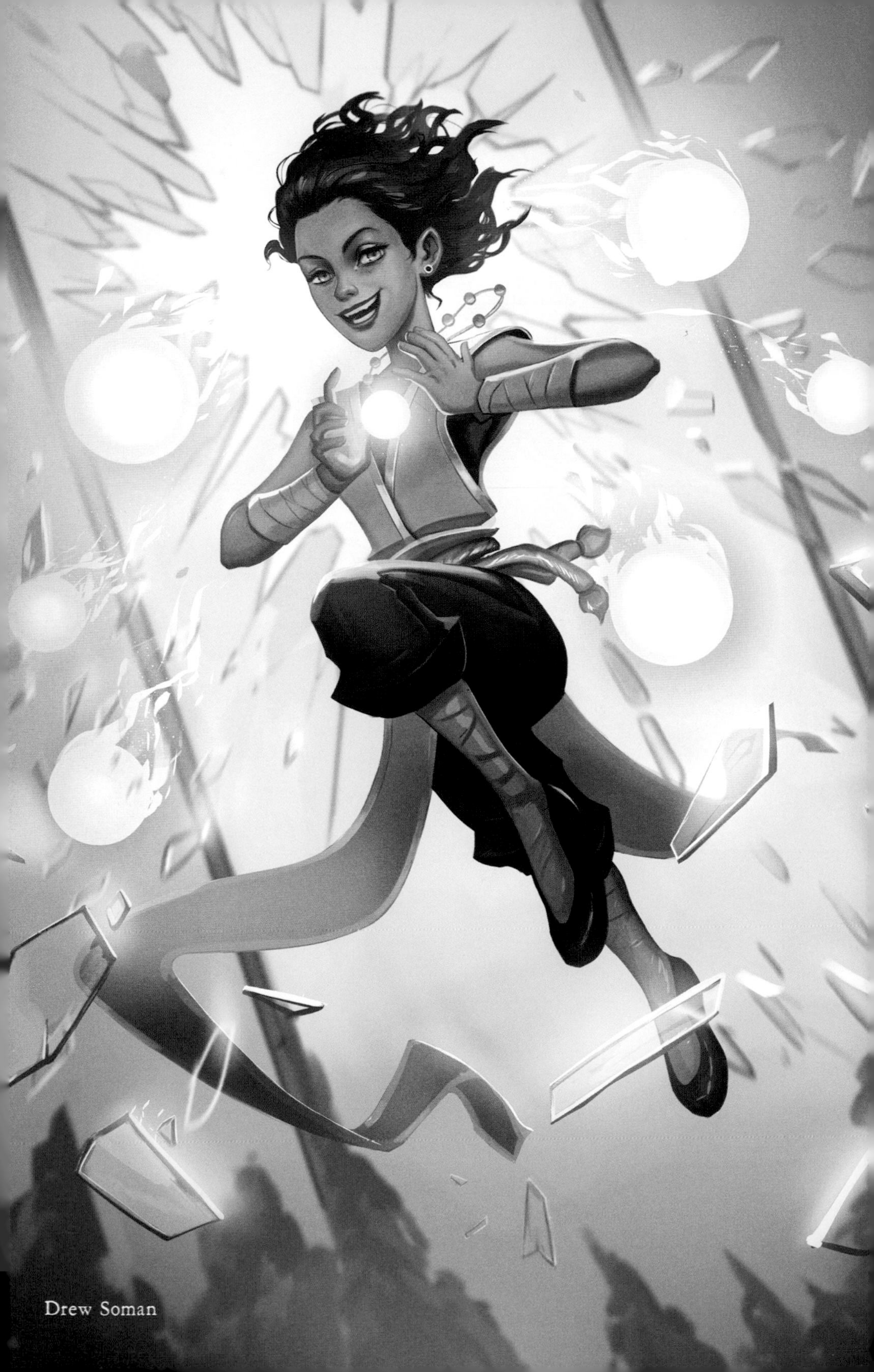

Drew Soman

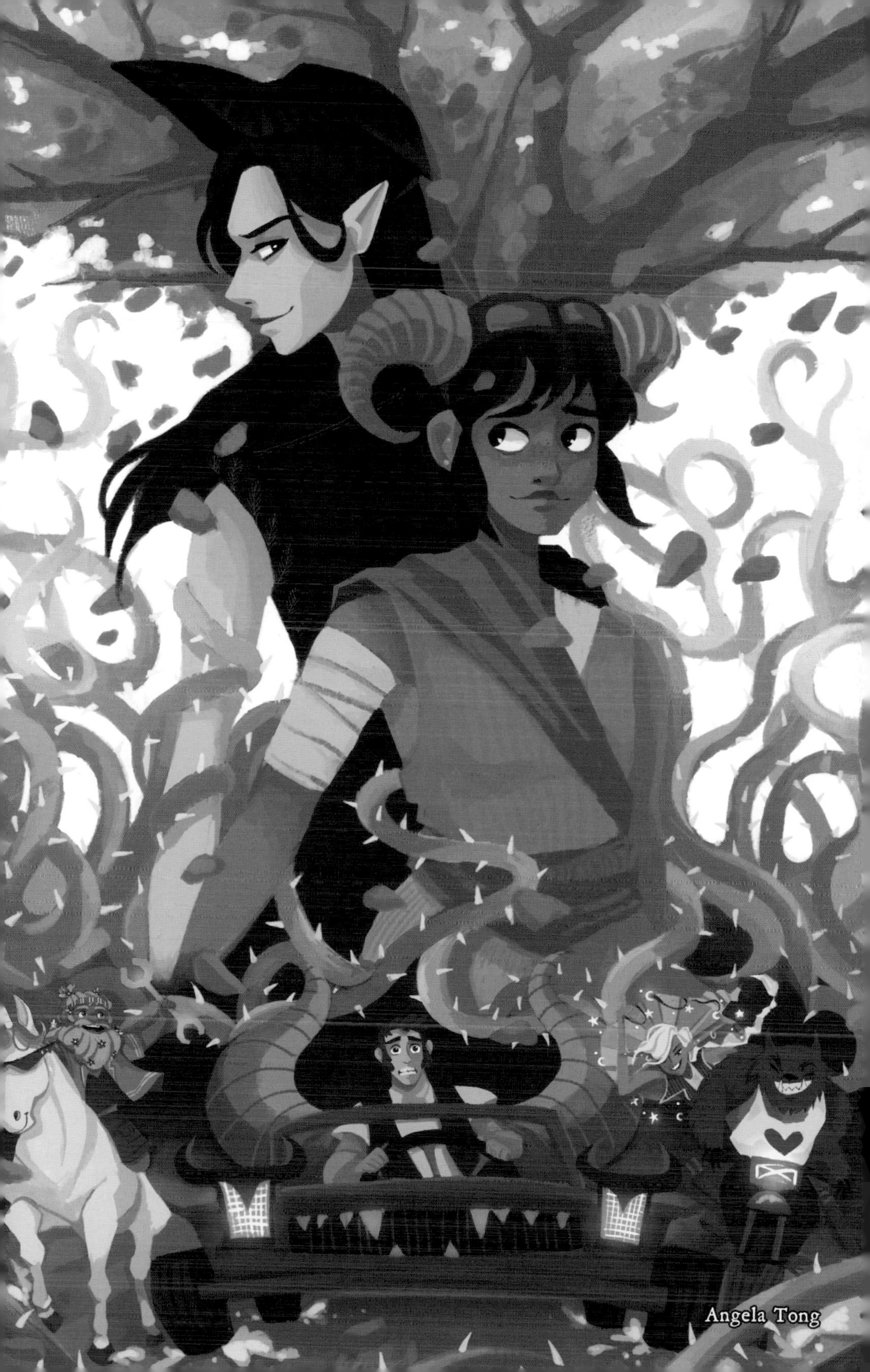
Angela Tong

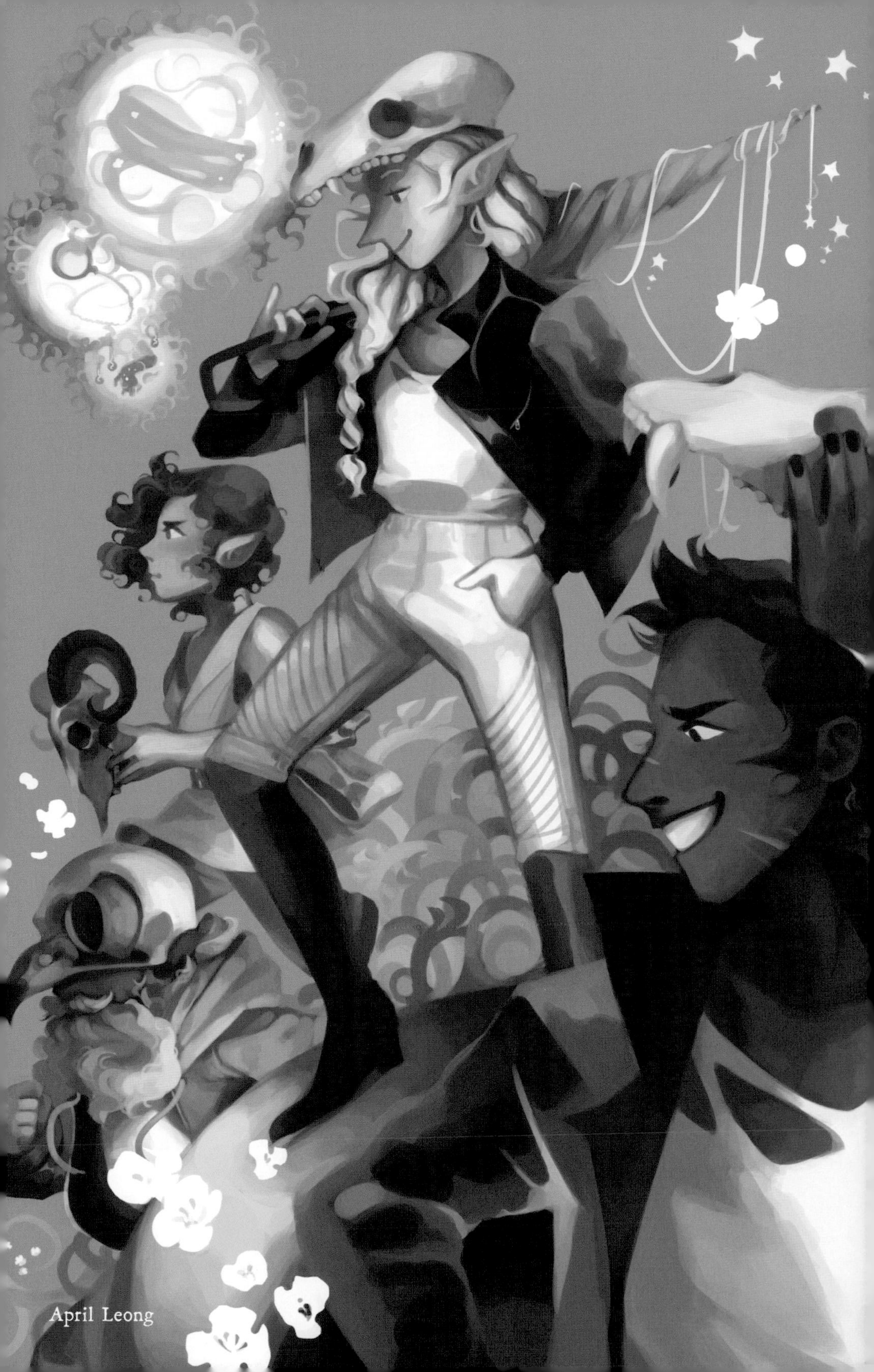
April Leong

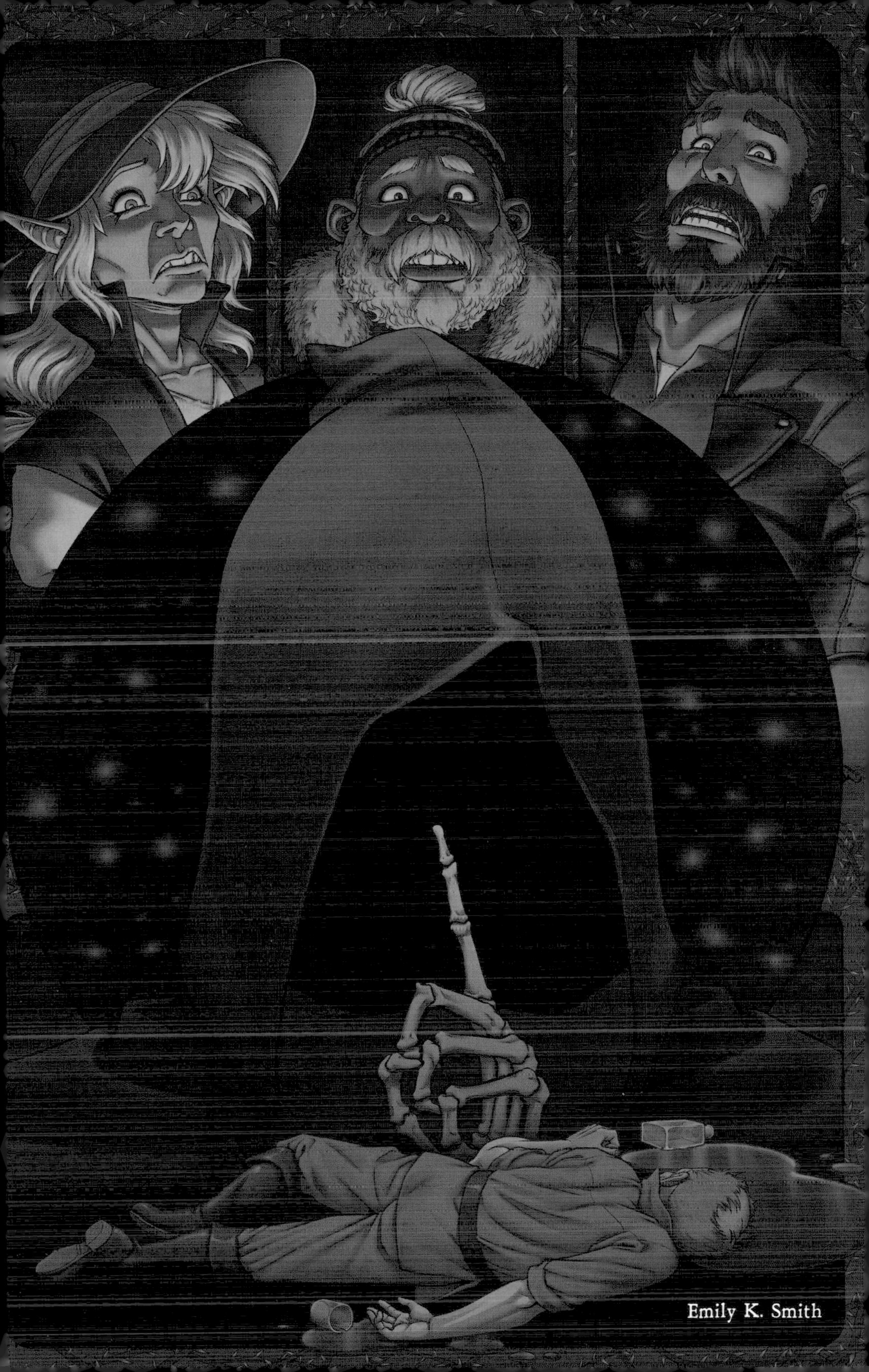
Emily K. Smith

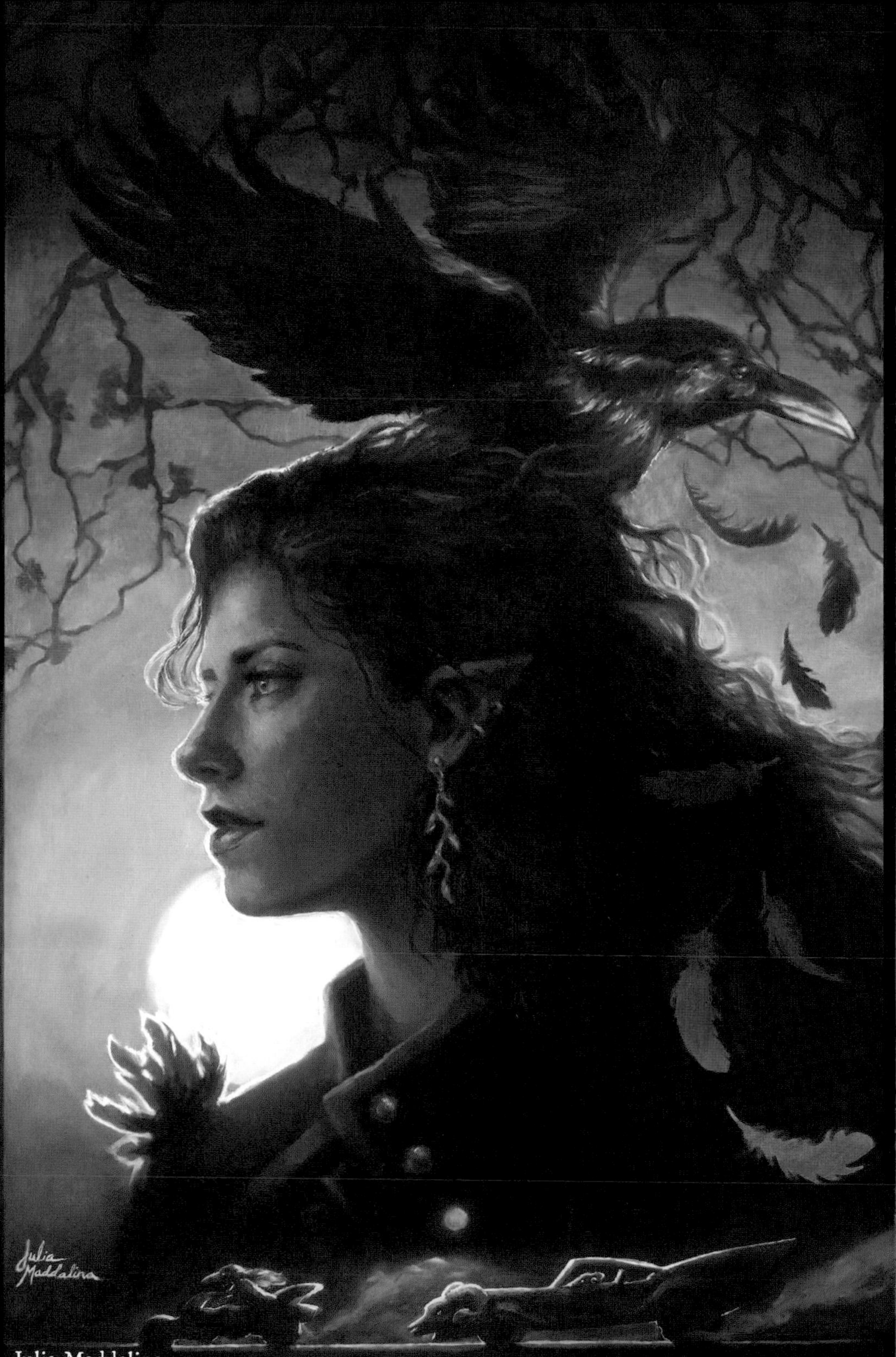
Julia
Maddalina

Julia Maddalina

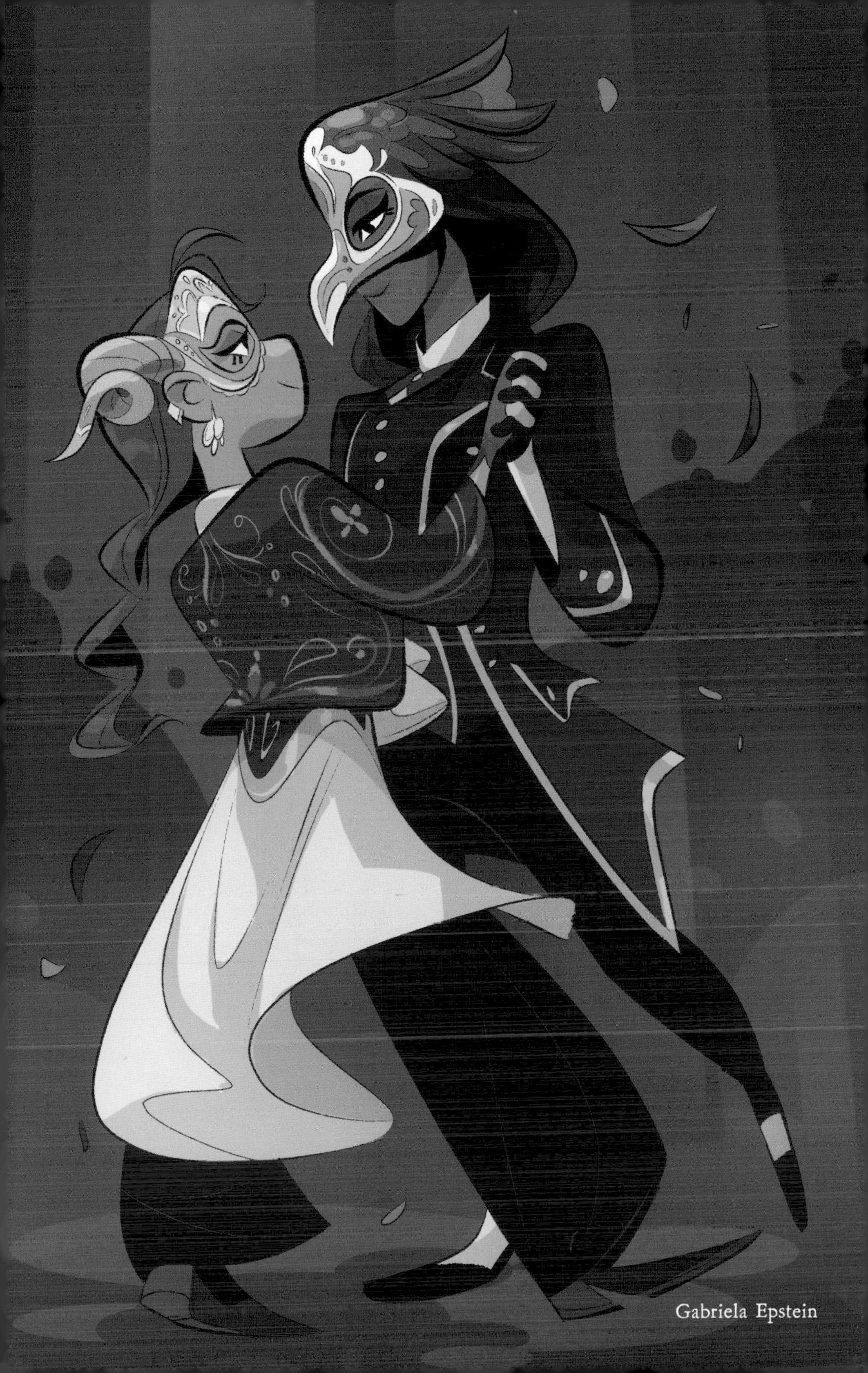
Gabriela Epstein

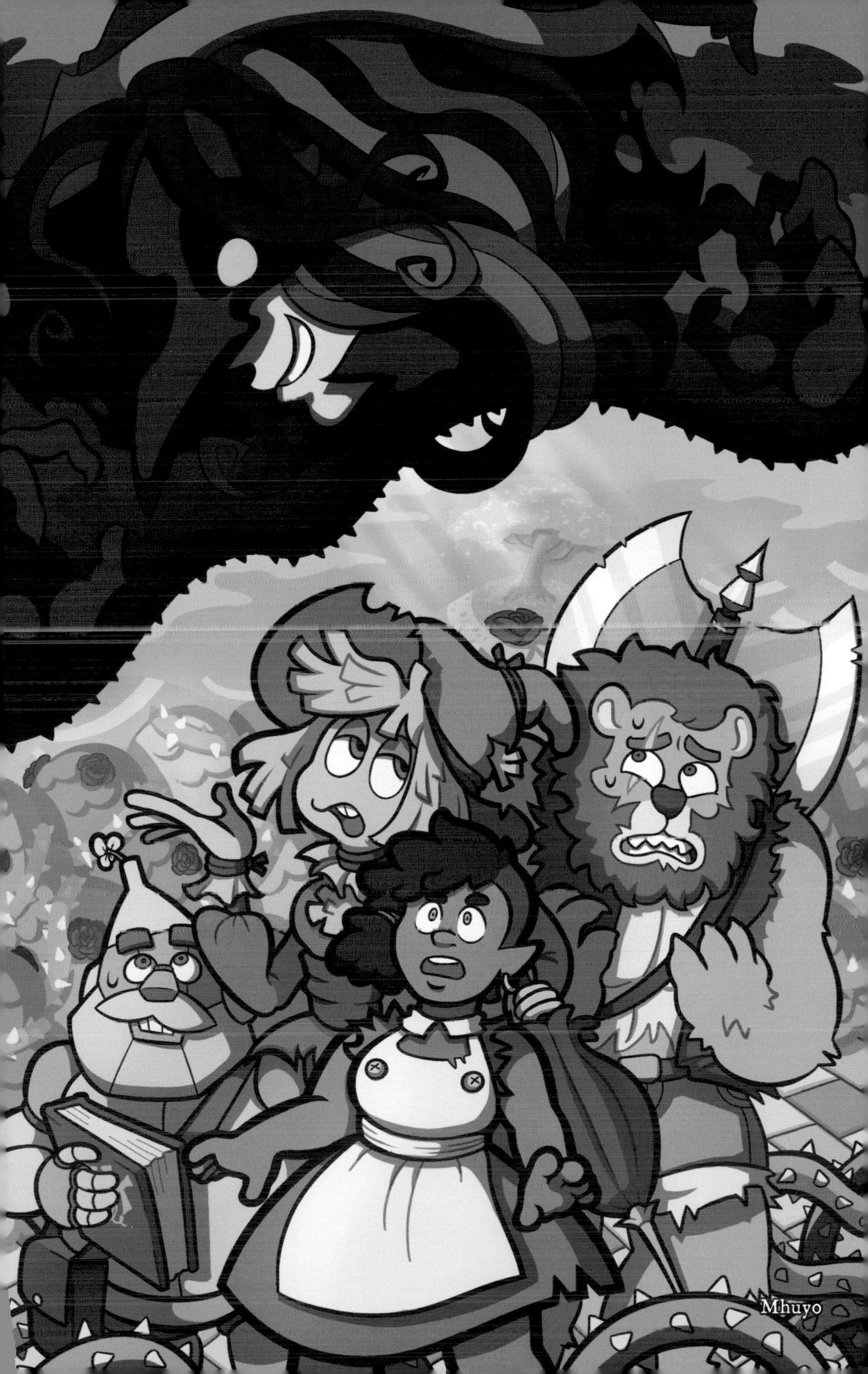
Mhuyo

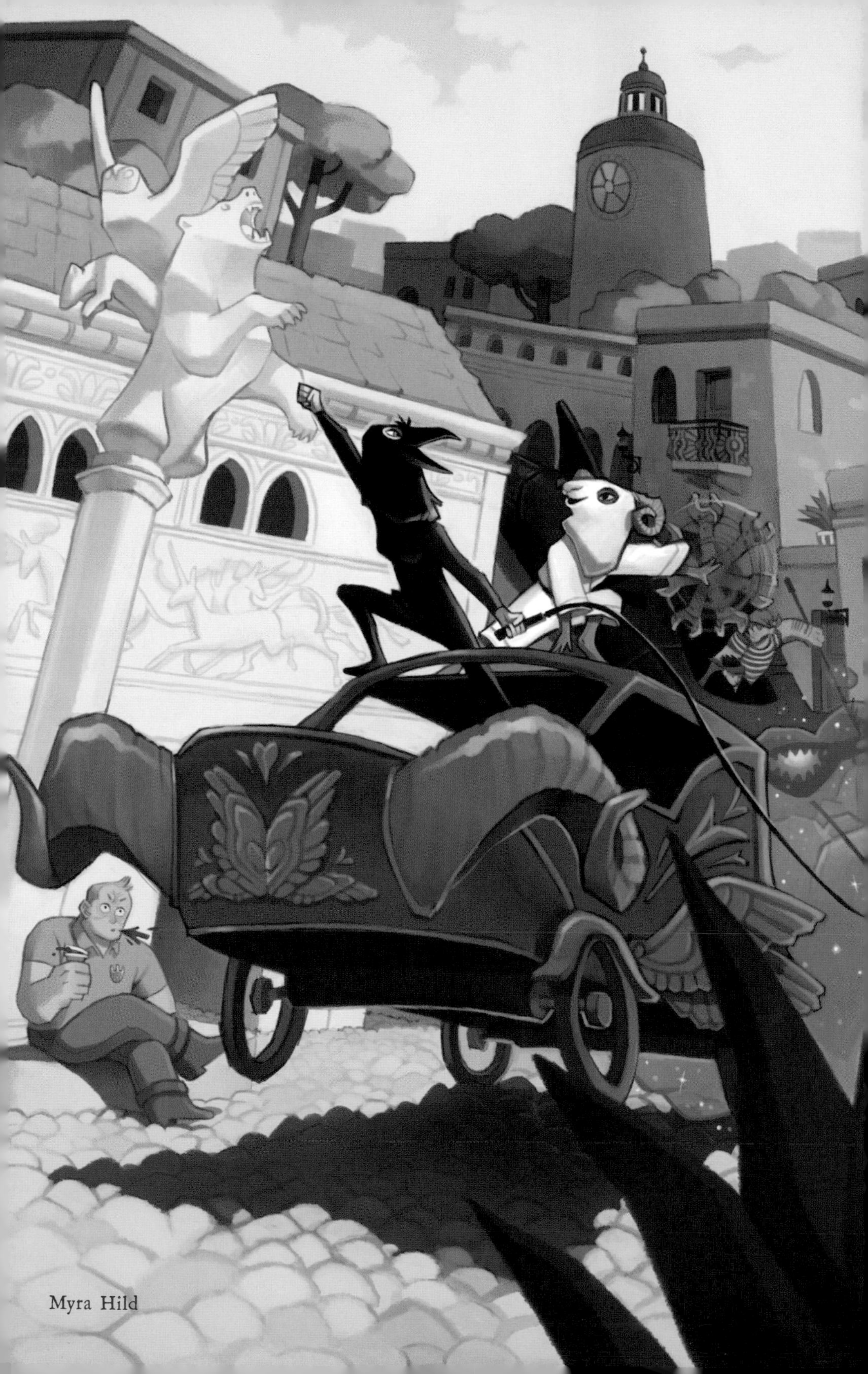
Myra Hild

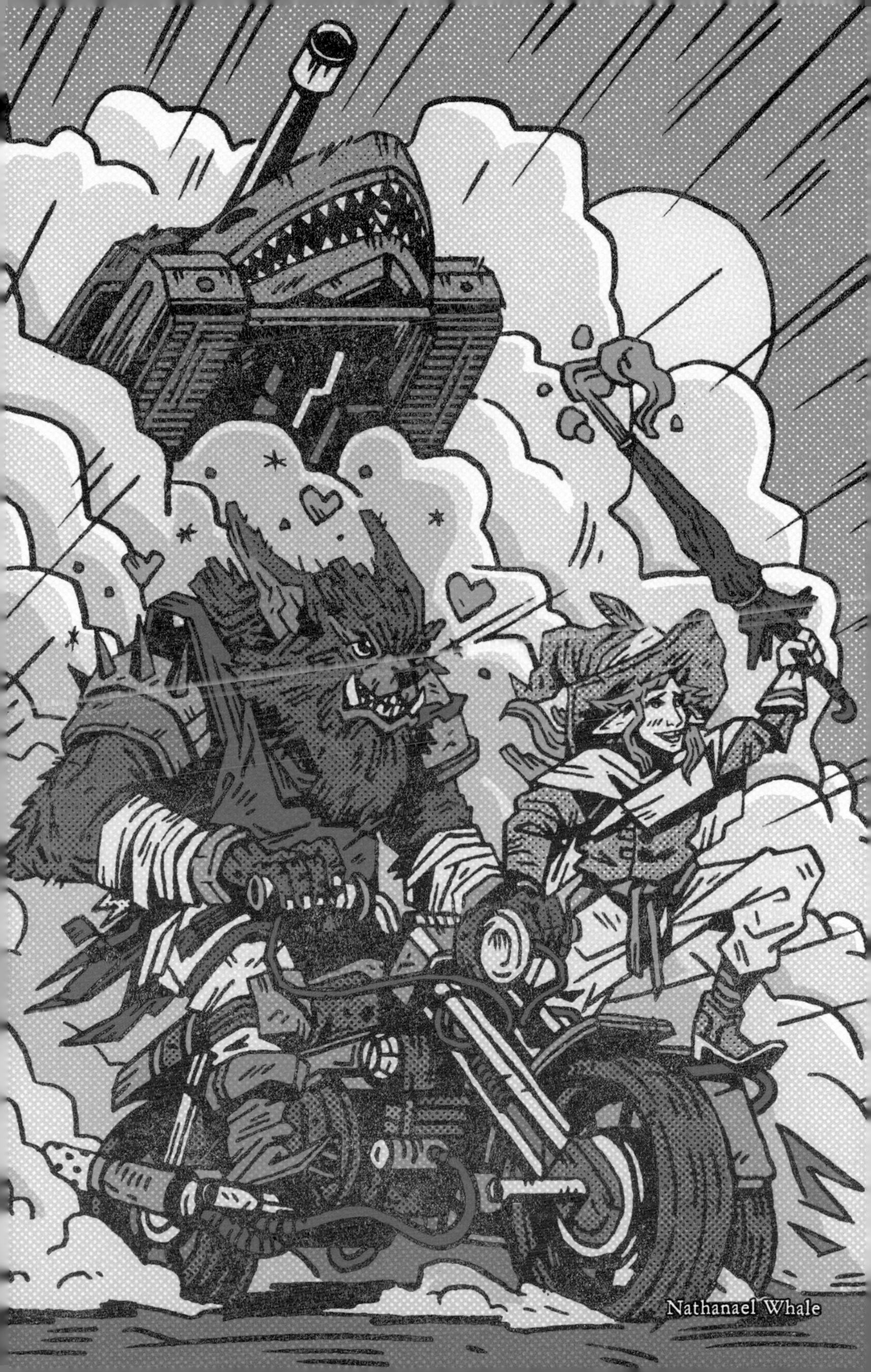
Nathanael Whale

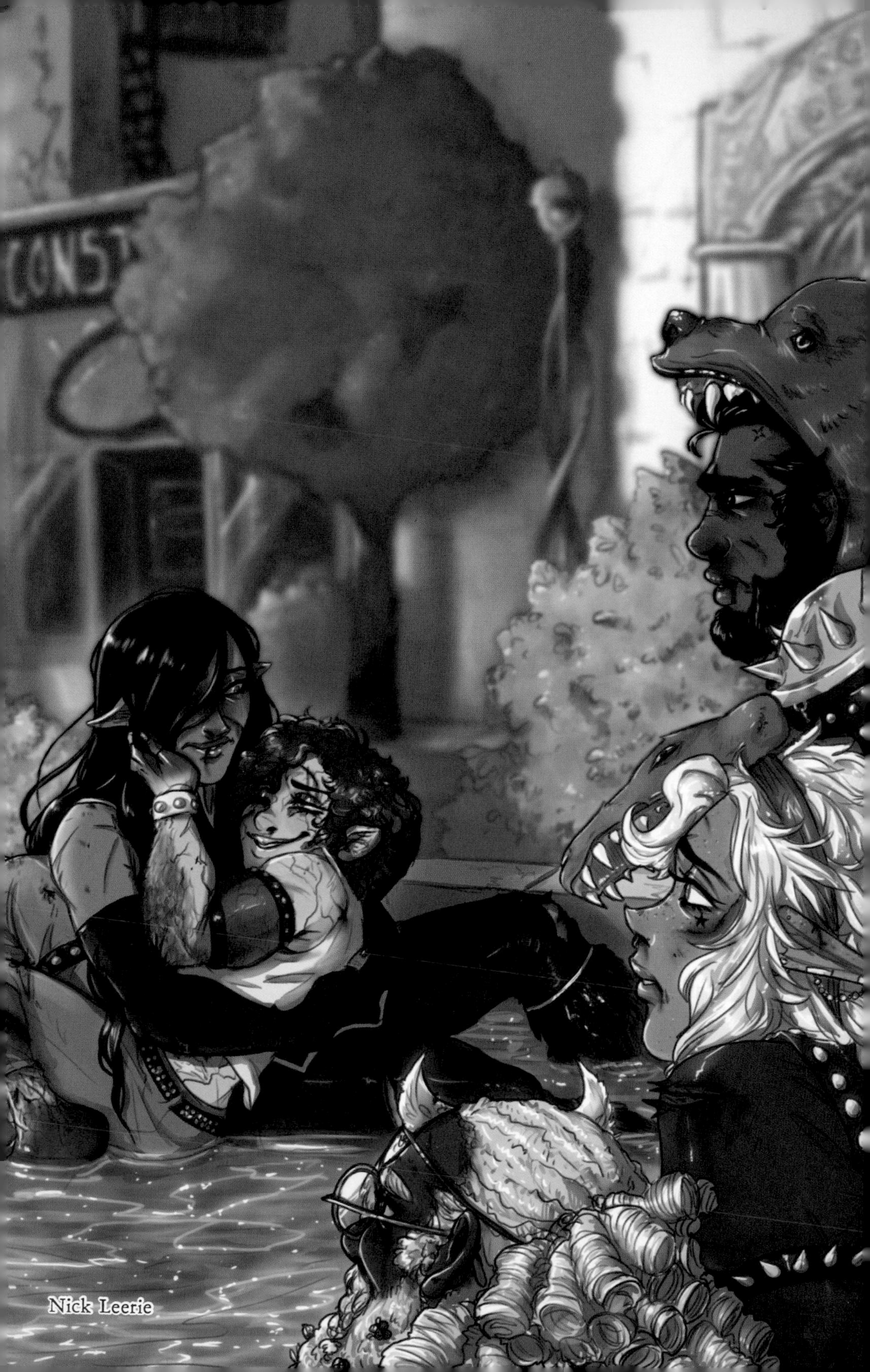
CONST
Nick Leerie

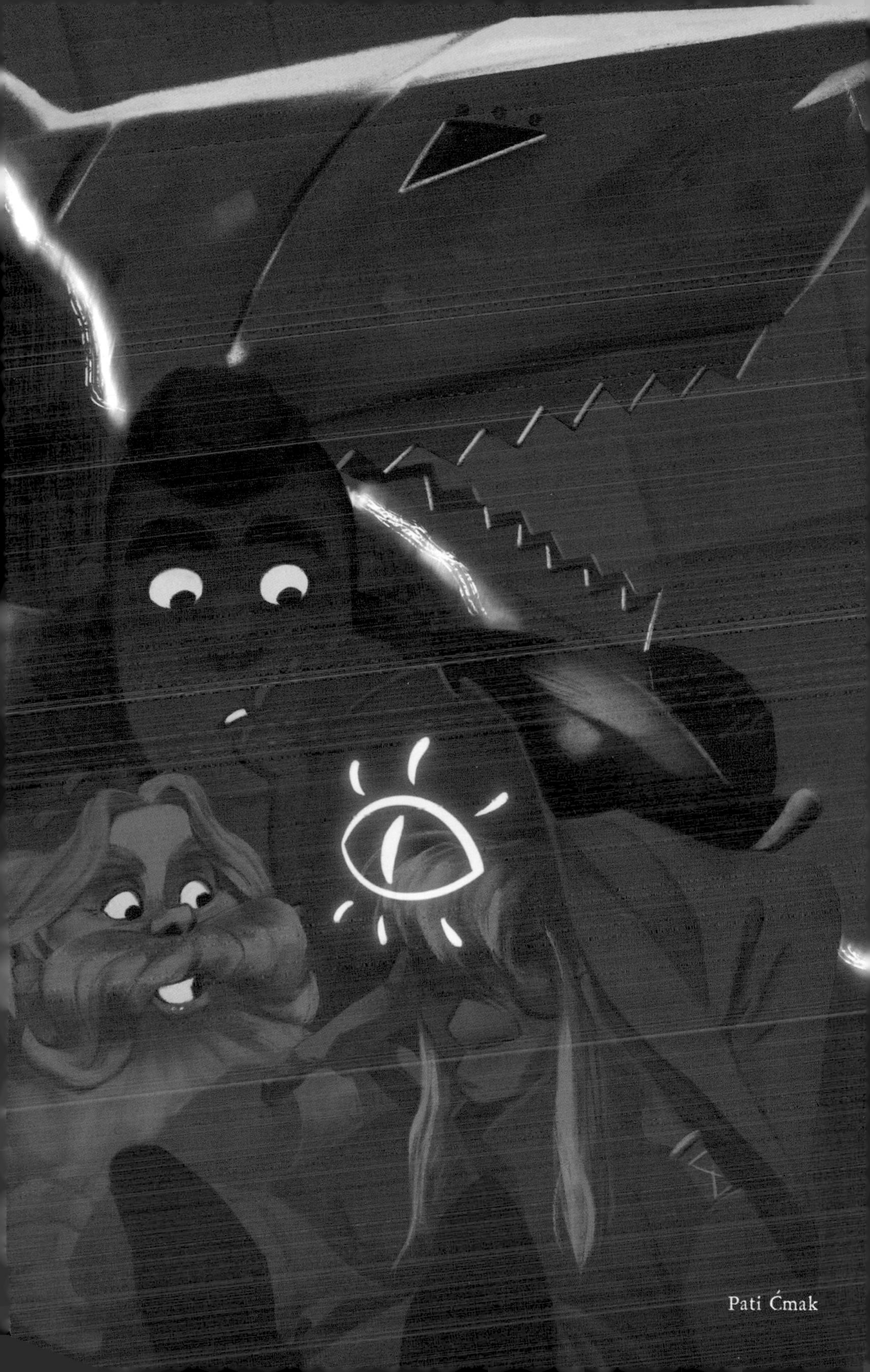

Pati Ćmak

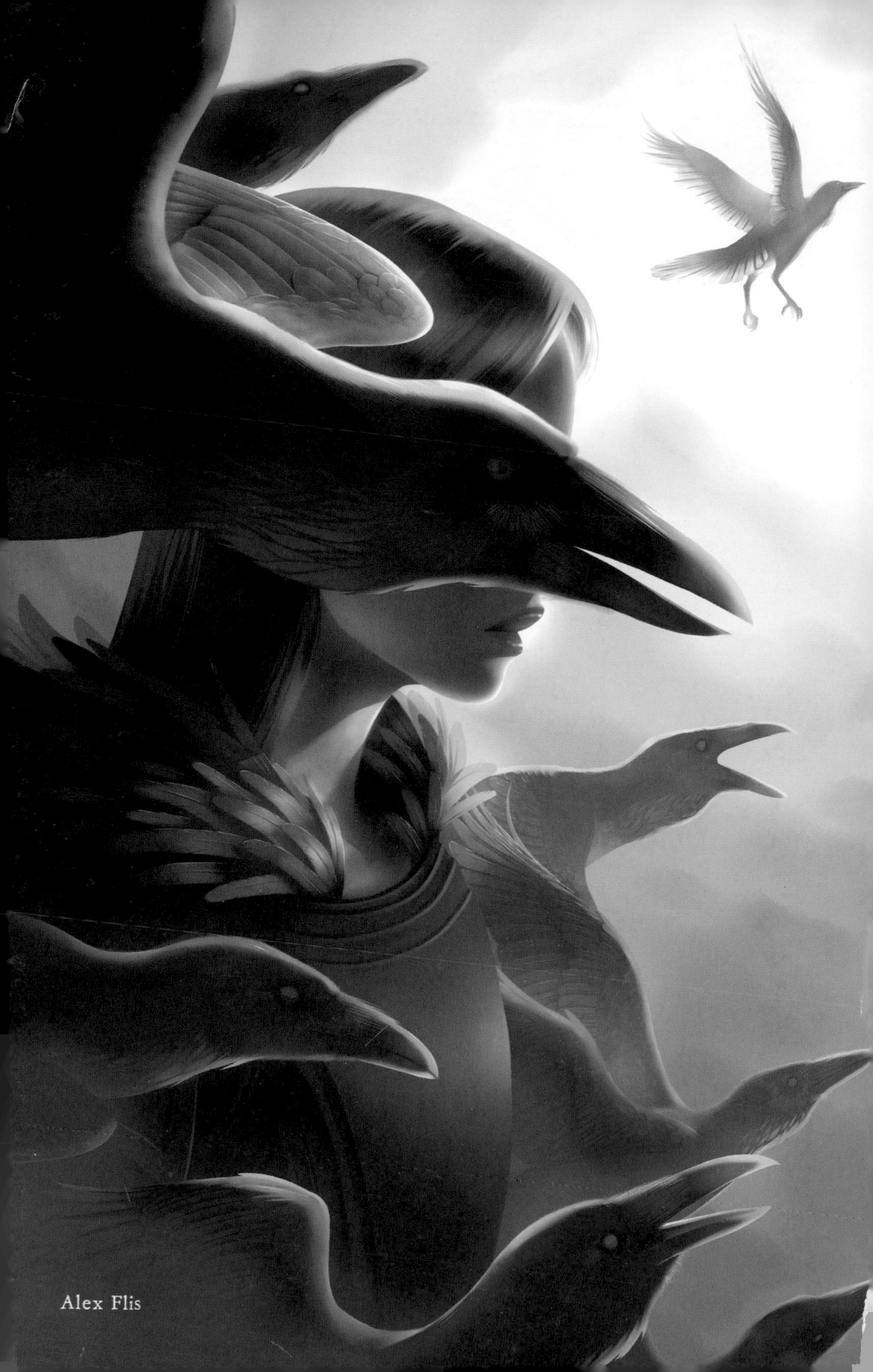

Alex Flis